Maria,

~~Happy to see~~ you again

thanks for all your help with

Enchantment the writings!

and Intervention 12/8/07

in Family Therapy

Using Metaphors in Family Therapy

D1526847

Enchantment and Intervention in Family Therapy

Using Metaphors in Family Therapy

by
Stephen R. Lankton
and
Carol Hicks Lankton

Crown House Publishing Company LLC
www.crownhousepublishing.com

Published by
Crown House Publishing Limited
P.O. Box 2223, Williston, VT 05495
www.crownhousepublishing.com

and

Crown House Publishing Ltd
Crown Buildings
Bancyfeling, Carmarthen, Wales, SA33 5ND, UK
www.crownhouse.co.uk

Originally Published in 1986 under the title,
*Enchantment and Intervention in Family Therapy:
Training in Ericksonian Approaches.*
Reissued 2007.
Copyright © 1986 by Stephen R. Lankton
and Carol Hicks Lankton

Library of Congress Catologing-in Publication Data

Lankton, Stephen R.
  Enchantment and intervention in family therapy.

  Includes bibliographical references and index.
  1. Family psychotherapy. 2. Crisis intervention
(Psychiatry) 3. Hypnotism–Therapeutic use.
4. Erickson, Milton H. I. Lankton, Carol Hicks,
II. Erickson, Milton H. III. Title.
[DNLM:1. Family Therapy. 2. Hypnosis.
WM 430.5-F2 L289e]
RC488.5.L355 1986   616.89'156   86-4240
ISBN:978-1845900830

13 digit ISBN: 978-184590083-0
10 digit ISBN: 184590083-9

This book is dedicated to Shawn Michael Lankton, who first made us a family, and to Alicia Michelle Lankton, who added yet another dimension.

Acknowledgments

We want to thank Barbara Levinson, Seyma Cahilman, Stuart Sugarman, and Jeffrey Zeig, the sponsors of the workshops whose transcripts appear here. Thanks also go to the families we saw and whose identities, of course, we have protected. We also want to thank Jack Moser, Susan Vignola, Lance Scalf, and their clients for allowing us to use transcribed portions of the work they did at our advanced training workshops. In addition, our appreciation goes to Ruth Wood for taking care of the shop all those times we were on the road. And speaking of being on the road, we want to acknowledge the participants in all our workshops, whose eagerness to learn and interest in this material inspired and shaped the content of this book.

Contents

Preface

The air is unseasonably cool for late August. The pine trees and palms are getting a workout they don't often enjoy. The leaves are falling as rain crashes into them like bullets. Visibility is reduced now but it will get worse still. The wind is gusting at 60 miles an hour. It is not dark yet; the hurricane won't make landfall for several hours.

The hurricane that is approaching the coastline has people darting about, taping some windows, boarding others, purchasing emergency supplies, and adorning their homes and offices with safety precautions that almost resemble holiday decorations. Neighbors are talking and helping, and strangers have a temporary common bond of survival. Tonight the winds will reach 130 miles an hour. Already the waves in the Gulf are four feet, practicing for their rise to 15. Then they will reach perhaps 20 feet or higher. And that is when they will begin making house calls.

The ocean gives and the ocean takes. It has given us many learnings and many opportunities to return and refresh ourselves physically and mentally from hundreds of trips to all parts of the United States and to a dozen other countries. This weekend the ocean will take. We can't avoid an occasional wave of fear or a tide of tears that well up momentarily as we bring chairs and toys indoors and pack emergency supplies. And even in this state of excitement—or perhaps because of this state of excitement—the ocean is giving us another chance to know ourselves and each other. And it is now giving us a chance to evaluate what is important to us in our home and in this office. Which things do you ultimately select to take with you when you know that everything remaining is in jeopardy? We're reminded of how fleeting and transient our material possessions really are and yet how deeply symbolic they are of our most treasured memories and values.

Each family in our neighborhood, spellbound by the storm, has its own unique approach to the coming crisis. Some shoot off to stay with a parent of one or the other spouse. Some have children come to stay with them. The locations they choose often have little to do with safety. Some stay here to stick it out unless forced to leave by "the authorities." Some work with their neighbors; some prefer the solitary approach. Some are brave and full of advice while others are fearful and full of rumors. While some families prepare amidst an attitude of directed calm, others shout and quarrel their tensions away. But the ocean and its wind will be unfair to each of them regardless.

Each of us learns from others and, in so doing, we teach others something about learning. When the storm has passed, some families will be untouched except for the common fears of anticipation, and others will have lost a great deal of property; some, I suppose, may lose loved ones as well.

It is now five days later. Evacuations are over. Tape has been scraped from windows. No one died this time—only a few pine trees and palms gave their lives.

Sitting in the lifeguard tower about seven feet above the sand, I (S.L.) watch the beach after midnight. The waves break about 30 or 40 yards out and they wash in every five seconds. They are about waist deep 15 yards out, and at the point of the breakers they are chest deep. The beach is almost entirely flat. The waves push an inch-thick white rim several yards up the beach. In the distance the hotel lights are barely visible. The shoreline is almost deserted. The storm removed a long section of the fishing pier. Sand has been pushed dozens of yards inland to cover sidewalks and streets. Some motels are open, but not in the conventional sense of the word. Foundations have been washed away or have fallen.

The storm only flirted with this beach. It passed 25 miles offshore and made landfall on the beach 100 miles to the west. It slapped the hands of many beachfront homes and it slapped a few in the face. Many homes were flooded.

I prefer to stay dry tonight. The ocean gives a peaceful calm again. Two young women run and actually dance about in the edge-zone where the water from the waves packs the sand firm. They don't want me to know they looked my way a couple of times. We don't verbally interact but communication occurs. They long for yesterday's songs and dream of to-night.

On what remains of the pier, men are shining a spotlight in the water. The illumination gives them a surreal appearance. They are hunting. Sharks weighing up to 900 pounds were caught this month. The men ignore the women and they ignore me. They look deeply beneath the surface. They dream of yesterday's shark and long for tomorrow's story.

Behind me the beach fades into sidewalks, bars, and parking lots. The "night owls" are cruising, kissing, drinking, laughing, disappearing. There is a different species of shark about. The automobile license plates read "Virginia," "Tennessee," "Florida," "Mississippi," and "Alabama." Some of them only long and never dream. They ignore me and seem to know from a distance that I live in a different time, a different world, a different night.

What all this has to do with Ericksonian hypnosis and therapy is not mysterious, only subtle. Motivation is different for different cultures, apparent even in the recent contrast between our experience of the relatively stable residential neighborhood and the shifting sands of the beach community. The bait is different for each different fisher. Each group has a goal determined by collective needs. The needs of individual members of each group are defined by an interplay of biology, personal history, culture, family, values, peers, expected sanctions, chronological age, "psychological" age, and environmental circumstances.

There are many equally powerful parts of the ecosystem at play in each family. In one family one level is apparently most influential to the functioning of the members, and in a different family it may be another level of the family system that is apparently most significant. Traveling, teaching workshops, doing therapy, we learn something from each place to which we go and from each family with whom we interact just as we learn something different each time we merge with the current mood of the ocean.

Paradoxically, in each location we learn something new about what we teach. This book is a composite assemblage of teachings from five different workshops in the U.S. Primarily, it has been created from what we feel are the most representative of several family therapy workshops we've conducted, some individually and some together. These took place in Boston, Massachusetts; Austin, Texas; Newport, Rhode Island; Phoenix, Arizona; and Pensacola Beach, Florida.

For the most part, the material is verbatim transcription, but we have, of course, taken editorial liberties to modify and rewrite parts of it to improve readability and protect confidentiality and anonymity of participants and clients as the material made its transition from spoken word to printed page. Oral communication often deletes words and in their place conveys information with timing, pause, inflection, face muscles, movement, gesture, and so on. Editing in this book has recaptured many of those verbal deletions and filled in the necessary referents and details. The portions we chose from the several workshops to reconstruct this transcript were those from which we feel we learned the most and the participants received the most. The topic of each workshop was the same: the framework for an Ericksonian approach to family therapy—enchantment and interventions in families.

We have molded our teaching workshops and written this book after noticing trends in therapy approaches where either the individual is emphasized and the social organization is ignored, or the social (usually, the family) context is emphasized and the individual's feelings, behaviors, or beliefs are considered inconsequential, thus discounting and neglecting the structure and organization of the individual roles. In our opinion, each of these apparently dichotomized views is of equal importance. They are merely different structures within a larger ecosystem. Family therapy, in our view, ought to concern itself with family organization, roles, communication, cognition, emotion, simple motor behavior, and out-of-awareness (or unconscious) experience, as well as environmental circumstances and developmental demands from the culture. A therapy that seemed to regularly intervene at each of these levels and consider them each important was that of Milton H. Erickson.

If the field of therapy is, in some ways, like an electrical circuit, Erickson was at times an inducer and at times a transistor in the circuit. At times he stimulated and sparked new information; at other times he changed direction in a way that seemed unpredictable to many. He might describe one case that dealt with hypnosis and involved one family member; then moments later he would describe a case relying upon a radical change in family organization but not using hypnosis at all. Some cases were almost sinfully brief while others were arduously lengthy.

He believed in the family. He was the center of a neighborhood. As Marshall McLuhan might say, he was tribal. He was often nonlinear in his approach to problem solving. And like many nonlinear thinking individuals, he left a flurry of ideas with little in the way of an organizing framework to help others grasp the contributions systematically. He left *that* work, we suppose, to his students and colleagues.

While most contributions to the Ericksonian literature to date have provided the professional public with an understanding of many of his techniques, it seems that there have been only a few helpful frameworks to making sense of the large portions of the entirety. This book is a continuation of our efforts to provide such order. It is a companion to *The Answer Within*, providing a systemic framework for understanding Ericksonian interventions in family therapy.

We have chosen to title this book *Enchantment and Intervention* to indicate our belief that hypnotic communication and hypnotic effects occur throughout the entire process of family therapy. These effects are achieved whenever such interventions as paradoxical prescription, metaphor, blocking communications, indirect suggestions, therapeutic binds, and so forth are used. This enchantment captures the family members' conscious attention, stimulates unconscious search and resource retrieval, and leads consciousness from confusion to an understanding that comes from within. Enchantment is a concept in therapy as important as empathy and, as we view it, it is intrinsic to the approach we learned from Erickson. Thus, "enchantment" is the foundation on which therapeutic interventions are structured.

We have intended to present and analyze specific interventions and then build them together systematically into ever more complex combinations of interventions. This book closely conforms to the sequence of teachings and training activities in our five-day family therapy workshops. The illustrations used in this volume are the actual workshop materials and overhead projector aids. But the detailed training of hypnotic induction, trance phenomena, and so on is almost nonexistent in this book. For that material the curious reader should consult *The Answer Within: A Clinical Framework of Ericksonian Hypnotherapy* (Brunner/Mazel, 1983). We designed this present book to pick up where the former leaves off.

After a brief introduction to Erickson in Chapter 1, Chapter 2 presents an ecosystems model and several means of assessment that lead finally to logical treatment plans for sessions. Each chapter thereafter addresses a level of the ecosystems framework provided. Chapter 3 focuses on disturbing the family organization with task assignments in particular. The Ericksonian interventions we call "ambiguous function assignments" are presented there. To us it is a unique and exciting explanation of one of Erickson's maneuvers that has previously been regarded as simply part of his eccentric creativity and, therefore, unteachable and unlearnable.

Chapter 4 considers in great detail the development of individual family members by helping them to generate emotion, behavior, and attitude changes. This is the longest and most detailed discussion of metaphor protocols to date. It presents the step-by-step formulas for the structure of metaphors that will have a highly predictable effect on each of those areas, as well as family structure change, self-image thinking change, and, particularly, specific emotions. What sequence and elements are necessary components to make a story convey challenge to a belief, enhance a self-image, build a behavior, or elicit sadness, anger, relief, fear, and confidence? These are the questions answered in this chapter with specific formulas that add accountability and predictability to the use of metaphor in treatment. The hypnotic effect of family members' communication on one another is presented here with ideas for using that force therapeutically.

Chapter 5 deals with changing that level of the system that can be viewed as more personal or interactional—increasing role flexibility. We detail many paradoxical interventions and tools to aid in perturbing the family at this level of the system.

Chapter 6 delves deeper into the individual subsystems in the family and concerns itself with unconscious resources and the use of suggestions and hypnosis in the family interview. Chapter 7, the family session, presents a live interview that demonstrates the final collage of the various component approaches and interventions as it helps a naive family with their serious problems.

Chapter 8 concludes, as we often end our workshops, with a group induction designed to provide both a demonstration of techniques and a learning experience that will complement and extend the training. We have chosen to add an induction that has never been in print previously. Perhaps more than any others we have done, it reflects a degree of excitement that comes from the stimulating atmosphere of an International Congress on Ericksonian Therapy and from a group induction where several members of the Erickson family were in attendance.

You, the readers, as professional psychologists, social workers, psychiatrists, family therapists, and so forth, are likely to be entering your offices and beginning face-to-face contact with families and their individual members at 8 a.m. or 9 a.m. local time, week in and week out. You may wonder how, using Ericksonian approaches, you can better help the client or family. That is what the training workshops underlying this book have hoped to offer: a conceptual framework that takes into account the variety of dynamics from the social level to the unconscious level that inevitably affect families, and builds in a practical way, emphasizing interventions that act at each level. Each new piece covered relies upon the preceding teaching of interventions and attitudes and builds an interdependency among the parts. Although the written word is not a substitute for professional training, supervision, and feedback, it is, nevertheless, an educational tool. This is the next best thing to being there, as they say. This book can be studied as a framework for integrating an Ericksonian approach into your practice and, perhaps, vice versa. We hope to convey a manner of approaching families and making the enchantment and interventions that were a part of Erickson also *a part* of you.

Gulf Breeze, FL   Stephen R. Lankton
September 1, 1985   Carol H. Lankton

Enchantment and Intervention in Family Therapy

Training in Ericksonian Approaches

CHAPTER 1

Meeting Erickson

I want to begin by giving you a definition of enchantment as we use it. Enchantment is to influence by or as if by charms and incantation; to thrill or enrapture; to allure; to delight; to fascinate or bewitch. To fascinate is to cast a spell over; to transfix and hold spellbound by or as if by an irresistible power; to command attention or interest by the artful, subtle, challenging, strange or piquant. Piquant means arousing pleasant mental excitement, engaging, provocative or agreeably challenging.

With that in mind I want to play a brief video portion of a family therapy session. This picks up at the end of the first interview with the family of a (diagnosed) 28-year-old schizophrenic son who has just returned home from 10 years of hospitalization. The son complains that his arms are too weak and his muscles are deteriorating. I openly interpreted that somatic complaint as a communication that there are standards about becoming a man, which are perceived by him as too high and seem, to him, to be beyond his reach. There is much that could be said about this family and this session but I want to just show you this following portion when my two-and-a-half-year old son is brought in the office to help me. I'll turn it on just prior to calling him and I think you will be able to garner the mood and events in the session. As this starts, I am telling the family a story about a recent dinner guest and her four-year-old son. The story illustrates a point about how children learn the attributions which are used by parents to describe them. [In this transcription "S" is for Stephen, the therapist; "Sh" is for Shawn; "F" signifies the father; "M" signifies the mother; "D" signifies the daughter.]

3

S: We are sitting at the dining room table and the two children were in the kitchen, 15 feet away, quarreling over some toy, and as a result of the child dealing with Shawn [my son], he decides to share. He gave the toy to Shawn and they were happy. And at that point the dinner guest said, "Gee, I'm so glad that Bobby [her son] did that. Usually, what he does is [gesturing with a right hand punch] hauls off and hits the other kid." I counted silently to myself when I heard her say that: 1, 2, 3, 4, ... When I got to 7, her son lifted his right hand, swung, and hit Shawn.

F: Ummmm. [Here he sits up and adjusts his posture in the chair and straightens his tie.]

S: Now, putting it the way she phrased it was the stimulus that created the idea that led to the result. The boy must have thought: "Oh, is that how I handle things? Of course!" If she had said, "I'm so glad that Bobby got back in touch with how cooperative he has always been," he would have come to think that instead.

   Now I want to show you one other thing. This will require that I get Shawn to come in before you folks find yourselves leaving. [stands and opens office door] This is metaphoric but I think it will be a good seed to plant. [enters hallway]

S: Shawn!

Sh: [from far away but with energy] What?

S: Come here.

Sh: Okay! [still with much energy]

F: [turns head toward sounds and smiles at the verbal response heard from Shawn]

D: [to family members] He's a cute little boy.

S: [reenters room carrying a jade-stone blade adz from New Zealand]

Sh: [comes running into the office and looks at all the people as he moves across the room to Stephen]

F: [to Shawn] Hello, how are you.

Sh: Two.

S: He's two, that's right.

D: [laughs]

S: [takes Shawn on lap. To Shawn] This is Sally. This is Sally's father, Peter. This is Sally's mother, Marge, and her brother, David. [to family] This is my son, Shawn.

F: [with a warm smile] Hi.

D: We played with your toys once, Shawn.

M: [interrupting] Excuse me. My father and Shawn have the same color hair.

Sh: [picks up two felt tip pens and starts to remove tops from them]

S: Before you play with those pens I want you to show them something. They want to learn something about dealing with their son better. [tone shift] If you are done with the pens, show them about having power, would you please?

Sh: I have two markers.

S: Do you have power?

Sh: Yes I do, really strong *power.*

D: [laughs]

F: [smiles and leans forward in chair]

S: Would you show them? Here I'll hold these [markers] for you and you can have them back when you are done. [handing the adz to Shawn] Show them how you get power.

Sh: I hold [the adz] real tight and say really loud: [lifts sternum, raises chest] *POWER*! [All laugh warmly.]

S: And when you grow up do you think you are going to have power?

Sh: [enthusiastically] Yes, I do.

S: I think so, too. Take those pens and go into the kitchen to mark with them, okay. Take this paper, too. [Shawn begins to leave.]

D: We were glad to have met you, Shawn. You want the caps [to the pens], too?

S: No. [to Shawn] Just bring them back when you are done with them, darling.

M: Goodbye.

F: So long. [wipes nose with right hand]

S: Now you are dealing with a child who is like a baby in some ways . . . and when he grows up he [Shawn] is going to think he has power.

F: [slowly and thoughtfully nods head, yes. Uses right hand to scratch the right side of his chest.]

S: I have simply used this wonderful physical object. He has been doing this [holds adz and raises sternum] since he could talk.

F: [raises chest and sternum "automatically" as Stephen displays it.]

S: We have a hundred such things as that around the house and office that we have used to raise Shawn.

It should be clear to all of you that Shawn is fascinated with that adz and that he is charmed. He has been aided, by use of it, to fix onto and hold a sense of power. As he grows up spellbound, as we all do, in various ways, he will realize more and more ways in which he has power.

Of course, this family is having many ideas about how this applies to each of them and to their communication and to their son. In the session on this video, Shawn held them spellbound. They were enchanted with this matter and they did not soon forget it. Each of them learned a lot of things from that session which were seeds for future sessions. In the same way Shawn's learning about the adz has been a seed and will be the foundation for future learnings. There is much to be drawn from even this brief glimpse of our family therapy but, for now, let's stay on the theme on which we began.

Many of you know that Erickson gave us access to tools from the oral tradition with a variety that no other clinician has done. He provided us with an understanding of the use of paradox, suggestions, binds, oxymoron, interspersal, confusion, and so on. But these are all techniques; these are all mechanical. There is something else that he provided that we must insist be remembered. Erickson gave us a nontangible quality we call enchantment. Enchantment is a quality of delivery, like fascination, that has a relationship to his techniques as empathy does to reflective feedback, and has as much to do with therapy as other terms like listening with a third ear, understanding, genuineness, and care. It is a part of Erickson's work that is not easily taught and may be as elusive as an attitude toward clients and problems. However, it's every bit as crucial to the therapeutic formula and needs to be placed in the list of Ericksonian Techniques lest it be forgotten.

I visited Dr. Erickson every three months for five-day periods for almost five years. But I did not return to study with Erickson again and again because I expected to be understanding or teaching his material, but rather because I was undergoing a pleasant spell. I was charmed; my interest was piqued. I was fascinated and enchanted. We want to resurrect these terms: charm, fascination, spell, and enchantment and keep them alive and well alongside empathy and genuineness. Every one of them is crucial and essential to this approach to therapy. We will focus on tools and on the treatment throughout this workshop, but please remember to keep vital this elusive and subtle aspect of interview management, treatment delivery, and human nature.

Most of you have some familiarity with Dr. Milton Erickson and his work. But there may be some of you who are being introduced to him for the very first time today. He was credited with the use of voice tone shifts that he employed in order to make a particular point and gain the attention of the unconscious for further learning. I hope that those of you who are able will listen to our voice tone shifts at various times throughout the workshop (represented in italics in this transcript). It is by employing what we learned from Dr. Erickson that we are more capable of teaching his complex approach as we understand it. He was a man who had very strong convictions that the people you meet *have enormous creativity.* You have a conscious and an unconscious mind and can be expected to *know more than you think you know.* Much of what you learn is learned unconsciously. You can *learn much of importance* without really being able to *recognize it when it is happening.* In this workshop *you will,* for example, as anyone would, possess the ability to *learn at a number of levels at once.* Owing to this multilevel operation of consciousness, you can *really expect* to continue to reflect upon a learning long after it has occurred, and with each reflection *gain still further learnings.* We will present, in the next five days, lectures, learning exercises, case material, videotaped cases, and so forth. It is our goal to provide, *in the context of family therapy,* the very thing that gained your attention and appreciation in our previous books. That is, this will be a systematic and programmed sequence of learnings. We will begin at the beginning, going through the diagnostic steps and the interventions one at a time. We will put them together into more and more complex combinations and finally we will present them in their totality in individual and family cases.

Erickson is credited with helping fuel and stimulate the family therapy investigations of the Palo Alto group of communication researchers that included Bateson, Haley, Watzlawick, Fisch, Weakland, and others in the 1950s. Family therapists have learned a great deal from these pioneers and much of what we take for granted came from the influence they had on the field. Understandably, in the last few years increasing attention has been given to Erickson's original ideas and he has been recognized as a prime mover and origin for many attitudes and interventions that are essential to us on a daily basis. Being an "active" therapist, giving assignments, using the communications and talents of the clients for motivating therapy, and approaching treatment naturalistically are a few of the attitudinal contributions he introduced when psychoanalysis was *the* accepted way to do therapy. Interventions that have come to fall into the categories of therapeutic binds, utilization, paradoxical directives, indirect suggestions, metaphor, anecdotes, and the clinical use of hypnosis and confusion in therapy have all been linked to Erickson.

That is what I wanted to learn and understand when I (S.L.) first met Dr. Erickson in 1976. I studied with him by traveling to Phoenix and visiting his office-based training sessions for five-day periods every three months. Airfares were cheaper then and my folks lived within driving distance. So I would stay with them and borrow their car. Each year the agency I worked for paid my way one time, my parents paid one time, and I paid the rest. I always would *have the feeling* that I learned a good deal and I would always *notice an improvement in therapeutic work* that I did after I left. In a few months I would want to return for more of that unusual learning. I didn't fully appreciate what I was getting at the time. But, within a few days after the training or therapy, I would *always* find that I was thinking and saying things learned in Erickson's office and repeatedly came to accept that *a new meaning will come* from what I think or thought I gained. This is, as you might suspect, still happening, *even this week . . . even today!* This is true for me and for my experience. I'd like to impart some of my understandings and experiences to you and help you better appreciate them.

I really never intended to be here or anywhere talking to people about

Dr. Erickson's work, although it's reasonable that I would be because I have some kind of a talent for absorbing other peoples' behavior and recreating it. And what I would do is I would leave his office and then not really understand at first what had been the important elements of what he had done and if anything therapeutic happened. For example, a woman came in from Tokyo one day, and she was there for therapy. But before he sent us all away, he asked her if she had ever been hypnotized. She had and said, when asked, that she could not speak or do anything in trance—unless, she wondered, she might be able to *do automatic writing.* Automatic writing is that ability to make written notes or sketches or references when you don't pay conscious attention to that part of your experience. *You are paying attention elsewhere.*

Maybe I should take you back for a moment. He was born in 1901 in a log cabin with a dirt floor, no running water, and no indoor plumbing. He lived on a farm and was really a rugged pioneer type, as were his parents. He attributed most of what he had acquired to his parents' way of life. They were practical, hard-working, and respectable folks. *You have to be practical and hard-working* in Wisconsin. His father, Albert, was also kind of enigmatic. When he proposed to Erickson's mother, Clara, she wanted to think about it. And Albert caught her underneath a tree a couple of days later and said, "You know, when I proposed to you I didn't ask you to make a *single* decision." And she accepted at that point, totally confused.

So, there were those kinds of stories. When Erickson was four years old, according to Lance Erickson's wife Cookie, he was carrying out two buckets to fetch water. And his mother said, "You can't carry two buckets full of water, you're too little." And he stomped his foot down and said, "I *will* carry two buckets of water." He was a willful young man, even prior to 1917 when he first got polio. And the reason I'm telling you that angle of it is that some contend that Erickson's hard work was a reaction to the polio. I think that is true but I don't think that's the whole story because he was clearly a strong and willful young man prior to 17.

Erickson was a strapping young man. There were some photos of him at this age. And when polio came, of course, there were no vaccines. He overheard the doctor say to his mother that her son wouldn't live to see another sunrise. He said he would "be damned" if that was going to be true. That was a terrible thing for a doctor to say to a mother. So he had people, without telling them why, move the dresser and keep the door open and keep the drapes at the end of the hallway open, so he could lie in bed and watch the sunrise. And he stayed up all night and he proved the doctors wrong.

And in a way, he has been proving the doctors wrong the rest of his life, in one way or another. So he turned conventional psychology upside down,

I think by bringing his strong-mindedness and his desire to do it his way, because he wasn't sure anybody else's way was going to be right for *him*.

And also there was a part of him that was the practicality and trickiness that he learned on the farm. You probably know the story that he developed double binds by bringing the cow into the barn pulling on its tail, since the cow wanted to resist. And he had a bet with his father. His father was pulling on the head. That is some brief early background of the man.

In 1947 Erickson had another bout with polio which left him in a wheelchair for most of the years after 1947. And speaking of proving the doctors wrong, he tells another story, when at 47 he was told he would have only another six months to live. And when they called him in late 1947 and said, "Dr. Erickson, you are living on borrowed time," he responded, "I can't think of a better time to live on."

He proved them wrong about the pain, as well as his interventions, which were quite different from the ones that prevailed. In that day, of course, there was a strong Freudian orientation and Freud's version of hypnosis was the only widely accepted one. Erickson was fascinated with hypnosis because he used it even before his polio happened, but was especially interested after it happened. He used hypnosis to control his experience of pain. So he was already playing and experimenting with hypnosis in ways he probably shouldn't have, prior to medical school and all through medical school, talking to and demonstrating for his instructors while studying with them. He started The American Society of Clinical Hypnosis, in 1958. In 1957, an American Medical Association journal was dedicated to the medical use of hypnosis. That was when hypnosis "came out of the closet" from a blow (or several) that it suffered earlier, the most severe of which was in 1896 when Freud published the studies on hysteria and illustrated some good reasons why *hypnosis was a terrible thing for people to use.*

Did our volume just drop? That was a very inconvenient place for the volume to drop on the words, "Hypnosis is a terrible thing to use." I have been selecting portions of my introduction to deliver with a lower volume and lower tone. I've been doing it purposefully to aid in the learning process. When the volume changes or the tone changes, the material that is delivered right then tends to be remembered by the unconscious for the sake of searching out the added meaning of the change in delivery. We'll talk about that later, but for now I should correct the inadvertent mistake by shifting my voice on this, *"Hypnosis is a wonderful tool to use."*

I'll tell you later why Freud didn't like hypnosis. He did it differently than Erickson did—by 100 years, for one thing. And he didn't have Freud's work to draw upon and reflect upon as Erickson did and as we do now. Erickson's approach to therapy was really different from almost everyone else's and it started with hypnosis. As family therapists you might not have been interested in hypnosis particularly, but you will be interested to know that Pavlov studied and used hypnosis, as did Freud, B. F. Skinner, Carl Rogers, Eric Berne, and Fritz Perls. So many who have developed their own approach to therapy used some version of hypnosis as a springboard. Most of the versions they used were similar—all conventional—and the overall point that we're making is that Erickson's attitudes and approaches to problems were quite different from the conventional.

So it's not really a digression to say this. Most of Erickson's well-known work was with hypnosis, but his family therapy and psychotherapy work was derived from his work with hypnosis. There's an exact correlation if you frame it the right way. Furthermore, the use of therapeutic trance in family therapy is a superb complement to family therapy. So let's start with what hypnosis shouldn't have been and I think it will help you better understand Erickson's novel approach to everything else.

In 1889, Freud went to study hypnosis with Bernheim and Liébault in Nancy, France. They were doing something called Suggestive Therapeutics. In short, it had to do with progressive relaxation and then speaking to the relaxed person with direct suggestions aimed at removal of symptoms. This is conventional hypnosis. Conventional or classical hypnosis is typified by direct suggestion and progressive relaxation. I say "direct suggestion." That means suggestions like, "Sit down, close your eyes" or "Your fever will go away." Those are direct suggestions. Those suggestions were aimed at removal of a symptom. And, of course, in 1896 Freud published the hysteria papers, and therein said that something was wrong with the hypnotic approach, that the symptoms would come back because this kind of hypnosis doesn't deal with the root of the problem.

Somehow it suppresses the problem. And that is exactly right. For some people, the problem will go away. Some people who are compliant enough will react favorably to this approach. Some will rebel against it. And it won't have any effect upon some people. And Freud found that in five cases. And that makes a good deal of sense. So hypnosis took a blow. It was supposedly not a good thing to do with families or the individual clients who comprise them.

In addition to that difficulty, there was Mesmer who was declared a fraud by the French academy. Remember American history when the East India company was formed? Benjamin Franklin had his fingers in all these things. Benjamin Franklin went to Europe to investigate Mesmer and find out whether or not Mesmer was "on to something" important with his animal magnetism theory. Franklin took two others on that investigation. One was Anton Guillottin, a doctor who had a unique surgical method for headaches that was named after him. The other was Lavasier, who was a French chemist. They decided that Mesmer was a fraud, that he wasn't being at all scientific in his approach. So hypnosis, because it was associated with Mesmer, suffered another bad blow.

Hypnosis was named after Hypnos who was the brother of Thanatos, God of death, and that's not good! So there were at least three blows: Freud's denouncement, the name suggesting sleep and oblivion, and Mesmer's fraudulent activities.

Hypnosis was brought into the United States by a man named Phineas Quimby, who brought a version of Mesmerism to Portland, Maine, and associated it with spiritualism of some kind. And that was not very popular with the growing scientific mentality. So, all in all, with Freud, Mesmer, Quimby, and Hypnos, hypnosis was not considered with much respect.

This did change. By 1957, the issue of the AMA journal we mentioned was dedicated to the study of hypnosis and in 1958 Erickson started the American Society of Clinical Hypnosis. He also wrote the entries on hypnosis for *Collier's Encyclopedia* from 1952 to 1962 and, in addition to other topics, the *Encyclopedia Britannica* entries on hypnotism and hypnosis from 1954 to 1973.

We said that Erickson's approach represented a significant departure from conventional hypnosis. For one thing, he would not necessarily require of people that they relax. Perhaps you know the case of the guy pacing the floor who said he wasn't a pyschotherapy client because he couldn't sit down and be still. He compulsively paced the floor. That was, in fact, his problem. And that kept him unavailable for psychotherapy. You probably know this case if you've heard about Erickson's paradoxical interventions. What did he say? What do you guess? Don't say if you *really* know. I want to hear your guesses. Does anybody really know what he said?

I'll paraphrase to the best of my recollection. This fellow says, "Here I am, I can't sit down. All I can do is pace back and forth, and that's my problem. I get so worried and so nervous. It's at times like this that I need therapy. But I can't sit down. No one is willing to work with me, of course, so they sent me to you. But I suppose it is hopeless."

Okay, now your guesses are getting closer. First of all, you think of some way of phrasing the paradox so it is acceptable to the person: "Keep pacing." That's not quite good enough, by the way, because that doesn't give you any therapeutic leverage. It does presumably prescribe the symptom but that is not enough in therapy. It's like catching the fish and throwing your rod in the water. So you want to add something to increase your therapeutic leverage to make some alteration. In this case it was to modify the direction of the behavior.

Erickson put another thing to it. He gave an interpretation or a reason, which you also ought to add to your paradoxical prescriptions. He said, "I'd like you to cooperate with me, if you are willing, by continuing to pace the floor and do it under my guidance and direction. And now I want you to pace past that red chair, making certain that you don't stop for a moment, and then pause and think, *'How very nice to sit in that chair.'* And just keep walking to the other wall. And when you get there turn around and walk past that chair, without hesitating for a moment to think, *'It would be nice to sit comfortably in that chair.'* " Erickson continued such directives until the fellow was allowed to stand in front of the chair and think about how nice it would have been if he could have sat in the chair. Then later he got to try it out just a tad. And, of course, soon he was sitting in the chair.

So, instead of progressive relaxation being a necessary prerequisite, Erickson would utilize whatever it was that the person was already doing. While the ability to relax is nice, he did not require it as the prerequisite movement into therapy. Instead of progressive relaxation, we have utilization, and instead of direct suggestion, indirection. So you can see, from the cow in the barn, how Erickson could quickly jump to making applications of those understandings to people.

As part of the utilization approach, we would have something like paradoxical intention. That's Victor Frankl's term for it. It is paradoxical symptom prescription, really. And Victor Frankl independently developed a similar technique, called paradoxical intention. So did John Rosen. Another thing that we could include with utilization is confusion. It is another natural phenomenon that can be utilized if you frequently call upon your doubts.

Now, maybe I should finish my story of the woman from Tokyo which includes an example of confusion. And another aspect of utilization that this story contains involves the use of trance phenomena. The term "trance phenomena" may be a little unfortunate because it obscures the frequently occurring, natural, everyday nature of these "life phenomena." Well, the woman came from Tokyo. Remember her? Erickson says, "Have you been in trance before?" And she says, yes, she's been hypnotized. He asks "What can you do in trance?" She then went on to report that she had a doctor in Tokyo hypnotize her and that he told her she was a deep trance subject. "So maybe I can do automatic writing. I remember Dr. Baker said that." Erickson asked, "Have you ever done automatic writing?" She said "No." "Can you do anything else in trance? Can you talk in trance?" She shook her head.

Erickson continued, "All right, close your eyes and I want you to realize that your left hand is going up to your face gradually. (Eventually her reticular activating system figured out what she was to do and the arm moved upward.) And when it does it will reach your face, so your right hand can move to your face and your left hand falls to your lap at the same speed that your right hand raises." And the other hand raised up to the face. Then he handed her an ink pen and told her to draw something from her unconscious on a sheet of paper.

And she did draw something, after which Erickson said, "Now your right hand will fall to your lap at the same speed that your left hand raises to your face. And when it does, you can open your eyes." And he shoved a piece of paper in front of her and said, "I wonder what this is." The woman looked at it in kind of a daze, from the surprise of the moment and being in trance rapidly and coming back out rapidly.

She said, "That is a mountain and a rainbow." So Erickson was playing on a little bit of doubt. He said, "Can you talk in trance?" She said, "No." He said, "I want you to close your eyes, and I want you to find that your left hand will raise up to your face . . . and when it does (and he waited for the hand to raise) your left hand will fall to your lap at the same speed that your right hand raises to your face. And when it does you'll sing aloud in Japanese." So she gets her hand to her face, at this point. There are about five or six of us in the room and she is singing in Japanese. Erickson said, "Loudly." And she sings louder. And now, "Your right hand will fall to your lap, your left hand raises to your face . . . and when it does it will come down, and you can open your eyes." And he put the piece of paper in front of her again and said, "Tell me what this is." And she said in a daze again, "This is a mountain." He asked, "What is this?" She replied, "A rainbow." Erickson said, "How many times have you been hypnotized?" The woman responded, "You mean here?" And he said, "Yes." She said, "One." "Are you sure?" asked Erickson. While she was in some doubt, he continued, "Can you talk in trance?" She said, "No." Then he asked if she could sing in trance. Now what happened then was brief but certainly was another interesting behavior to have noticed: She put her right hand on her cheek (unconsciously) and said, "Maybe."

Now here we have the use of confusion to create amnesia. And we have the use of naturally occurring trance phenomena, such as catalepsy, that people have all of the time and just aren't aware of. We also have amnesia all of the time—not constantly, but frequently. Throughout the day you can have amnesia, as you know, when you try to find your car keys or your socks or something that you put down carefully while you were on the phone, and cannot find again. So this was a simple example of using those kinds of things which people take for granted and don't use in therapy too frequently, because they seem too easy.

Well, that may not be a profound enough example, but let's list some of the other interventions involving indirection. We have indirect suggestion, itself. Metaphor is another one, not the version of metaphor that the dictionary has in mind—not a comparison in using like or as—but rather a story with a dramatic element. It is not a story that is boring. It is a story that captures attention, although Erickson would bore people on purpose sometimes, and he knew that he did, as one of his techniques. He would call anything a technique if it worked. Somebody asked him how he hypnotized folks. He said, "Well, I learned a new way for each individual. Sometimes I use the waiting technique, and I wait . . . for them to go into trance."

Anecdotes belong in this list of indirection techniques. We're just telling you these words which seem similar to you because we use them in sort of a special way. An anecdote is a little slice of life that illustrates something, as if you were to say, "That's like catching a fish and letting go of the line." You could think of that as analogous, therefore allegorical, to the point I wanted to make. We would call that an anecdote since there wasn't a story or a dramatic touch to it. It is even a little short for an anecdote. Usually an anecdote goes on for a few moments.

If I wanted to indirectly encourage amnesia in this essentially natural way, and these techniques are very natural sounding things, then . . . I'll give an example. First, I'm thinking of the rationale for you to use amnesia in family therapy since we are talking about family therapy instead of hypnosis. I can think of some but they all sound more like hypnosis than family therapy because amnesia sounds like hypnosis. If you had a situation where somebody had an affair and the other spouse is not going to let bygones be bygones, that might be a good time to therapeutically use some amnesia. Or if one spouse had an anxiety attack in 1957 and he is not going to go out any more because he keeps remembering the anxiety attack, that would be another useful moment. Or let's say they had terrible quarrels for a couple of years over money and now what you'd like to do is help them focus their attention elsewhere and have amnesia for those events. A little bit of help in forgetting the pathways that bring those events to mind would be real handy.

We had a couple who traveled from Australia. The wife wanted to have an orgasm and the husband had had an affair twenty-nine thousand years ago. She was going to be damned before she was going to forget this. It really made her mad and it still makes her mad. And she was going to squeeze out every little drop of blood she could get. Anyway, she did not seem like a nice person and it was a long way to come for therapy. So one of the things we would want to do is help her have amnesia. Now you could say, "Why don't you try forgetting about it, putting it out of your mind?" That would only alert her to its presence. It would be the best way to make sure she wasn't going to forget it. So you can't simply or directly say, let's put it out of your memory. You need to somehow say it with indirection and with anecdotes about how people forget. It might sound like this:

All of you have been in situations where you've been in a grocery store and you just know there is something you want there and your unconscious is holding onto it. And you know you know it but you can't get to it. And it's a learning of some kind that can be applied in other ways. And let me tell you another example of the same thing. I was at a party the other day and I shook hands with four people who I met at the door and for the life of me, I didn't recognize two of them later when they came up to me. And the other two, I wanted to say their names, but there was something about it. And everyone has had this experience and sooner or later everyone learns that this is an experience that you can use in a directed way in your life. Perhaps you don't know what I mean. So, let me give you another example. . . .

Now I'm not even using the word forgetting. I'm simply calling to mind anecdotal experiences we've all had that have to do with losing some material from consciousness. And that is not the therapy but that kind of attitude creates the therapy in an ongoing way. You are helping people in a natural way remember their own experiences, indirectly suggesting that they have them. You're not eliciting compliance or rebellion with direct suggestion.

There is another interesting category of technique and I'm not sure if we should put this under utilization or indirection. Maybe we should have another slot and put in a category called strategic homework. There are different kinds of homework assignments that Erickson gave. You know some of them. Let me take the one that you probably do know for starters and this one involves developing some skill. That is the homework where you say, "You and your husband really need to just talk to each other more, I think, so at dinner time I want you to put everything down and sit at the table with nothing more than a glass of water each and drink it slowly. Whoever drinks his or her glass first has to get it refilled. And then you have to sit there and go through it again." So, if you want to get out of this assignment, you have to gulp down two glasses of water.

The assignment continues: "The goal here will be to talk about anything you want to and drink your water. And terminate the activity *when and if* you both finish your water at the same time." All right, so they will do it. Now they won't finish their water at the same time. But they'll sit there at the table and they'll talk a little bit. And it's skill development. It is not very subtle though, because they are engaging in a practice they are supposed to be learning. In fact, it is going to alert them to their uncomfortableness. So, don't do that. That's the kind of task I thought I learned when I learned homework tasks a long time ago. Then I met Erickson.

He might instead take somebody to go to the restaurant. There is a case story that you might have read. He took a young man who had a phobia of buildings.[1] He said to the guy, "Everyone's afraid of certain people—men you'll be intimidated by and afraid of, and women you'll be intimidated by and afraid of sometimes, as we all are. And by the way, which of these categories of women would be the most anxiety-producing for you to be around?" Then he named "a mother with a baby nursing, a divorced woman who is physically attractive, an 80-year-old woman who is being helped across the street," and he named a total of 12 categories of stereotypes.

Of course, the one that this guy was most threatened by was the divorced attractive woman. Anyway, Erickson then arranged a date. "Now you will pick us up tomorrow at eight o'clock. My wife and I and your escort will be here at eight o'clock and we will go out to dinner." They went to the Loud Rooster, I think it was called, in Phoenix, so it gives you an idea what they had in store for them. And, of course, Erickson had a friend who was attractive, divorced, and female. So there they were together. This fellow had to drive. Now he's being thrust into the position of being in control; Erickson is sort of doing it—but he's in the back seat. This guy is the one who is taking the couple out for dinner. And they go to the Loud Rooster, and Erickson has prearranged it.

The waitress is in on it too. Every time this man makes an order, "Would you like water with dinner?" "Yes sir, tall glass or a small glass?" "Uh, a small glass." "Ice or no ice?" "Uh, ice." "One or two cubes?" So everything he says he has to go through a checklist of all the jillions of possibilities. And if he just wanted a steak, "All right would you like an eight ounce or a ten ounce?" The categories of different ways of being cooked, mushrooms or not. So this was a terrible ordeal for this man all night long.

When he got through his dinner, the man made the mistake of telling the waitress that he liked the dinner. She said, "Did you like it very much?" And he said, "Yes." "Did you like it very, very much?" Yes, he did. "Did you like it very, very, very much?" Well, he did. "We have a rule at this restaurant: if you like dinner very, very, very much you have to shake hands with the cook." All right, he'd do that. Now, "Do you want to go through the side door or the back door?" So all evening long, it was that way with this man's homework. Erickson's idea was that if the man could live through that, he could live through anything! Now that's a more interesting version of homework assignment. And it is *still* pretty straightforward.

Another version of the same skill development is that Erickson might ask a person to go to a geriatric facility and speak with a couple of friends of his because "the person who normally visits them is ill. You'd just be the perfect person of all the people I have on my case load to go do that for

---

[1] The discussion of this case can be found in Haley, J. (1973). *Uncommon therapy: The psychiatric techniques of Milton H. Erickson, M.D.* (pp. 65-68). New York: Norton.

me. I couldn't ask anybody else, but I know you value these kinds of things and I know you will probably help me out. You have time on your hands."

And so now this client is making small talk with somebody in a non-threatening situation. Learning to make small talk and not be threatened by it is what this shy person needs to do in order to get socially active. But sending him to a discotheque to have small talk would be the wrong maneuver. So here we have a much more interesting version of homework to develop skills. It's where you distract the conscious mind so that the context will, regardless of the fact that it is not the context in which the person needs the skill, build some piece of the skill. This is important: Don't try to get the whole "ball of wax." You need only help family members get *some piece of the needed skills* for their age of development. In order to distract the conscious mind, there are some things that have to happen. There has to be a reason given and it has to appeal to the person's values. It's a good idea sometimes to have other distractions involved, as well. But now what you have is unconscious skills being built and brought into the foreground, while consciously the person is not being threatened. There is no threat to the integrity of this person's self-image, which already says, "I'm a shy person."

I want to give another Erickson example of this technique. Let me paraphrase for you a story of a case named Harold[2] who said he was "a no-good dumb moron and homo." When Erickson told the story, it sounded like he said "homo" as though he had been criticized by his peers. These may have been attributions by his peers but Harold had also done some fellatio on what he called "punks."

Harold lived alone in a shack and had been sleeping in his clothes and bathing in a ditch. So he says that he is a dumb moron and he's never going to be anything else so don't try to change him. Erickson's initial therapeutic engagement with this young man was to agree that Harold was a dumb moron and that he shouldn't try to change him, but would he not agree that therapy could work towards the goal of having him achieve and have all of the happiness in life that he's entitled to, but not a bit more? Harold agreed to that.

During the first session Erickson talked about how a person keeps a tractor clean if he wants it to do good work and get the full value out of it. The next session, this man came back *groomed,* so Erickson had a little feedback on whether or not the use of metaphors would make a difference in behavior. Erickson spent this second session telling the fellow what kind of apartment he was destined to have someday when he lived on his own. Please recall

---

[2] For a discussion of this case see Haley, J. (1973). *Uncommon therapy: The psychiatric techniques of Milton H. Erickson, M.D. (pp. 120-135).* New York: Norton.

that Harold was bathing in a ditch at this point and he had escaped from people. Erickson described what kind of apartment he would have: because Harold had broad shoulders he would have 30-inch doors instead of those 26-inch doors; because he was right-handed his door would open this way instead of the other way; and because he was this tall, the sink would be a certain height. Also he would want to make sure the mirror in the bathroom was a certain length so he could see his whole head in it; and he would want to make sure the windows were a certain height, and so forth.

Erickson was indirectly building up this man's body image and his self-image. Obviously, body image is a part of self-image. But it was his self-image in the sense that he was a person who would have an apartment. Erickson had Harold conceptualize himself that way. It was all linked to the feedbacks of the "finer" qualities of his body. But Harold's going to have to get in shape just a little bit. He's going to do manual labor because he's a moron. Erickson thought Harold had better exercise so he could get good muscle development. When asked to do some jumping jacks, the man "failed" the "jumping jack test." Erickson thought that he did not jump correctly.

Erickson suggested that Harold listen to music in order to get some rhythm, so he would be a better exerciser, so he could be a better manual laborer; after all, he was a moron. So now with listening to music (and listening to music in a special way to make sure he'd do it), Erickson had him take dancing lessons so he could get the movement and rhythm together. And that was his first relationship with a woman that wasn't demeaning. Now you see, he really has a homework assignment to develop a skill of relating to a woman in a way in which he had to adjust his self-image a little bit. Erickson was already working on this in several ways.

But Erickson was not saying, "You *should* feel okay about yourself and you don't need to have this not okay attitude, because you *are* okay. And in fact, part of it is that you think that you and women don't get along well. So, I'm going to help you find a context in which you can get along well with women. How about taking dance lessons?" "Oh, no I couldn't do that" would probably have been the reaction. So the conscious mind was distracted. He's utilizing a person's personality, meeting the family at their own model of the world. Erickson's way of joining the system was with utilization techniques. Now Harold was consciously thinking that he was learning rhythm, so that he could exercise, so that he could do his thing as a manual laborer.

Well, that wasn't going really well enough, Erickson concluded in one of the early sessions. If only he had listened to the music a little closer, Harold might progress faster. So Erickson asked him to take piano lessons, too; that would help him really appreciate the perimeters of the music. He began taking piano lessons as well and did yard work in return for the woman who taught him. Another thing that was creeping up on him was the skill that he was building. He was taking piano lessons so he could dance and taking dancing lessons so he could exercise. He was exercising so he could do manual labor because he was a dumb moron. And he was in his own apartment by then and was performing a valuable service for a woman.

Some time went by—several weeks. And the real acid test was whether he was ready to stop dance lessons and piano lessons. Could he go to the barn dance and pass for normal even though he was really only a dumb moron? Erickson warned him, however, that he didn't belong there because it was a dance for regular people, not for people like him. Yet, it would probably be okay if he paid a little retribution for going. To paraphrase Erickson, he told Harold to notice that against one wall there would be a lot of women who weren't dancing, because of shyness or something. He should dance with, say, six of them, or maybe a half dozen of them. That would pay back his "crashing" their party. And that would be fair.

So, again, Harold was *not* going to the barn dance to realize that he wasn't such a bad guy. That would be a violation of his concept of himself. He went to the barn dance for his skill development, but his conscious mind needed to be distracted. He went to the dance and came back to the next session to report, "I was dancing and I looked against the wall. I saw a bunch of men lined up against the wall. They were too shy to dance. And I realized *I'm not as bad off as I thought I was.*"

Now at that point only, Erickson sat him down and asked him to memorize that experience that he was having. And that's also an indirect suggestion when you think about it. How do you really memorize an experience? You must do a lot of searching to make sense of that directive. Erickson had Harold "think into the future of all the times that you are going to want to use that experience, in various things you'll undertake in the course of your life. Close your eyes. Your conscious mind doesn't need to understand it exactly, but let your unconscious magnify, revivify, and memorize that experience."

Erickson, no doubt, named some things people do in the course of their lives. He didn't recount that part of the case, but knowing how he did things, he used metaphors to elaborate. So I'm sure he told Harold stories. While Harold was thinking about how he could use that sense that he's not so badly off, Erickson no doubt mentioned a few other contexts. At the very least, that is how we'd suggest therapists operate in a case like this. Harold graduated from college eventually. This is a lovely story.

The case of Harold illustrates one kind of homework assignment. A real important part here, to the degree that it's necessary, is making certain that a person engages in the assignment, but that the conscious mind is not threatened. The therapist doesn't need to go to elaborate ends if the family doesn't need it, of course. The case of Harold was very elaborate but Harold had begun by firmly stating that he was a dumb moron and "don't try to change me."

There's another kind of strategic homework. I really like this one. If you hate it, why don't you just pretend. About a year ago now, it finally dawned on us. Let me give you some background. We have several tapes of Erickson's work. On them there are many case stories that he tells *and* they all come out so perfectly. It frustrated me, really, that all these stories of Erickson's came out perfectly. Even the ones that at first glance seem to have ended wrong seem to ultimately end perfectly. I don't mind that he did great . . . I mind that I can't. How did he know? What did he pick up on? He never explained. And it is not fair to write it off that he just knew how to do that.

Let me give an example of part of this. I have a friend from England who had lunch with me. He had been working all day trying to figure out what would be the formula to calculate the volume of the remaining portion of a sphere if you removed a cylinder of any radius from the core of it. That bothered him all day long and I couldn't be of much help. But the real solution came, by the way, when you make the radius one. I remember that much. So simple, too—it should have occurred to me.

So maybe Erickson was just that kind of a person. For him, sitting around working was playing with integral calculus as it applies to human beings. I wasn't satisfied with that explanation, however, because he really was a down-to-earth sort of man. Even David, my English friend, would tell you how he did what he did to solve the problem if you asked him. Erickson would never tell you,—not in such a way that you understood. Let me give some examples.

One man wrote and shared this with us and said it was an example we might want to use in teaching. He saw Erickson one time and Erickson asked, "Would you take your shoes off?" So he took his shoes off. At this point perhaps he was thinking it would be more comfortable. So he took his shoes off and thought, "why not?" Then Erickson asked, "Now would you take your socks off?" So he took his socks off. He was in over his head, now, right? Then Erickson said, "Now wheel my wheelchair up on your foot." So the man . . . you know, the momentum is going in that direction . . . so okay, he wheeled the wheelchair up on his foot. Now after all of this Erickson asked, "Does that hurt." And, the man said, "No—er, not very much." And Erickson said, "It wouldn't hurt *at all* if you didn't do it!"

So let's look at this thing we call "ambiguous function assignments." We need an assignment, and the function, to the family or its members, must be unclear. The part that is distressing to those of us who have studied Erickson is that these assignments come to such a neat conclusion. What bothered me was the question, "How did he know it would come to such a neat conclusion?" And, how come all of them did? You never hear of one that didn't end therapeutically. I can only think of one that didn't turn out as he might have suggested and even that turned out fine in the end. There is some ambiguous function to this exercise and the point that you learn stays with you. The family or selected members learn the point and it stays with them.

It might have just been Erickson "goofing" in the sense of the word that means something like "jesting," or "making fun." After all, he was a fun-loving man. I feel I need to give you examples of these things. What kind of a fun loving guy was he? This example is very subtle. One day when we were in Erickson's office, one of his dogs was barking louder and more persistently than usual. Now, he had an intercom that he would use to speak with Mrs. Erickson for phone calls and so on. Sometimes she would pick up the phone and sometimes it would be him and he'd ask her to take down information from the call or whatever. So on this particular day the dog was barking, barking, barking in the back yard. Also you need to know that Mrs. Erickson had called on her husband or interrupted him six times already that day. In my memory, that was more than usual. And you need to realize that with the quality of the intercoms and his voice, the interactions sounded like *shouting* over the intercom. Now Mrs. Erickson was not bothering him but the dog *was.* And he hit the intercom button and shouted, "Make that darn dog shut up, Betty!" So is this fun loving or what?

That's one example and another is when I called about a wedding ceremony that we had spoken to him about doing for us. He couldn't come to our wedding and we had wanted him there. So we thought maybe we could bring our wedding to him and he could speak. We suspected he would say something profound. He indicated that he would be willing.

One day just before we went to Texas where we would be doing some training, I phoned him. I asked if we could use the opportunity to fly to Phoenix several days later for the promised wedding ceremony and he said, "Yes, I'll see you at 10 a.m. on Thursday." We discussed the time of day. I thought he began teaching by 10 but he said that at that point he was beginning teaching at noon. He said his health was worse but that it would be fine for us to come for this event. I said it would be wonderful and hung up.

Then I realized I was nervous. I always was nervous when I spoke to him. I realized that in my nervousness I forgot to mention our two friends who wanted to accompany us (and who had actually urged us to use this particular trip to call him about the ceremony). They wanted to go with us. So I called him back to ask about bringing the extra people. (There was a limited amount of space in Erickson's office and it was important not to drop in with a crowd.) Mrs. Erickson answered. She tried to talk me out of coming altogether. She really worked to protect his time and energy. I *assured* her that I had received his okay to come and that the question was whether or not to bring the others. She thought there might be too many scheduled students and eventually, she put down the phone to check the appointment book. Now, Erickson had been listening on the other line the entire time. I didn't know that and fortunately I had been very courteous when speaking on this call. When Mrs. Erickson put down the phone, he said, "I bet you're glad the last time you called you got *me* and not *her!*"

I didn't know if I should laugh or not. I was always so shocked at his voice, even on the phone. Well, those are two examples of his humor and a third one follows. It is about Barney, a dog. Barney belonged to a schizophrenic man, Fred. Here is how the story goes.

Fred, upon release from the hospital, was urged by Erickson to get an apartment near his office. This was so he could walk to the office. Now here is an example of one of the assignments I spoke about: Erickson wanted the man not to have to be alone, so he suggested he get a dog. And where do you get a dog for a chronic institutionalized man? As Jeff Zeig says, a home for chronic institutionalized dogs—a dog pound! There you get a chronic institutionalized dog. There the man got Barney. Afterwards, Erickson announced that he could not keep dogs in his apartment but he would be able to leave the dog at Erickson's house. However, Erickson would not be willing to feed and clean up after the dog and so Fred would have to come by daily to do these chores. This is not only clever, but it is aggressive and demonstrates to what extent Erickson was willing to have involvement with his clients. It shows how much he was willing to have responsibility and take risks with family development, too. But that is not the humorous part.

The funny part is that Erickson got a fly swatter and a horn. He taped the horn to his chair and chased Barney around with the fly swatter in his wheelchair. When he caught up with Barney he would swat *at* him and say, "Fred's dog!" And he would honk the horn, terrorizing the dog. Whenever Fred came to the house, the dog was *so glad* to see Fred.

Erickson would write Fred letters signed "your dog Barney." I'll paraphrase as much as possible. "Dear, Fred. Last night that old codger chased me in his wheelchair and scared me, just scared me to death with fear. I was lying at the foot of Kristina's bed. And you know how nuts and crazy, just crazy out of my mind I am, about Kristina. (Here we see Erickson using the client's own words: "nuts," "crazy," "out of my mind," "fear," "scared to death" and so forth.) And then before I knew it there was that old codger with his fly swatter and I had to tuck my tail between my legs so hard that it was 20 minutes later before I could untuck it." He wrote about being chased through the house, the absence of the lady of the house, being scared, frightened out of his mind, bizarre, and so on, until he finally fell out of the kitchen door just before that old codger caught up with him. He would conclude the letters with some mention about how glad he would be to see Fred, who would give him some safety from the old codger. And, he would sign them "From your dog, Barney." Fred would get these letters almost daily from Barney.

When Fred visited, Erickson would sit on a couch and break a dog biscuit with pliers, since he was partially paralyzed, giving half of it to Fred. Fred, in turn, passed it on to feed Barney. He was teaching Fred to be in a different role than victim. He was attributing all the crazy thoughts to Barney and teaching Fred to nurture via indirect means. This was very strategic. And, here you see another example of his humor.

Now we want to talk about these assignments in more detail so that they will be something you can recreate. When we do, there will be more examples. For the time being you have two or three examples. Now, how did it happen to turn out so great for Harold that he went to the barn dance and so on? It turned out so well in every one of these stories. How about the depressed woman who Erickson gave roses to and told her to drive in her car until she saw a woman grappling with several children she couldn't handle. She was to find this overwhelmed, haggard woman walking on the street and then give her the flowers with some believeable reason such as, "I have to drive to Tucson and these will wilt in the car. Won't you please help out and take these flowers off my hands?" Now why would Erickson have her do this? She had no idea. The purpose was totally ambiguous to her. But what if she didn't do it? It turned out that she did it. But what if she didn't? What if the man didn't put the wheelchair on his foot? I'm sure they would have been great stories anyway. They would just have had different endings!

We finally figured out the components we think go into the successful outcome of Erickson's assignments and the effect of the intervention. The effect or the purpose is different from customary interventions in that you don't teach the family a skill. Because, you see, the family doesn't know how it will turn out and *neither does the therapist!* Erickson couldn't have known in every case. There must be some way of assigning a task other than that which we usually expect. We tried to get a better name, but "ambiguous function" was the best we could come up with for now. The assignment is quite specific but the function is ambiguous and unstated.

For the sake of clarification, we are supposed to be examining Erickson's approach and rationale for indirection, metaphor and anecdote with families. I think we have just about satisfied that. Are there any questions? What happened with the woman and the flowers? Oh, she handed them to a stranger and the stranger *beamed* at her with a huge smile. Obviously, Erickson hoped she would learn that she could get a smile from somebody.

We gave a similar assignment recently to a husband who came from Michigan to be a client in our advanced demonstration workshop. People who had been with us long enough to know our jargon were the participants and we saw clients on closed circuit T.V. that was broadcast live from the suite down the hall. One of the men was this very depressed husband. He said that he had no feelings and felt like he was behind an "invisible shield." He couldn't feel the world. (I'm sure there is more to say about this case.) We had to work with the roles he and his wife played in his family, but only he was present. He was so emotionally remote from his wife that he hadn't even told her why he was making this trip to Florida. They were in a "marriage of convenience" but it didn't sound very convenient to us. He actively rejected any affectionate overtures his wife made because he didn't want to get too close to her. He didn't think he was in love with her and didn't think he wanted to be. He didn't share his feelings with anyone or rely on anyone for support, even though he was a psychologist himself and might have been expected to endorse that value.

The assignment we gave him at the end of the first session was that very assignment with the roses. We bought the flowers. Carol presented him with a dozen roses and the instruction that he was to give them away, one at a time, to whomever he selected, as long as at least three of them were given to men. Carol suggested some places he might go and told him to say to the person as he gave each rose, "I'm not feeling too good myself but I hope this brightens your day."

Well, the man felt very unpleasant when he left the session. It was, in fact, fortunate for the therapy that he did feel so badly after the first session. He made a detailed report of everyone he gave flowers to and what they said and did, but he wouldn't tell them that he felt badly. However what he had done can easily be seen from a behavioral viewpoint. Three times he interrupted the task and went back to his bedroom to sulk on his bed because he didn't want to do it. But he knew we had paid for the flowers and he owed it to us to do the homework. Also, he was in Gulf Breeze to learn something. So each time he would go back out and continue with the assignment. Everyone responded to him as the woman had responded in the Erickson story. They all told him that he had "made my day" by giving out the rose.

So here is a man who is being forced to make social contact and share something. Although he is feeling badly, he is interacting and he is getting positive social consequences. So, this is an elaborate behavior modification scheme to change the reinforcement contingencies on his behavior when he is feeling rotten, at the very least! If he had gone a step further and told each person that he felt badly, it would have been even better. However, it doesn't altogether matter, since he was feeling it and he was obsessed about saying it and was thinking those words. And while recognizing those feelings and obsessing about sharing them, he was getting the reinforcement contingencies changed radically.

Without our prompting, he sent two of the roses home, one to his wife and one to his daughter. Consciously, he didn't know why. He had been making no sexual, tender, or romantic overtures towards her and had been rebuffing hers. Now remember this case because when we come to am-·biguous function assignments with families I'm going to want to show you several aspects of this example, elaborate, and show you in detail how we use ambiguous function assignments.

So far we have been relating stories about and covering Erickson's attitudes toward problems, use of history and use of family, and short-and long-term treatment decisions. Now we need to discuss his rationale for the selection of family members who would and should attend the session. And, you're not going to like this because my answer is kind of simple. On second thought, you may like it. I like it because this always has been the way therapy worked for me. I think his decision on how much of the family to get in the office came down to this most of the time: *What is practical and possible?*

Erickson was from the farm. If you need wood you chop it. If you can't get the horse in the barn, even by pulling on his tail in the opposite direction, I guess you leave him out. So practicality made Erickson's decision for him most of the time on who from the family he could get to a session. If it was practical and possible and efficient, he wanted the folks there who were involved. He frequently saw couples, and the couple with the child or children who had the presenting problem. But he would also often see only individuals and still do family therapy. I can illustrate that for you, I believe, to your satisfaction.

He wouldn't force the whole family to come in if there was a huge resistance against doing it, usually because that would be contrary to his first tenet which was to join the family in a way that was acceptable to them. There is one little twist in that. He would join the family in a way that was acceptable to them but he would not play the role that they had intended for him to play. I think that added feature is a very important second tenet if you want to succeed, even with individuals, but it is crucial if you want to succeed with families.

Family members create a dual, triple, or quadruple induction on the therapist. They may, for example, have Dad saying, "It is Johnny's fault," Mom saying, "Yes, it is that Johnny's fault," and little sister saying, "It's not my fault, it *must* be Johnny's fault!" Your attention is being directed by three hypnotists towards Johnny. So, it is much more important in family therapy not to accept the role that is given. This idea will get more emphasis later, but for now, I want to underscore that you need to hold an attitude that allows you to create a balance. On one hand it allows for a role that is acceptable to the controlling members of the family but is not the pre-scribed role that reinforces the self-imposed limits they have created on one another. Some of the real devices to keep you from that dilemma are re-framing and relabeling, paradox, and therapeutic leverage.

As for Erickson's short-and long-term therapy, how might you go about making a decision about the question of duration? Let's say that we have three categories of Erickson's work: short-, *very* short-, and long-term ther-apy. There are many examples of each and sometimes I suspect that some overgeneralizations are made about Erickson's work by people who are familiar with only a handful of cases of one type or another. In fact, there was a conference of a prestigious hypnosis organization a short time back and one of the speakers actually said, in response to a question about his views on Erickson's work (and of course I have to paraphrase) that unlike Erickson *he* preferred to get his clients cured and out of his office; but Erickson would call families up and urge them to return for years. He went on to imply that Erickson had some difficulty letting his clients terminate. Perhaps he was speaking of a different Erickson! This allegation does not fit the facts that are published and it does not jive with the philosophy of the man I knew.

I will give an example of *very* short therapy.[3] An alcoholic with no other family came to the office with his war memorabilia in a scrapbook and Erickson tossed the scrapbook into a waste basket. He said, in effect, "That is what I think of your reliance upon the war memories." Now before I tell you this next part, you need to know that Erickson investigated the method used by this man to get intoxicated. The man would drink a beer with a whiskey chaser and repeat the process one drink at a time. So Erickson told

[3] Erickson, M. Personal communication, August 17, 1977.

him the next time he went to the bar to buy three whiskeys and three beers at once and line them up on the bar. When he drank down the first one he was to say, "Here's to that damn Dr. Erickson, may he drown in his own spit . . . ," or words to that effect. Erickson led him through what he was to say with each of the drinks. These were a string of angry and hostile remarks that he was to associate to Erickson for having tossed out the scrapbook. That was the end of the therapy. The man left the office. But he came back sober three months later and thanked Erickson for doing it.

Now that is very short therapy, and Erickson had some reasons to believe that it would work and that it was the most practical. Disrupting the symptom will usually cause its demise. The more a symptom has a firm pattern to it, the more the entire behavioral pattern will "fall apart" when you get the family to change just one component in the sequence of events that leads to it.

You could make a mechanical analogy about this. If your automobile has a bad brake lining, you *can* still drive it; if your power steering fails or your brake lining is almost gone or several spark plugs are disconnected, you *can* still drive it. It's just more difficult. The mechanical functioning on an automobile is not as "tight" as it is on a microcomputer. In the computer operating system, or mother board if you have one, if little resisters or diode fuses go bad on the circuit board or a bad ground connection on the memory board, etc., you won't be able to use the computer. One byte out of place—one tiny byte—16 bits of binary information that occupy the width of about 26 electrons, I believe it is, on a floppy disk that contains your operating system, and the system is kaput. Now that is a firmly patterned operational machine and it all has to work very quickly in the right order. It is much tighter than an automobile.

The same is true for patterns with people. When there exists a firm pattern that can be disrupted, and the family members are not candidates for therapy, then brief contact may be indicated and perhaps only with the available member(s). Rather than lose the whole war trying to recruit that kind of "family" into therapy, Erickson *would do* what was practical. Now the difference between that very short therapy and short-term therapy is that in short-term therapy both of these factors apply, but there is one other: the family members are more willing to come to therapy. And what can be done with more family contact is that more resources can be retrieved.

I don't know if you understand this use of the term retrieve, yet. Here's an example. We can talk about courage for an afternoon and we can talk about tenderness for an afternoon. How about the case of the wife who had a ringing in her ear and the husband who had phantom limb pain. Their session is discussed in, and is also available on a tape that accompanies,

Erickson and Rossi's *Hypnotherapy: An Exploratory Casebook.*[4] Erickson has only seen the husband before and only once previously and the couple is willing to sit in Erickson's office and take the therapy that is given and be recorded for publication. Erickson responds to their request for relief from their symptoms by saying "All right. Now I am going to give you a story so that you can understand better." He proceeds with a story about when, as a youth in premedical school, he passed by a factory with pneumatic hammers—12 pneumatic hammers banging away. He went into the factory and the people there were moving their lips and talking but he couldn't hear what they were saying. So he went to the foreman and received permission to sleep on the floor that night for an experiment, because he was "interested in the process of learning." The 12 pneumatic hammers banged through the night and he did get some sleep. The next morning when he awakened he could hear the workmen talking, as he put it, about that "damn fool kid." "What in hell was he sleeping on the floor there for? What does he think he can learn?" Erickson's ears had made an adjustment. And the listeners to this story can understand that consciously and can retrieve the similar *experience* from their own lives and do *that* unconsciously.

Erickson also tells of his three-month canoe trip down the Mississippi river. He had taken this trip to rehabilitate himself after a polio attack, by the way! He said that he felt his ribs "fighting with canoe ribs" all day, and at night he was happy to sleep on nice firm *ground.* He longed for the comfort of the *ground.* Then someone invited him into a home and it was difficult for him to adjust. He said, "Everywhere you look, your looks come to an end." He was used to looking into the wide open spaces. His eyes had to adjust. And he was offered a bed, but he longed for the comfort of the ground.

Now you don't really know what he is talking about here. But I guarantee that as a listener you are encouraged to do a lot of thinking. This is indirection with metaphor. You are doing a lot of, "What's he talking about?" What he *is* talking about is how people can adjust their sensory perceptions and their preference for how they experience things. He continued to elucidate how people living on a farm don't notice the smells of the farm but once they leave and then return, then they notice the smells, and then they go away. When sufficient resources are retrieved and arranged, and there are some psychodynamic learnings as well, the problems are resolved.

To return to the couple mentioned earlier (the wife who had ringing in her ear and the husband who had phantom limb pain)—since this couple

---

[4] Erickson, M.H., and Rossi, E. *Hypnotherapy: An exploratory casebook.* New York: Irvington, 1979.

was willing to be in therapy, he could do short therapy with them. His short therapy included a disruption of the symptom, as in this case where he was teaching her how to tune her ears to not hear the ringing. *But* the process worked by retrieving resources. Erickson did not just disrupt the symptoms with this couple. In brief therapy, by using anecdote, indirect suggestion, metaphor, and homework, we can help families retrieve resources they need.

With this couple, regardless of whether the therapy is defined as short or brief, Erickson helped in several ways. As a result of the resources retrieved, the roles changed. The woman stopped infantilizing her husband; the man didn't have to have a symptom to have something over which his wife could not exert control; she learned to tune out and not have a ringing in her ears, and he learned to notice pleasure and not pain in that phantom leg. In order to be very effective, we need to be able to see families or individuals long enough to retrieve resources or else we need to see families who have a tenacious symptomatic pattern that can be disrupted. Fortunately, most people who refuse to come into therapy *do* that because of the rigidity of the family and therefore *do have* very redundant sequences of behavior leading to a display of the symptoms.

There was one case where Erickson seemed to make a mistake. And it illuminates this previous point. This turned out all right but was failure if judged by Erickson's failure to successfully join. The family came in wanting *him* to talk their daughter into getting an abortion. He would not do that kind of thing, of course. He angered them and they left after half an hour of quarreling. As they went out of the door, Erickson, in desperation, added the final word, and I'll paraphrase again: "I'll tell you one thing you won't have to do if you get an abortion!" Since this was an inimical challenge, the family stopped to answer it with a defiant, "What's that?" Erickson continued, "You won't have to think of a name for that baby!"

The story ends two weeks later when the family came back and apologized profusely for being rude and awful. On the way home they began thinking about what they would name a baby, and then actual names came to mind and that led to thinking about what a baby might be like, and that led to other thoughts, and so forth. So we see a double learning here. Erickson disrupted the symptomatic pattern, that is, the firm redundant argument, by telling them what they didn't have to do. This, we see in retrospect, was taken up by them because they were susceptible to the challenge. He disrupted the symptom pattern by reminding them of what they wouldn't have to do while having the symptom. It is like *me* telling *you,* "I don't have to remind you that you'll want to take a break pretty soon. It goes without saying that certain bodily functions are in need of self-regulation in the morning due to biological programming and reinforced by practice.

I don't need to remind you of this." Also, by doing this, certain resources are retrieved, since awareness is focused on various things. The focusing of awareness does build resources. That is all we need to say.

Finally, the differences between short- and long-term therapy are apparent. With families who are amenable to therapy and the context of therapy, of course, you can have more sessions, retrieve more resources, and guide the use of those resources. Again, I think Erickson's decision about this was based primarily on doing that which was practical. You can read *that* learning between the lines in his case reports. You can actually read it in print in some places.

The case of Sandra W.[5] is an example. This woman was hallucinating naked men dancing in a corner of the ceiling. She came to see Erickson and said something to the effect that, "You have probably noticed the naked men dancing over my head. They are there all the time; I can't get rid of them. They are not dangerous but they are a nuisance; I have to go to the bathroom in the dark. They are always there." She also told him that she had short episodes (of psychosis) where she would go to China floating on a cloud or to her castle at the bottom of the ocean. These catatonic episodes would last for up to two weeks. She explained that she was irate that her husband divorced her when she told him about all this and one of her bosses had fired her when she told him. The current boss seemed similarly inclined.

Sandra wanted Erickson's help, not to stop hallucinating, but to stop others from bothering her. He explained that he knew this woman was not a psychotherapy candidate. She didn't want these behaviors changed. She was only there because she was about to lose her job as a school teacher. You need to know, briefly, that what he did with her was ask her to time distort so she could have a three-minute break that would seem to her like a two-week break for a trip around the world. Erickson asked her in the trance if she understood the phenomenon and would agree to carry it out. She agreed and the arrangement to do so was made. She could then conduct the trips to China or the bottom of the ocean during a coffee break and maintain her employment.

This is a lesson about the actual understanding that Erickson shared concerning the rationale for short therapy. However, for your interest, let me just tell you about the part of the problem that concerned naked young men. He asked Sandra to let them float over his empty closet and leave them in the closet. He told her that she could come and check on them

---

[5] A discussion of this case can be found in Erickson, M. (1980). Hypnosis: Its renascence as a treatment modality. In E. Rossi (Ed.), *The collected papers of Milton H. Erickson on hypnosis, volume IV: Innovative hypnotherapy* (pp. 70-75). New York: Irvington.

whenever she'd like to see if they were there and if they were okay. She did come back once every week for the first few weeks. That checking became every few weeks, then every few months, and finally not at all.

She had no more of those catatonic episodes, although she did come back—I think it was a year later—and demanded that since Dr. Erickson had helped her with the naked men and the trips around the world, could he please help her with the psychotic episodes she was having (she used the word psychotic). I really shouldn't tell you about this session because Erickson's intervention here does defy the laws of nature and logic. We'll have to add to the list of interventions: creative and bizarre. All right, since you begged. Erickson asked her to take her psychotic episode and *go into trance* and *then put her psychotic episode into a manila envelope* and mail it to him. Then she was to *come out of trance and proceed to conduct herself in a normal and healthy manner.* So he gave her a way to discharge the craziness. It involved going into trance, which would reduce the strain on her conscious mind, of course, and then release the tension in this unusual way. God knows where he came up with that idea!

The next day Sandra did come to Erickson's office in a hypnotic trance and gave him an envelope. She said, "She'll want to know what happened to this." Then she left. A couple of weeks later she called and Erickson told her that he had something that belonged to her. She replied to the effect, "Oh, that is where it is! I wondered what had happened to that psychotic episode." She added that she thought he had been involved in it somehow. Every couple of months she would send him a manila envelope and that continued for over 10 years. That enabled her to work and maintain checking accounts and so forth. So Erickson felt justified in the amelioration of the symptoms rather than the cure of the individual in this case, because that short amount of therapy was all that was reasonable and practical to try and accomplish.

Erickson's work is so simple and natural, not to mention so much a part of him, that the subtlety may escape you. It is so simple that I sometimes wonder why I'm teaching it and then I recall that it was anything but simple when I first visited him. It dawned on me in a metanoia one day and has, for the most part, been very understandable to me ever since. Before we look at some video examples to compare and contrast this approach with some of the other prevailing ones, I want to finish something that I started when the workshop began, my reason for visiting Erickson.

As you recall, I said that I would visit him and then return to my caseload and do with my families and clients (for whom it seemed appropriate) what I had just watched him do, like with the woman from Tokyo. I wouldn't know what part of what I was doing was the important part. That is, was the important part the hand moving up and down or the fact that it was then being followed by the other hand? Was the important part challenging her about the picture or would just asking her about the picture work? Was the crucial feature for that amnesia this or that or what? If I could determine what was essential, then I could generalize the learning to others and help them create amnesia in family therapy in areas where it was called for, for something other than singing in Japanese (which I haven't had to use, yet!). I also didn't know about inflections and nonverbal delivery which are absolutely essential to the effectiveness that Erickson achieved.

When I heard these things from Erickson, I would go back to my office and attempt to recreate them just as I had heard him do. You may need to know that I don't recommend this for anything other than learning! I did that with a few families that would tolerate my being sort of unusual; I mean, *I would* talk in his tone and inflections! Remember when people came to self-actualize and it was still trendy to be in therapy? This was before economics changed the kind of families that come to therapy. One divorced mother of four, for instance, had myasthenia gravis and she was interested in *anything* I might do that would could help her. What could I do that would help her regain control of her bladder? What could she do or think or feel that would forestall the muscle deterioration and tap into any spirit of healthiness that she could find inside? How could she do the very best with her kids and what do you even tell your kids?

I did my learning with these kinds of families and couples. They were a bit interested in what my trips to Phoenix had been like. They would listen and they would go into trance. Then, bit by bit, I would subtract a component and finally do it in my voice and my tone. Eventually, I left the mask of Erickson behind and became able to recreate to my satisfaction the important components.

One further word about learning these therapy skills: Begin with those families who you already know how to succeed with, the ones that seem "easy." In other words, begin with the ones who you understand and *who you trust.* I say the families *who you trust* and that may seem backwards to some of you. But the thing is, you are learning, and if your learning is met with punishment it only impedes the process of developing clarity and understanding. So if your unconscious is taking risks beyond that which you comfortably know how to do, make a *safe* learning environment for your unconscious: work with families you *trust.* For example, you may trust people who are not "trustworthy" in the social sense, but you understand where they are coming from and what you can expect from them. In that case, you *do* trust them. Perhaps you trust them to be rude, or trust them to make excuses, or just the opposite. But you can work with them because you "have their number," as the cliché goes.

As for families that you don't trust and who surprise you with the way they avoid responsibility, or whatever, don't try to learn these techniques and help the families, too. You won't be able to assess whether or not the surprising results come from their deviation from the norm or from your interventions. The result will be that you will get your interest and your creativity punished, or frustrated at the very least.

Work with these techniques with the families who you trust, who you understand, and who seem somewhat "easy" to you. You know what I mean by "easy" families; interview management and treatment planning are understandable to you and no one in the family is likely to act in an extremely unreliable manner. You realize by now, I hope, that using these interventions will force you to use a new or different way to view families' and people's problems. Looking at familiar families in this way will make some of them seem understandable and others will be on the fringe of making sense. Soon the families with whom it seemed harder to construct treatment plans will become "easier." Then the boundaries that separate the families that seemed "easy" from those that are "hard" will expand. In other words, if you make it a rule to follow this simple injunction, more and more families (and individuals) will seem accessible and actually easy to treat with these techniques. The range of "seems easy" will get larger and larger.

Do you recall that this has been a tangent? I was talking about being able to recreate what Erickson did with clients that I chose to *trust* and learn with. I would then observe myself and decode what I took to be the significant differences in my own presentation. Finally, I observed myself and worked with various ways of breaking down portions of therapy until I could explain a framework for it without confining it. That is how I came up with all of these cognitive mind schemes for various therapeutic episodes. These are what I'll be sharing. And when I share them, you'll see that the pieces fit together nicely and overlay one another. They create a tapestry that includes all there is to follow as near as I can determine.

On the personal side, these cognitive mind schemes or this framework bring me a lot of comfort when working. For instance, there was a woman I was working with at a large conference. I had never seen her before and the audience of nearly 2,000 professionals and video camera demanded success. I approached the event with the attitude that I didn't know what to do for this woman and that I would merely do what one does to help a unique person develop a trance and use her resources to *control the pain.* I was going to stimulate her thinking so she could put herself in trance. My conscious mind had no ideas of what to do other than these principles and techniques that I'll be sharing with you. In fact, I had a little dialogue with myself at one point that went like this: "What are you going to do with this woman?' " I don't know but all of these people want to see some action."

"Well, I'm going to do just what I teach, because that works!" "I hope, for everyone's sake that it does." All I could do is follow these guidelines. What I am offering is a framework that allows ample room for individual creative expression and regard for people.

Ten years ago, when I first began to develop and apply these ideas, I didn't know what the important components were. Then, eventually, I learned to decode portions. I didn't need to do certain things but I did need to drop my voice down, for example. I want you to appreciate those subtle things that Erickson makes seem so easy when he does them, in contrast to the following common example (videotape) from the media which is really very typical, unfortunately. Even though you are going to think it quite humorous at first, it is really typical of what many hypnotists do today.

So what follows now is from the Charley's Angels show.[6] The "F" and the "S" represent the other two Angels, and the "K" is for Kelly. I assume you are familiar with this show. . . . The "T" represents the "hypnotist" named Terrance.

> F: This is Miss Osling. The daughter of L. Bruton Osling, Osling Oil.
> We called about a consultation with Madame Dorien.
> T: [with a voice affectation of authority, pomp, and mysterious
> power—this affectation continues throughout] Oh yes, won't you
> come this way. Many, many people seek out Madame Dorien for
> escape from this troubled world, for reassurance that there is life
> after death. Humm?

So here we see I have written on the overhead "authoritarian" and "therapist takes the power dimension in the interaction." This voice tone is not especially different from one I have heard from a famous psychologist who has worked and lectured on self-image and hypnosis. I forget his name or I would tell you. His most recent tape, which I heard, said something to the effect of "Listen to my voice and my words will be the most important and profound words you have ever heard." I want to say, "Give me a break! Who does he think he is kidding." But he *is* utterly serious with that. Now the thing is *this* tape is not much different than that which passes for hypnosis and has been called hypnosis for many years. Of course, you have to buy my premise that this is like traditional hypnosis. Let's watch more and I'll let you decide.

> F: Oh obsolutely!
> T: But not all who come here are sincere. Oh, yes, we get the scoffers,

---

[6] This program was a rebroadcast on the ABC television network on February 12, 1981.

the mischief makers, who in their time waste the precious strength of Madame.

So this is his way of using indirect suggestion only he doesn't know it. *He tells them to comply!* Do you see that? It is a very important point. In a way the indirect suggestions are used for the induction of the relationship, but as you will see, the so called "official trance" will be all direct suggestion. No wonder clients keep coming back to the office . . . and their symptoms keep returning to them in classical hypnotherapy!

> *F:* Oh you don't have to sell me. Back in Detroit I was so scrambled even my psychiatrist gave up! But would you believe, just four sittings with a medium and I got it all together!
> *T:* Then it is your friend here who is troubled.
> *F:* Oh, yes. Her father died last year.
> *F:* Perhaps I should interview Miss Osling alone.
> *F:* Oh, great! I'll wait outside.
> *T:* Please relax, Miss Osling. Feel at peace with the universe. I am Terrance. You may call me that.
> *K:* All right, Terrance.

Now here we have another indirect statement about his power and your powerlessness. I'm going to write, "client is powerless" on the overhead. Here we also see the *direct suggestion* of "feel at peace with the universe." That is a pretty tall order! If she could do that, why would she be seeing him?

> *T:* What is your first name, Miss Osling?
> *K:* Kelly.
> *T:* You seem tense, Kelly. I'm going to play some music for you, to help you relax. [music] I want you to concentrate on the music. Listen very carefully so that you will always recognize it. Are you concentrating?
> *K:* Yes.

On the overhead I'm writing "use of mechanical devices to induce trance." Erickson observed that it is better to have people *imagine* the occurrence of music than to actually listen to it. That way people will begin concentration that is inward. Maybe I should mention one other thing. Some hypnotists try to measure hypnotizability by how much performance of a certain kind they get from subjects. Erickson believed that almost anyone, excepting those with severe mental difficulties, could be hypnotized. His definition is essentially that hypnosis is a state of heightened awareness and inwardly directed concentration. So, we like to say that anyone who can be *socialized* can be hypnotized. That is, normal socialization includes times when you are absorbed in a thought or projecting about the meaning of life, or what you will do in 10 years, or what if you had been a merchant marine, etc., and these are part of the clinical trance state—these *are* trance states of normal life. Well, Terrance has used abnormal, that is mechanical, means to stimulate trance, not knowing that it is the least efficient of the alternatives.

> *T:* Listen to the sound of my voice . . . and the music . . . concentrate . . . concentrate. Count back from 100 . . .
> *K:* 100-99-98-97-96 . . .
> *T:* . . . and when you reach 90 you will sleep and hear only my voice and the music.
> *K:* 92-91-90 [closes eyes] . . .
> *T:* Sleep. Can you hear me Kelly?
> *K:* Yes.
> *T:* Good. From now on each time you hear the music you will sleep and answer questions about your loved ones and hear only my voice. Do you understand?
> *K:* I understand.

Now here the scene fades and I will skip ahead to show you the action that comes from this during the subsequent seance. But before we see that, notice this form of progressive relaxation. It is not uncommon to have a person count as a means of implying that small increments of relaxation will occur. Here we see the reliance upon counting as if this alone will automatically establish deep relaxation and "sleep" with *any* subject. Also, we see the direct suggestion of when the eyes would close, and so forth. So I write, "progressive relaxation and direct suggestion." Let's summarize what we have about this type of traditional hypnosis. We see an authoritarian approach, implications of the hypnotist having the power, demands for compliance, use of mechanical aids, progressive relaxation, and direct suggestion. In addition we sometimes see, as we do here, the association with the "spirit world" and the financial exploitation depicted here.

Now the tape takes us to the seance and our focus goes to what subjects think of *their* experience of trance. Of course this spirit meeting, on the show, was *not* presented as *real in the context of the show*. So I take from that that the hypnosis *was* presented as real or believable, at least in some way. You see, the producers surely had a psychological consultant who would oversee this part of the script. I also wonder why the APA or some other organization does not make them desist, unless it is because *most hypnosis is done this way* all over the country—even today.

Well now, what follows is not hypnosis. It is the response of the person to hypnosis. This is the training that many of your families have had before they come to your office. This *is* what they expect from the trance experience. Everyone, at some level, will expect this. Some more than others will realize that what is on TV is not real. Some won't! Well, let's look at it now and I'll continue to summarize.

> *Room:* [indistinguishable "spirit" noises and music, then the same music begins that Kelly heard before]
> *K:* Please, please, please! Please, Beemish, don't make me go into the dark closet. I promise, I promise, I'll be good. Let me have Lillibeth! I get so scared in there alone. Oh, please, Beemish, let me have Lillibeth for company. Beemish, Beemish, Beemish!
> *F:* [whispers to Kelly] That was sensational.
> *K:* [obviously awakening, looks around the seance room silently]

Now I'll skip ahead again to the scene after the session and to the reunion with the other Angels in the car. You see here the typical notion that people will be oblivious to the trance phenomena that occur. Furthermore, you see from what just happened that the people can be stimulated into *negative* unconscious material that has emerged.

> *S:* How did it go?
> *F:* Oh, she was great. Kelly, you really were. [pause] Kelly, do the bit again.
> *K:* What?
> *F:* You know, the little girl voice.
> *K:* There wasn't any little girl.
> *F:* I'll tell you, it gave me goose-bumps. Come on do the little girl's voice.
> *K:* I don't know what you're talking about! Nothing happened at all. If you really must know, it was so dull, I think I went to sleep!
> *S:* Hey, Kelly, calm down. We know you're tired. I'm tired too!

Well, it would appear that the emergence of this negative unconscious material is affecting Kelly's usually sweet disposition. There is a typical attitude, even among supervising professionals, that trance experiences will awaken these sleeping demons. Here is where your families come to develop a conviction of that sort.

Here I'll skip ahead again to later that night. We pick up on Kelly asleep with a doll and dreaming a nightmare. We see that we now have depicted a *spontaneous* emergence of this unconscious material.

> *K:* Beemish, Beemish. [dreaming of being put in the closet as a little

girl] Don't make me go in the dark closet, please. [We see her
dreams of the matronly servant pushing her into a closet and taking
away her doll. Kelly is apparently remembering being terrorized at
three or four years old.] [The phone rings and Kelly picks it up.]
Hello. [The music we heard before in the office and seance is
playing and the voice is that of Terrance.]
T: Kelly, Beemish wants you. You will come here at once. Do you
understand?
K: [Silently puts down phone and walks toward door. We then see
Kelly driving in her nightgown in the car and then sitting in the
office with Terrance.]

Well, I have to say, it is a darn good thing that she doesn't sleep in the
nude because, as you can see, she drives right to his office in her nightgown.
Again, we see here the notion that people are oblivious in trance, will do
things against their will, and can be expected to be powerless against both
the hypnotist and their own boogie-creatures.

Certainly interspersed with what we *do* want to show—that is, examples
of direct suggestions, demanding compliance, therapist's having the power,
and so on—we also see the use of relaxation rather than joining clients at
their model of the world. These other things are associated with myths that
almost everyone will bring with them about hypnosis. So take a look at
Erickson now by contrast.

And again, you probably think that I'm joking, and I wish I was. There's
a lot of hypnosis that goes on like this that's clinical hypnosis. And therapists
are also apparently under the impression that they have to be this way,
although there are permissive suggestions that are recognized as different.
Kroger[7] wrote a book, a very well documented, huge book that covers many
facets of hypnotherapy. There's a single bibliographical reference in his
chapter on indirection, on indirect suggestion, which happens to only be
seven pages long, I think. And the reference to Erickson is the pantomime
technique. And Kroger is one of those fellows who *has* worked real hard
to promote a reasonable understanding of hypnosis for many years. And
yet he still promotes a lot of these antiquated ideas.

What follows is the "Nick" videotape. Erickson is working with this
person and it was recorded by Herb Lustig, M.D.[8] In this written transcript,
"E" will represent Erickson and "N" will represent Nick, the man whom
Erickson met the night before at a party. Nick seemed to need help in life

[7] Kroger, W. (1977). *Clinical and experimental hypnosis in medicine, dentistry, and psychology.* Toronto: Lippincott.

[8] Erickson, M.H. (1976). "The Artistry of Milton H. Erickson, M.D." Herbert Lustig, M.D. (producer). Philadelphia, PA.

adjustment and agreed to be a demonstration subject for this taping. There is another person present, Monde, who Erickson has just been working with while Nick observed.

> *E:* Did you know you *went into* a trance while I was working with Monde?
> *N:* No. I thought I did. I wasn't sure.

Well, right away Erickson has Nick in a "No-Set." That is, he is not sure and will err in favor of saying "no." This is not the greatest situation for suggestibility. Listen how Erickson seems to just throw out the past tense verb to get Nick to say "yes" and admit that he is having experience with hypnosis.

> *E:* And this is the first time you *had any* experience with hypnosis?
> *N:* Yes.
> *E:* So, you're going to *find* a lot of new things out about yourself only you won't *know* what you're going to find out until after you have found it out.

Do you see how he is turning the attention in to Nick. It is the subject who will find things out and he will find them from *himself,* not from the therapist. Also, we hear indirect suggestion. This is like telling Nick that he must listen to the whole presentation before concluding. This is, I hope you agree, far more impressive for its subtlety.

> *E:* All your life you've known that you could lift your hand and lower it. But there was something you learned *long* ago, and that was that you couldn't lift your hand, that you didn't know it was your hand. You were an infant, and your hands were just objects.

Now, I don't know about you, but if I had just heard that discussion from a person I didn't know, I'd be sitting *absolutely* still right now. And, in fact, that is what Nick is doing. It is *essential* that you *notice what is happening with the subject.* Nick is sitting how? Right, *perfectly* still. And what is he doing? Huh? Right, *nothing!* You can count on the fact that in order to do nothing, you have to be still and stare at something real or imagined. And it is *this* personal orientation exhibited by Nick that is being utilized.

Nick is willing to do very little. Consider that even the night before this man accepted the invitation of a perfect stranger to be a filmed subject. That doesn't sound like wise problem-solving behavior to me! Nick began the session with "No." He seems to be retreating from different experiences and concluding something about his self-worth when he does. Do the others of you here who have analyzed this tape agree? Okay, I don't suppose this is irrelevant information. Look at Nick's belt buckle and tell me if that image on there is the symbol of the leaf of a marijuana plant. If that is so, and it appears to be, we might assume still further that Nick is the kind of person who makes sure that he collects a little "kick" when he withdraws and forms these conclusions.

Anyway, notice how Erickson will now use the two features of Nick's presentation: current behavior and personality orientation. Listen to what Erickson is about to say:

E: And one of the first things that a person does when he goes into a trance is he looks at some one spot. He doesn't need to move. He doesn't need to talk, doesn't need to do anything except let his unconscious mind *take over and do everything.* And the conscious mind doesn't have to do anything. It's usually not even interested.

So do you observe here that Erickson said nearly every word in that context? He said, "One of the first things *he* does . . . ." That is, *he* and not she was to receive this therapy. There is certainly more than one thing to do since he said *one of the first* things and implied that there will be more things. Finally, and most importantly, Erickson has implied that Nick has *already* achieved the first step. You cannot use the same words with someone else and necessarily achieve what Erickson did here. You must do the same *process.* That is, you must *utilize* the client's behavior. Do you realize how *different* that is from relaxation!

So far, for Erickson's tape I have written: "gives the power to the family members," "uses indirect suggestion and anecdote to stimulate thought," "does not demand compliance," "utilizes the family members' ongoing behavior," and I have placed anecdote and indirect suggestion under the label of "Indirection" and made another main category called "Utilization." These two categories will subsume most all of the techniques, behavioral and strategic interventions he is associated with but the other category called "Principles and values of treatment" is of crucial importance in this therapy. It is there that I've written "family member has the power," "indirectly suggest," "utilize the family member's behavior," "tailor comments to the family member's personality," and "positively frame experience." Well, that is quite a list to expect you to infer from only a few sentences. How about watching some more.

E: And while I've been talking to you, you've altered you respiration; your heart rate is altered. I know from past experience that your blood pressure is changed, your pulse is changed, and your eyelid

reflex is changed. And you really don't need to keep your eyes
open; but you can *close* them now.

Here we have witnessed indirect suggestions to ratify the trance and to
establish eye closure. Let me ask you, if Nick had not closed his eyes would
that have been resistance? No. Eye closure was never demanded, as in the
previous tape. This is all indirect suggestion, even the sentence that says
"but you can *close* them now." That is, you *can* close them now. That is
not to say, "when you reach 90 you will close your eyes." All right, let's
watch more.

[Nick's eyelids flutter as he closes his eyes.]
E: That little flutter is learning to get acquainted with yourself at another
  level of being. Now first of all I'd like to have you enjoy the comfort.
  I'd like to have you discover that your sense of comfort continually
  increases.

Now here, Erickson obviously means something vague. He says that the
"sense of comfort continually increases" and from that we can't say that
he means just in this session. So we see his learning framework for this
trance. Now pay special attention to this next part. The question you ought
to try to answer is, what is he getting at when he says this next thing and
the anecdote to support it?

E: Now in the back of your mind, which is a common phrase, we
  know a lot of things, and sometimes we have trouble getting those
  things into the front of our mind. We can have a name on the tip
  of our tongue, but we can't say it; we don't know what it is but we
  know that we know it, but we just can't think of it, but it's there
  ready to be said. That's because the unconscious is hanging on to
  it.

Now I'm going to skip a few comments that were directed to Monde. It
seems that Monde has gone into a trance, too, and Erickson wants to tell
her that either of them can modify his words to fit for them as individuals.
But I want to pick up the tape again right here. Now, remember the question?
Why does Erickson raise the idea about the "back of the mind" knowing
something? Any suggestions? The answer is in what he follows that seed
with. When you listen for that also listen especially for the tone shifting
(represented here as underlining) that is happening.

E: Now, I know there is some reason why you came to Phoenix to *see*
  me. You had some purpose in mind but exactly what that purpose

was, I doubt if you *have very much of an understanding.* Usually you don't *know why,* but your unconscious mind does *know a great deal more.* And your unconscious mind in *knowing* that *additional material* can let it come to your mind slowly, gradually, in such a way that you're *not disturbed,* you're *not distressed,* in such a way that you *become aware* that you can *handle* things and *understand* things and *discover* there are some things you dislike and some that you like and that there are many different understandings that are possible to you.

Do you hear the tonal shifts here? You see, Erickson says at the conscious level, "Usually you don't know why." He makes an excuse for not really being aware of something. But to the unconscious he says, "Know why!" And this continues on for many sentences: The verbal vehicle is not the whole message.

Now, I want to refer you to an article in the *Collected Papers, Volume 1* called "Two-Level Communication and the Microdynamics of Trance and Suggestion."[9] In this paper Erickson says that he uses two tones of voice. One is normal for speaking to the conscious mind and one is soft. The soft voice, he says, he uses for speaking to the unconscious. The softened tone makes the words spoken with it different than the norm and, therefore, it suggests that a meaning out of the norm is intended. Unconscious search results.

E: Since this is really the first time I've met you, really talked to you, I can't really know very much about you, but your unconscious does know much more about you than you do. It's got a whole background of *years of learning,* feeling, thinking, and doing.

Also notice that many times you have heard a reference to the differences between conscious and unconscious mind functions. This is another and final feature to add to the list on the overhead. We call that one "conscious/unconscious dissociation."

Do you appreciate my commentary on what Erickson's doing here? You do, oh good. I think without it you might miss what he's doing because it comes so easy for him or seems to come easy. This was after *decades* of studying each of these things as techniques. So it's clear that he thought them through and tried to write them up.

---

[9] Erickson, M.H. and Rossi, E.L. (1980). Two-level communication and the microdynamics of trance and suggestion. In E.L. Rossi (Ed.), *The collected papers of Milton H. Erickson, M.D. on hypnosis, volume 1: The nature of hypnosis and suggestion* (pp. 430-451). New York: Irvington.

CHAPTER TWO

System Dynamics, Assessment, and Treatment Planning

FAMILY SYSTEMS FRAMEWORK

Is there a particular Ericksonian attitude, theory, and behavior towards individuals and families formulated within a *systems* framework? Many family therapists would be satisfied with a formulation of his diagnosis and intervention strategies that relied upon general systems theory, ecosystems theory, or cybernetic-type theory. However, Erickson himself never offered such a formulation. He did not do so in my personal contacts with him, nor in writing, nor in face-to-face contacts with any other student of whom I am aware. If one looks in the indexes of Erickson's collected writings, or article titles of any book written by Erickson (and co-authors), or any edited collection of articles authored by Erickson, not a single entry will be found entitled "family" or "systems," etc. It is intriguing that he is well known for his creative and pioneering contributions to family therapy (witness books by Watzlawick, Fisch, Haley, Madanes, Hoffman, etc.) and still not a single entry in books *by him* refer to "family."

Uncommon Therapy and *Conversations with Milton H. Erickson, Vol. 2: Changing Couples* and *Vol. 3: Changing Children and Families*, each by Jay Haley,[10] are notable exceptions, but the former does not contain an index and is not considered in the above observations. It is noteworthy,

---

[10]I am referring to Haley, J. (1973). *Uncommon therapy: The psychiatric techniques of Milton H. Erickson, M.D.* New York: Norton; and Haley, J. (1985). *Conversations with Milton H. Erickson, M.D., Vol. 2: Changing couples & Vol. 3: Changing children and families.* New York: Norton.

nevertheless, due to the extensive emphasis it provides for a family developmental framework. The books by Haley are all about families and make extensive reference to various aspects of the family by means of the cases presented in them. The emphasis on families was added by the editor and not by Erickson. Erickson's parlance is shown by the entries in the index that reflect the language he used. That language was psychodynamic. Of course, the language of systems theory just didn't exist! He couldn't use it. Projects such as the one which first took Haley to Phoenix have resulted in the scant vocabulary we have even today.

Therefore, since there is no preexisting linguistic framework, we must project onto Erickson's work a set of ideas that will unite, all inclusively, Erickson's interventions in a suitable family therapy theory or framework. I suspect that, as we have, you will develop a set of attitudes towards people and their problems and gain a level of proficiency in formulating interventions consistent with Erickson's approach; then you will begin relying upon a conception of the interaction and influences of a number of human systems in order to place his work in the framework of a systems theory. The elaboration we offer will show experience interlocking in a mutually influencing matrix that can be understood to span from the internal experience of single individuals, coupled partners, family structures, informal social networks, socializing institutions, families of origin (real and imagined), and sociocultural and economic environments over time. We prefer to think of this as an ecosystem approach to human problems since the theory offers more than that of the so-called general systems theory. Specifically, it offers an understanding of the historical influences on the populations of individuals and families, and on the environment, too.

You have a page in your handouts [Illustration 1] you should look at now. The point here is that we can take an exact replication of Erickson's material on hypnosis and use it at individual levels, in waking state therapy, or in couples or family therapy.

The trick to doing therapy easily and successfully is merely understanding something about a dynamic that relates at different levels. Now these arrows in your hand are only going in one direction, which is a little bit inaccurate, of course. But I think you'll see the logic in writing it this way. It especially makes sense for a child being born into a family. The family organization is already a function of another level up here, which are the cultural mores that dictate the range of family organizations that are acceptable. It is certainly in flux right now, so we have group marriages and homosexual couples, single-parent families, serial monogamy, spouse swapping, singles condos, and whatnot. So the range of family organization is certainly broader than what would have been accepted before.

Nevertheless, once there's a family organization of some kind pushing at those boundaries or staying solidly in the middle, *they will delineate the degree of role diversity that's possible.* Now, you know this. You all know what I mean. It's just a matter of making words make sense here. You know, "Chris, you don't like potatoes, give them to your brother," teaches her about what she likes and what she's supposed to do about something when she does or doesn't.

We have a little boy who has red hair. Carol and I both had red hair when we were infants as well, so I presume he'll end up blond. If he doesn't, this child has to fight society. Nearly everybody we see has one or two things to say to him, one of the major ones being, "Where did you get that red hair?" So what's he going to think? He's a very smart child. He's always going to be alerted to the fact that everybody sees his red hair first. Most of the people do. Strangers do. And then the people who aren't bright enough to let it drop there have to tell us what it means to have red hair:

System Dynamics

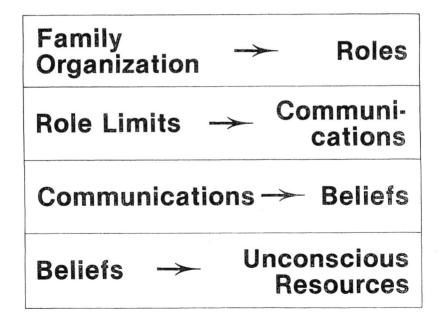

Illustration 1

"Oh, he's going to be sensitive," "He's going to be irritable," "He's going to be angry," whatever. So we lean into his ear and we say, "Whenever you hear people say that, that's an opportunity for you to make an improvement on what they don't understand."

Those are roles that he learns to play from a larger society, but the family does it too. Basically, he's very smart. You've already heard me say that. That's a role that he's getting trained into. I could have been a person who sees all stupid, klutzy things he does and then say I have a son who's a klutz. And I could prove it. I'd hold him up and he'd klutz. And instead I hold him up and he would say "hi" to all of you. And then when you'd laugh and you'd applaud, he would applaud. And then you'd applaud and laugh and he'd do something else.

And you'd go, "Wow, what a smart kid". And it is due to a couple of things. His expectations have been shaped by our attributions and reinforcement, and the ones that *you get* that predispose you to notice certain things, now that I've said them. So they come true for you and they become true for him and we are all reinforced. And we all think we are simply commenting on reality, when in fact we are *inducing* reality.

And so he's going to be smart. It will be real tough for him not to be smart. He may be smart in a way that is different for him than it was for us. We were at the Hilton in Albuquerque and there was a flute player. Shawn had his baby bottle. It was his one-year birthday party. He was sucking on the baby bottle as the guitar player and flute player came to the table. And he was really fascinated, having never seen a flute player before. And he started copying her. I leaned over to Carol and said, "Look at that, he's modeling the flute player's behavior." She's one of the few people who can notice those things and say "Right," instead of "Oh, bullshit." And so we both knew that he was demonstrating *that* degree of trying to learn.

I saw a child in the airport who was sitting with his mother. He was about three, maybe. He was sitting on his father's shoulders with his hands on his father's jaws and his father was chewing gum. The boy was flexing the muscles in his jaw, while he was holding on to his dad's face. He was learning a certain thing about what men do with their faces. So kids will do that sort of thing all the time, whether or not you notice it, and what you make of it will, of course, determine what kind of role you teach. The natural dynamics of any system can be characterized, for convenience, as that routine activity which has the highest frequency of occurrence. In the individual we refer to this as "personality."

We recently worked with a family we like to use for examples of brief therapy. In this family it was okay for the children to be infantilized, for them to be helpless, for them to not grow up. It wasn't okay for them to get assertive and aggressive. One of the teenage children was babysitting for us and someone took the lounge chair from the porch of the condominium on the beach where she was staying. Carol asked what happened to the chair. She whined, "Oh, those people over there took it." And Carol said, "Why didn't you tell them to give it back?" She said, "Oh, I couldn't do that."

Well, why couldn't she do that? Because every time she came up to Mom and Dad and said, "I don't want to go to church tonight, I want to watch Kojac," she learned the roles that were acceptable to her and the ones that weren't. Now those roles then delimit the degree of communication she can make. So she learned to play the subservient, victim role, but not any assertive roles. The same girl, by the way, tipped a plate of spaghetti onto one of our dining room chairs and said, "Oh, I always do that." So keep that in mind. The kind of communications that she can make and can get away with determine the kind of belief system she formulates, i.e., "I'm the kind of person who always spills something and makes a horrible mess." And once she's formulated those belief systems, then the unconscious resources to the contrary won't ever pop up, or if they do they are considered a conflict and she goes for therapy.

So if she won't *get* aggressive impulses, she believes she's not the kind of person who can have them, so she doesn't have them. A person who believes he can't be confident in front of a group spends a lot of time making sure he notices the opposite of confidence when he is in front of groups, right? A person who believes he has ringing in his ears hears that ringing that we all have and doesn't notice the times when it is ameliorated. So you stop noticing. Or you know the people who "just can't stand it when somebody does that," they have a belief system that says, "This range of experience from other states of consciousness are the only things I can notice." And although there are jillions of others, they fail to notice them. They fail to notice how they can be relaxed.

And you know this in a bunch of different situations. You have depressed people who can make sure they don't laugh at a joke or something that is pleasant or humorous. You have the person who thinks all men are horrible, rotten people. She has never met an honest one in all her life. She's failed to notice perceptually the men who do things that are trustworthy. She doesn't see Mr. Rogers, for example. And if she does, her belief system modifies it into something else. But basically what she does is she just doesn't notice. She distracts herself to something else. She remembers George who was rotten instead of Mr. Rogers who reminded her of George.

So now the problem is—and these things are mutually interactive, of course—if I'm *always* experiencing a certain low threshold of some kind of agitation, then my belief system has to acknowledge it or I have a conflict of some kind, and my belief system includes thoughts like these: "I have a problem" or "I'm always having these thoughts of trying to murder my children." You know, "I don't know what to do about it and that is why I come for therapy." Well, that's a function of the family allowing a person to play a role and worry about something instead of confronting the problem directly. And that family member communicates about it in a way that's off target and then has a belief system that there is something wrong with him or her—and that's okay—rather than thinking there is something wrong with Mom and Dad *and* having impulses of anger or something that is disallowed in a role that they normally play. S/he can believe there are angry impulses to injure the children. So you are getting a problem to manifest itself here as an interplay of pressures going both ways. You may get a person who has a problem with other areas, say the communication that occurs because of roles that she plays and feelings she has. This is what we get as the presenting problem.

Or maybe it's "my son ran away from home" and it's a family organization problem that is presented. So the problem can be presented in any level. Communication includes feelings, of course—"I have so much anxiety I just can't stand it . . . something has to happen here!" We're allowed to make those communications. There's nothing wrong with our belief system. So if you see Albert Ellis, he says, "No no, *this* is the problem" [referring to "beliefs" on the overhead—Illustration 2]. If you see Moreno, *this* is the problem [referring to "roles" on the overhead—Illustration 2]. If you see Jay Haley, *this* is the problem [referring to "family structure" on the overhead—Illustration 2]. If you see Fritz Perls, *this* is the problem [referring to "communication"—Illustration 2]. Eric Berne would certainly emphasize this level of communication being the problem. Each therapist tends to favor a certain position on how to interpret the difficulty and all of them are right because through their successful interventions they have to shift *everything.*

Erickson seems to have developed a range of interventions that do different things to different levels and he used most of them in the course of total therapy with any particular family. I've labeled those around the side here.

By contrast, Perls is listed only in the communications area that includes behaviors and affect. *E*motion, by the way, is movement outward. But he was not very concerned with the cognitive area. He would call it "Elephant shit," I suppose. Perls would try to break into an explosion of core feelings to change the way you present yourself in social presentation. So he would try to bust into the unconscious areas and have you change your communication. And to heck with your belief system. Stop doing it and it won't be a problem anymore.

By the way, I think all therapies *reserve the right* to say some things about your thinking are wrong and some things about your thinking are right. All therapies will explain it in a certain framework. I need to say that because

Erickson thought that something about the unconscious process is much more valuable than the conscious process. So before you write him off because of that, think about it for just a minute. All therapies do that. Albert Ellis says some of your thoughts are rational and some aren't and the therapist gets to choose which ones are which. Fritz Perls says all of your thinking is wrong, so forget it—it's just thinking. Eric Berne would say that there is some thinking that's Adult and there's some that's contaminated. And if it's contaminated then it's the same as those irrational beliefs that Ellis lambasted, but he's nicer about it. And furthermore, some of it comes from different ego states and therefore contains a different orientation to life in the first place.

System Dynamics

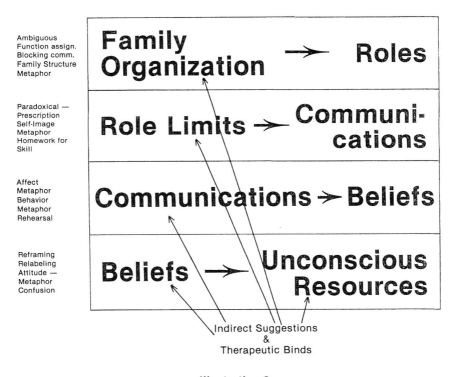

Illustration 2

There is primary and secondary process in psychoanalysis. The cognitive behaviorists, like Beck, for example, have a way of putting it that I like a little better. It is a little more systematic in the sense that it is not a good or bad thought; it's a discriminative stimulus and what follows is not useful. *That* determines that it's a nonuseful thought. But again, there are things that are good and bad about your thinking processes.

Erickson seemed to more highly value the unconscious because he said the conscious mind contains a set of limiting beliefs. What he meant by *limiting* is that "therefore I can't have these unconscious resources." You know the people you run into and you say: "Why don't you try going dancing a little bit more and getting out?" "Oh, I make such a fool of myself when I go. Oh I couldn't do that, I'm so uncoordinated." So they won't let themselves have the natural gracefulness that the body was certainly made with in the first place, because their belief system continually finds ways of only choosing those ungraceful moments to remember and recreate.

So *reframing* or *relabeling* and *attitude metaphors* [Illustration 2] are what you could use to urge the person to conceptualize a belief differently. Actually, another thing happens here—*involvement* of some kind, just plain *active involvement*. If you do a debate where you defend topic X, you tend to change your belief system in favor of topic X.

For retrieving unconscious resources [Illustration 2] metaphor and indirect suggestions are the things that stimulate unconscious activity. An example is if I say, "A taxi driver told me something the other day that was interesting. I can't get it out of my mind. I just thought I would share it. He said that he had someone in the back of the car the other day who was rambling on. He was hardly listening at all but he heard the guy say:

"There was this old man who was sitting on the side of a hill. And some passerby came with a back pack over his back. And the passerby saw the old man looking over the city and said, 'Hey old man, what kind of people live in that city down there that you are looking at?' And the old man said, 'Well, tell me stranger, what kind of people live in the city from which you came?' The passerby said, 'Well, it's funny you should ask me that. They were backstabbing, backbiting, untrustworthy people. They would steal from their own mother. I had to leave the city. They were terrible people. They were liars and con artists. It was disgusting.' And at that the old man said, 'I'm sorry, but I'm afraid you are going to find the people in this city to be just like the people you left.' The next day another passerby came and saw the old man sitting on the side of the hill looking at the city. And he said, 'Hey old man, what kind of people live in that city down there?' And the old man said, 'Well what kind of people lived in the city that you left?' And he said, 'It's odd you should ask me about that. I was just thinking about how sad I was to have to leave. They were so kind and tender and warm and they would give you the shirt off their back. They were always willing to help a friend. I was sorry to have to go.' And the old man said, 'Well, I am pleased to tell you, you are going to find the people in this city to be just the same.'

"Anyway, he left me with that. He said the guy had to get out of the taxi and leave then. And this was rattling around his head, he wanted to tell me about it. And ever since he told me, I've been wanting to tell somebody else."

Now you see, hearing that metaphor you start doing a lot of thinking and doing things that are difficult to describe: comparison contrast, memory association, congruity checking, identifying attributions to the memory you are having, and so on. And that's unconscious experience. It is caused by indirect suggestion and metaphor.

For example, your unconscious mind certainly knows a lot about confidence that you couldn't explain consciously. I doubt that anyone here could articulate consciously how to begin to feel a sense of confidence. Usually you don't notice. It may begin with an alteration in your body posture. Everyone's heard the phrase "breathing deeply, sigh of relief." But a conscious mind never really knows how your unconscious can go about regulating your body experience and change it to be more comfortable.

Now, if I keep talking like that, you keep having more and more unconscious associations to those words—unconscious processes—too. And I'm not changing your belief system, not changing your communication, your roles, or anything. I'm simply retrieving unconscious resources—in this case, confidence. Or you are retrieving them, using my words as a stimulus.

All the arrows going toward the unconscious in the diagram are saying, "There needs to be a good deal of stimulation of resources going on at different levels." So Erickson sent the "moron" to the barn dance so that he would have to play a different role. Erickson worked to change Harold's body image so he would believe it was possible to get an apartment. He had him dance and take music lessons so he would have to learn some new communications and a different role.

But the role really gets solidified when it's something the client conceptualizes as a role. Until then Harold was just retrieving communications of how to be with a woman and not be threatened. Then he went to the barn dance and realized, "Wow, I'm not so bad after all." I have a different role. It is handy to give people something that will justify for them the change in their role—rites of passage of some kind. The use of a middle initial you've never used will do it. I haven't talked to Bob or Mary Goulding about this, but they probably would agree and maybe even explain it this way. They have suggested that a number of people change their names so as to present a different role to the world. There's a man I know whose name was "Twig," and Bob Goulding asked him to change his name to "Forrest." Changed his family tree!

Any questions? [Question about paradox] Yes, it seems to me that Erickson's use of paradox is more gentle than some I've seen. Paradox tells you to keep doing what you are doing for a different reason. Therefore, the role is changed a little bit or the family organization is changed. Consider the case of the girl sucking her thumb.[11] The parents bring her in to Erickson. She's been labeled aggressive for sucking her thumb. They are a very religious family and aggressive is an important word in this family. Erickson tells the parents, independently of the girl, to give it four weeks, to do exactly what he tells them to do, and he guarantees it will change.

What the parents should do is no matter what the girl does, ignore it. That's not a paradox with them. That is setting some kind of limits on the family transactions. In other examples of paradox, Erickson tells many people in their twenties to disconnect themselves from their parents. And sometimes if it's a real pathological family, he does more. He told one woman to leave home. She was living with four aunts and her mother.

She was to leave the house and get a new apartment, not to tell them the phone number or *address*. And *that* limits communication. And then there were assignments: She was to room with two other girls and was to drive at random around the city in a car, at least two hours every night. You know what that will do, don't you? That will make her go through normal teenage socialization, cruising the streets and making commentary on all the things she sees and being socialized by those girls a little bit. That is what every teenager tends to do at some point.

To return to the thumb-sucking girl, Erickson brought her into the room alone. He instructed her that she keep doing it and do it better. That is paradoxical now. She's got a role where she sucks the thumb and she *is* the bad kid. The paradox is to keep doing *exactly* that, but *do it better* because if *that* is what she thinks is irking the hell out of her parents, he's just going to laugh at her. If she *really* wants to irk the hell out of her parents and get back at the school teachers on her back, she'll get saliva in her mouth first, so she can make a nice sloshing sound. He tells her all the best ways to suck a thumb to get the flabby portion of the thumb here in the mouth so that it will pop when she pulls it out. And to twist the hand around so she gets some attention for it. And not just to do the hit and miss things, but to sit down methodically for 20 minutes in Dad's study when he's working, in the kitchen while Mom is preparing the meal, in the family

[11]For a discussion of this case see Haley, J. (1973). *Uncommon therapy: The psychiatric techniques of Milton H. Erickson, M.D.* New York: Norton, pp. 195-202.

room while people are watching television, in the sewing room where Mom is sewing, and in every class that she really hates the teacher—20 minutes. Not a minute less.

Well, then Erickson brings the parents back and he begins to tell them and remind them that their agreement is that he could solve the problem in four weeks but they have to do exactly what he says and that is ignore it, no matter how good or how bad it gets, ignore it. So, they go home and call him up and they say, "Hey, she didn't suck her thumb the whole way home. This is great, whatever you did." And he reminds them no matter what happens, ignore it. The next day they call up and say "Well, things are much worse. She sat sucking her thumb for 20 minutes in the kitchen, 20 minutes in the study. It is 20 times worse than ever before. We are going to stop coming to therapy." And he reminded them no matter what happens, ignore it.

Well, what happened here is like what happens with piano lessons. Twenty minutes became 12 minutes, and then it became eight minutes, every other day. And then she would forget to do it. And in three weeks she wasn't doing it at all. So, look at the roles. First, we've got the role of "I'm a person who is accidentally sucking my thumb and can't help myself, and I'm sorry I am irritating you. It's my unconscious aggression." Next, we have the role of "I'm going to really irk you guys with this and do it really good." So it's the same behavior, but because it has different motivation it becomes a *different role*. It is the same conduct but a different role. Now *that* is a gentle beginning to change.

It could be exactly the same behavior. But the paradox in this case exaggerated it. Nevertheless, the paradox prescribes the same behavior, so the role is different because the motivation is different. It's different if I say, "Eleanor, I'm going to knock your brains in here." If you know that this is an illustration point that I'm making in a workshop, that defines it at some level as a different role. I'm still a nice guy making a point. It is very questionable to bring up an example of violence, but still, it is the same behavior but it has a different motive so it *is* a different role. By contrast, if you see Eleanor and me in the lobby and you don't know me from anybody and I say the same thing in the same way, then you wonder if there is a crime about to happen. So it is the same behavior, but if the motivation is defined by context or otherwise, then it changes the role that is being played.

Self-image thinking, another intervention on this chart [Illustration 2], is aimed primarily at the area of the role and its influence on communication. It changes the role radically. It is really teaching family members to think about themselves in a different way: positive, goal-directed, visual rehearsal. This amounts to systematically going through the body image and telling each family member good and bad things and what they mean (or what they *can* mean). Having people visualize themselves acting out certain capabilities is helping them think of themselves playing a different role.

There is a metaphor called family structure protocol that we teach and when you hear such a metaphor you begin to think about reorganizing the family. That goes on the chart at the family reorganization level and it involves getting the major family hypnotists to think of reorganization of the family. Self-image thinking can be done through guided imagery or metaphor, directly leading a person to it. I'm only including Ericksonian techniques here. You can include psychodrama here, assertiveness training, many techniques you already do and should continue to do.

For the communication level of the chart, there is the behavior protocol, emotion protocols, shaping in general, and shaping congruency. Virginia Satir, for example, emphasizes shaping congruent communication. Also, Fritz Perls could be seen doing this. Erickson would have you do that too. He would have you rehearse the way you would do things but we have no special terms for it, of course.

Now, for changing beliefs, I've already mentioned reframing, relabeling, attitude metaphors, or actively involving a person. And indirect suggestion works because you are needing resources stimulated and retrieved at every step. Indirect suggestion is the stimulus that helps create search for more meaning, more material, more experience, and will link that meaning and experience to the area in which you are trying to have it apply.

One other thing we need to do here is show you diagnostic parameters [Illustration 3]. We are looking at basically the same information here [Illustration 4] on this "Case Presentation Format" sheet. We use the latter

DIAGNOSTIC PARAMETERS

1. Structure and organization of social network and family.

2. Stage of development of family system & next likely stage.

3. Psychological age of individuals in system.

4. Sensitivity and flexibility of members to others in system.

5. Needed and/or available resources.

6. Pattern and function of symptomatic behavior in the system.

Illustration 3

Case Presentation Format

Client ID: _____   Marital status: _____
Age: _____ Psychological age: _____
Children _____
Stage of family development: Next logical stage of development:
_____

Family Structure:
Who talks to whom: _____
How involved (time): _____
What's avoided: _____
Typifying affect: _____
Usual roles: _____
Role compatibility: _____
Parallel to F.O.O.   _____
Disagreements on values, identities, actions: _____
Loyalties, scapegoating, myths: _____

Function of symptom: _____

Available needed   First Phase: Second Phase: Third Phase:
    resources: _____
                      _____
                      _____
                      _____

Treatment contract: _____

1. Self image thinking and anticipation framework changes:
       Goals: _____
       Metaphors: _____

2. Attitude restructuring and perception changes:
       Goals: _____
       Metaphors: _____

3. Family structure changes:
       Goals: _____
       Metaphors: _____

4. Emotional role and affect changes:
       Goals: _____
       Metaphors: _____

5. Age appropriate intimacy and task behavior changes:
       Goals: _____
       Metaphors: _____

6. Changes related to increasing discipline and enjoyment of living:
       Goals: _____
       Metaphors: _____

Illustration 4

for all members in the family in supervision groups. Take a minute to peruse it. We tried to make sense of the different elements that Erickson seemed to take into account—the structure and organization of the social network in the family. Take a look at the visual map in the handouts that refers to the same ecosystem information. This chart looks like ET without a neck [Illustration 5]!

What do we know about the private self of this individual? What do we

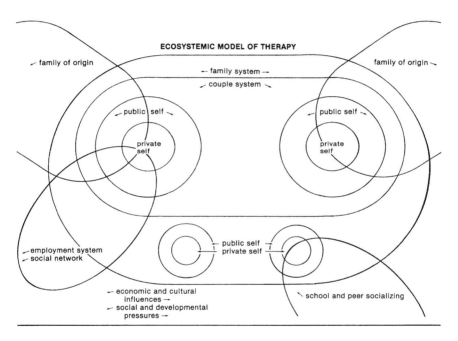

ECOSYSTEMIC MODEL OF THERAPY

Private Self	Public Self
biological-chemical system	behavioral options
muscular system	task related behaviors
emotional system	intimacy behaviors
cognitive system	symptomatic pattern sequences
beliefs	social role system
thoughts	public self-image system
imagery	
content	
sequence	
self-image system	
residual	
central-bodily/social	
scenarios-value system	
emanated-goal system	

Illustration 5

know about the public presentation of this individual? And what is it that happens between the individuals in the couple system, which is the larger unit to define reality? Also, how is it with the children's level of organization, which has lesser impact on the way to reality (unless one of the children is playing the role of one of the spouses, or there are younger children still and you have a multiple layer here)?

As an example for this hypothetical person, let's use words like, say, dominant behavior and friendly-dominant behavior and that which is hostile-dominant. Then we can ask, does this person generally have dominant-hostile behavior aimed at a spouse who has submissive-hostile behavior, such as self-effacement [Illustration 6]? This would be like Mohammed Ali saying all the time he can do things better than you can. That is dominant and hostile. And people playing complementary roles with him (e.g., a wife, especially) will likely be self-effacing: "Oh, you are right, you do things better. I wish I could do things as well as you." There are only two choices here. Either he and his wife would relate reciprocally in that dominant/self-effacing manner or she would behave dominantly as he does and they would mutually criticize a third person. And in that case, God help their children. Probably what happens in his family is that the men are elevated and the women diminished so that the boy will be as good as Dad: "We men are so pretty, we deserve two watches, and you don't deserve any. And just ask us if you want to know the time!"

So I want to know the person's general personality orientation with others, and I want to know the nature of his or her private experience. Does this person (in the Ali example) have a typifying affect of hostility? Does he have narcissistic thought process going on all the time privately—what he can get for himself and how he is better than anybody else and how he can beat up any other boxer in the ring? If he is having these kinds of thoughts all the time *what is being avoided in his private experience as well*? Is tenderness being avoided so that he can keep competitive thoughts going and act competitively?

I don't know when I first see someone but I want to know the private experience of the individual and I make some professional guesses about it. And that includes the biochemical system, which I have no business monkeying with in the sense of intervening, because I am not a doctor. I can think about it though and we intervene with the muscular system, the emotional system, and the cognitive system, which includes beliefs, thoughts, and imagery. We intervene with regard to the contents and the sequence of activity within these systems. We pay particular attention to intervening in the self-image system, which includes residual self-image ideas from childhood, central body image, and then social scenarios that will reflect the person's value system or goal system.

So, does Dad use excessively dominant behavior to overly involve himself with his son [in Illustration 6] who is encouraged to model after Dad and do the same behavior to Mother and sister? And what is the relationship back to the father's family of origin [Illustration 6]? Did he have a father who was always demeaning and critical of him? Or did he have a father who did the same thing that he is doing to his son, which would be represented as overinvolvement on this illustration. And then what happens in the social network? In the speculatory case of Ali he has to go out and beat people up from time to time to keep this justification going. And if he doesn't take out his tensions in the wider social network, then he can do worse here at some level in the family—or on the psychological level, because there is an interplay and balance between these various systems and levels of interaction.

There is an interesting case we supervised where a woman came in for therapy *very* anxious and self-critical. She was going to get married and the husband-to-be wanted to have 350 people there. He was sort of a local coach-hero in town. And he wanted everyone in the city, it seemed—the whole population of Pensacola—to come to his wedding. She had anxiety attacks which brought her to therapy with one of our colleagues, Dr. K. So I asked about the criticalness of this woman's husband-to-be—that was my first question, in fact. And sure enough he was known as an overly critical man. With an overly critical type such as I just outlined, it is okay for the partner to stay submissive and self-degrading and have self-critical thoughts and, of course, *anxiety*.

But this woman came in wanting to *get rid* of anxiety. If she wants to get rid of anxiety, we had better either *buffer* her against this criticism [pointing to Illustration 6], or, if we can influence him in some way, get *him to stop* doing this. But if he stops doing this, then he feels insecure. And he didn't want that. *And* he is better at getting rid of his insecurity and she is smart enough to put her experience aside so that he won't feel insecure. You can't tell them this because they will just say, "What are you, a social worker?! You are making something out of everything here." So here we see the importance of a complete change involving the entire ecosystem.

Another point here is that, in the fiancé's position as a rehabilitation counselor, he has a very positive relationship with the people that he counsels. He is dominant, friendly, takes care of all their needs. And you know what? He doesn't think counseling works! Isn't that odd? So in other words, his private thoughts would, at times, go something like this, if he were to articulate them: "These people are all stupid. I'll help them along and pull them up by the straps and pat them on the back and send them out. But they are not as good as me because they can't handle their life." Or the more humane version of the same, which is, "We just have to cope with

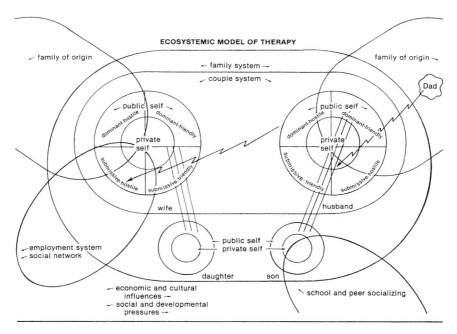

ECOSYSTEMIC MODEL OF THERAPY

Illustration 6

our problems and solve them. It's that simple, life's tough sometimes." Now we can't say that *he* does this, only that *if* a person were acting in these other ways, he would likely be doing that. Is he typical or different in that way? Either he does or he doesn't and *that* information, as well as how he really does whatever he does, is *vital*. But then, all of this network information *is vital*.

So he's not criticizing his clients, but he's doing the same thing to them. He infantalizes them in some way. He's overinvolved and infantilizing these people he works with. What are you going to do as the therapist? He won't come to the therapy because he doesn't think therapy works. So you have an interesting problem on your hands. If you want to do family therapy with this couple, it seems there are only two good choices. One is to teach this person (wife-to-be) some kind of private self-experience. Before I teach this wife to be more dominant and friendly, I had better teach her a way of buffering her private experience against that criticism. That will change the reinforcement contingencies on that criticism (from husband-to-be) and it will change the symptom.

Consider the "Lucy-Snoopy transaction," for example, where Lucy says,

"You stupid dog, you just lay around all day," and Snoopy kisses her on the cheek. That's the end of her criticism. She runs away. That will change the reinforcement contingencies and cross that transaction, thereby stopping it. So I can do that, but if I do that, I'm going to create a divorce here, or else he is going to take his insecurities out on his case load. I don't know which is worse but we have the same difference. We have an ecological problem on our hands. So how could this case be solved?

We weren't directly working with this family but we were offering supervision to Dr. K. in a monthly study group. He works at the university and so has a lot of students looking for field placement situations and similar sorts of experience and places to research for written papers and so forth. So I suggested that he use two of his students, people from the wife's social network, who wanted to study vocational rehabilitation.

They were to call up the coach-counselor-fiancé and enter into his social network. They were to say, "Dr. K. spoke about you with praise and suggested that we contact you to find out if it is possible to become involved in helping you in the vocational rehabilitation counseling program. This would help our field placement. Would that be okay with you?" Do you see how this would feed his narcissism, thinking that Dr. K. thought he was a great guy. And he was going to have two students thinking he was a great guy. They wouldn't need to know otherwise, by the way. Everyone wins in this case: The students get a field placement that they learn from. The fiancé could now affiliate and be supportive of the work done with Dr. K. because he thought Dr. K. thought *he* was a good guy. That would bolster his self-esteem enough that it would be possible to get his fiancée to respond differently to his criticism without freaking *him* out and feeding his insecurities. What he might lose from her (towards building his self-esteem out of insecure feelings) would be supplied by these two students and his image of Dr. K. as someone who approved of him.

I would then ask him if he was willing to come in for therapy to help *coach* his wife-to-be over her fears. And at some point my conversation would start to mention things like, "Every good coach should know—I don't need to tell you—what every good coach knows. You reinforce people for their good behavior and they'll do a better job. And there is praise and there is reinforcement. In fact, some praise goes like this. . . . We find something to compliment about the person. . . ."

So that way Dr. K. could have a treatment plan that would cover both the interventions in the broad social network and also the goals for the office. The goals for the office, of course, would include the behavioral learnings on how to praise and compliment, but also any new ones that came from deficiencies in behaviors that might be needed as the wedding becomes a marriage and treks off towards childbearing decisions.

The actual talk in the session would be indirect suggestions about all the things he "didn't" need to talk about, because, presumably, the coach already knew it. In the meanwhile, therapy would be used to actually inform the coach of things he didn't know, which is how to praise and reinforce and so on. This would probably result in some of each session being used to resolve the insecurities or whatever private experiences reinforce this whole gestalt that is here at a number of levels of dynamics [on Illustration 7].

Essentially, family therapy could be done with only the wife-to-be in the office, but if he had refused to come in under those conditions, I don't know what else could have been done to help the system creatively grow into marriage except to work with *only the woman* and have her carry the proper changes back into the family in the right order. So there are two things you can do. You can either do the family therapy with a single individual or you can attack another element of the system with interventions that will cause a ripple effect throughout the entire system. In this case, it happened both ways. This husband was encouraged to come into therapy when the threat had been reduced enough so that he could come. Does that make sense? I think that is kind of a nice example.

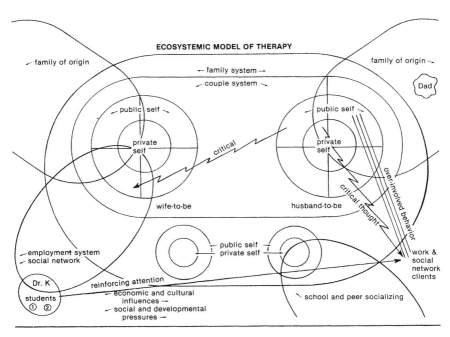

Illustration 7

So let's go back to the words on this chart again [Illustration 2]. What is the structure and organization of the entire social network, not just the family? Sometimes it is not necessary to go that far. What is the stage of development in the family system and the next likely stage? This is the stage of development of the system where the couple in my example are about to become married. They are going to be fully independent now and are going to make certain compromises about how much independence they give up. So those are the things that need to be negotiated between them *and with their social network*—actually, the entire ecosystem—and done for the most part *unconsciously*.

And the way they do it will depend upon their psychological age. So you need to treat each person as if they are that age. If you are dealing with Richard Simmons, as a speculatory example—he wouldn't be likely to have just one psychological age. Richard Simmons probably makes more money than any of us, so his ability to handle finances is certainly at a more mature level than his social-sexual development seems to be. Now I mean no offense if you are a Richard Simmons fan. Furthermore, I don't know if this is a stage personality or a real person that I am talking about. I imagine it is a stage personality. I certainly hope so. He is so expressive that he *does* make a good example. Now, let's just *assume* that the character he plays on the exercise program is the real person. How old is he approximately in chronological time? Someone said maybe 45.

How old is he socially? Eleven, okay, you are generous, sir. How old would you say he is *sexually*? Yes, there seems to be something of a discrepancy here but some general agreement—it sounds like you are saying between three and five. If you are to most efficiently retrieve resources, you ought to appeal to the psychological age that best represents each family member's level of achievement! There need not be only one.

We have a somewhat similar case where the father initially refused to come in until we appealed to his community role as a clergyman. Before we give this case, we need to underscore something. Answer this question: How do you get all this diagnostic information, anyway? How do you figure out how the interaction of these levels operates in the family? The answer is easy. It is . . . what? That is right, you observe the family in action.

OBSERVING AND USING FAMILY INTERACTION

Don't get the idea, just because you read that Erickson was identified with hypnosis, that he simply put couples and families in trance and told them stories. He was very clear about the importance of getting each member's opinion and getting each member in gear. He demanded interaction from time to time. He asked mothers to sit on their children; he had husbands confess affairs; he also had individuals move from home and not let others know their whereabouts; and he had people take separate vacations. He had individuals buy and give gifts to others and he had them go to restaurants. It is unthinkable that he did not use that interactional information to provide diagnostic information like that we just covered.

When a family comes in we try to get them talking to each other rather than to us, and we set up encouragement and interruptions in the process to help test the strength of the set patterns of interaction that emerge. For instance, a couple came in recently and the wife had been crying just before the session. We are going to show a tape of this couple later when we look into induction and reorientation, but we just want to show with this example how a pattern emerges and then is tested. The wife had the day off and had planned to go horseback riding while the baby was in the nursery. But it rained and she didn't go riding. Consequently, she saved eight dollars. So she planned to take her husband out for dinner when he got home and, I guess, she planned to do it on eight dollars! She took over an hour getting "fixed up," as she put it, and she did not tell him anything about her plan.

Now when he came home, the husband thought he was coming into a house where dinner would be waiting on the table. It wasn't, of course, and he was angered to think that he had to clean up and go out to eat. Also he was worried about spending money and he knew eight dollars wouldn't go very far. To make the financial situation worse, they were coming to therapy right then. She cried the entire way to our office. When they sat down, I asked who wanted to speak first about the events of the week. He looked at her expectantly but she said, "No you might as well go first." He said, "No, you go ahead." And she again said, "You might as well tell them your side." So he did. But you see a pattern here in this short opening gambit. She had needs—but that was not enough to motivate her speaking for herself. Her husband looked to her to speak—that was not enough. Then he turned down her suggestion that he go first and told her, in words, to go first—that was not enough. She intended to illustrate that she was hurt or wronged but to do so with a martyr-like role and a self-effacing maneuver.

Now the question we have is this: Will she maintain that strategy inflexibly, or under what conditions will she be likely to do something else? If Carol or I align with her, will she still refuse to speak for her hurts? If we leave her alone, will she ever do it? Once she does speak for her hurt, will she surrender it immediately if one of us aligns with her husband? What happens if we both align with one or the other of them? What if we disagree with both of them? This interview management is done very quickly by our choice of words. Carol might say to her, "You and I will allow your husband to go first *for now* and *we* will just sit here and evaluate what he says about this whole thing." In this choice of words the alignment has supported the wife.

Now we observe, what does she do when she has Carol's support? Does she discard it? Does she flirt with Carol? Does she play "na-na-na-na-na-na" with her husband? Does she attack men in general? Does it make any difference? Does she act like that is not enough? Throughout the interview we change our alliance at our choosing and act as free agents on the side of mental health—not on the side of any particular family member. If one aligned member tries to use the identification to "get even" with another member, we will disaffiliate just as quickly as we moved in. We are not manipulated by the emotional or logical displays *or the symptoms* of the clients.

I think that you can see how, in this way, we can soon discover who talks to whom and what the typifying affect is in the communication. We can see what the roles are and how flexible these roles have remained, and we can find out much about what the other members do to further the continuance of the roles. The live interaction is essential for diagnosis of the existing state and the needs.

There is another aspect of interaction that provides a dual function for our work. The enactment of assignments we construct before and after the interventions let us know how well the resources have been retrieved and let the family know exactly what we want of them. Let's look at the tape of the family where the father was, in fact, successfully encouraged to attend for the first time. In this tape segment you will see the father, mother, and the IP who suffered from bulimia. We have altered the names and other aspects so that the family is not identifiable but we have not changed any detail that will be relevant to the learning here. The father is 58, the mother is 49, and the daughter is 25 years old. This family was seen at an advanced supervision workshop by the therapist, Lance Scalf. The situation in the workshop is that therapists and families work in a suite adjacent to the conference room. What they do and say is broadcast on closed circuit large-screen TV. Carol and I can have constant contact via an intercom with an ear plug in the therapist's ear. That way the therapist can carry out the plan we have all created but we can direct the show inconspicuously when we need to do so.

Now in this segment you will see the therapist leading the family in a rehearsal of the paradoxical homework he has assigned. Perhaps I need to introduce the family to you a bit more. The parents referred the 25-year-old daughter for her bulimia. They have many problems, however, not the least of which is that the father has just lost his job. The father and mother have not had sexual relations for years. The daughter here is just recently out of the home and now the father and mother are living alone in the house.

This is obviously the stage of family development when the couple need to reunite. To make matters more interesting, each member has now displayed some physical, read that "psychosomatic," illness. This includes the daughter's bulimia, the father's "near" heart attack and colitis, and the mother's irritable stomach. The therapist had originally planned a far too grandiose session. He expected to do a number of things in this session leading to a reduction in symptoms for each of the "hopelessly ill" members. However, we insisted that he avoid playing the role of "savior" begged of him by this family and, in fact, not deal now with getting rid of the daughter's bulimia. Instead he should spend the entire session on one *obstreperous* issue: touching.

He should introduce it in a logical and metaphoric fashion, use trance with the entire family to correct their attitudes about touching, help retrieve comfort in touching, and finally, prescribe that each of them continue to get sick as a way to receive love and caring but do it in a more systematic and less random way. They were to get ill one day a week each and skip days. On the seventh day, they could rest since they were a very religious family. In order to ensure that the family understood and could carry out the instructions, he was to rehearse it with them, after trance, in the therapy session.

He would show them how to nurture the "ill" person and that is the segment you will see here. Note how terribly depressed the father is and also be aware that this couple have not had sex or even kissed in four years; and the father and daughter have not touched in an affectionate way in at least seven years prior to this. The trance with the entire family was done to challenge and correct attitudes about support, helping each other, taking nurturing, and how to touch. Since the husband appeared depressed, possibly suicidally, and since he didn't even wish to come to the session, here at the end of the interview we've asked the therapist to get him on the couch and have him be the major receiver of touching for this "practice."

In the following transcript the father is identified as "H," the wife is "W," the daughter is "D," and the therapist is "S." It begins with the father reclining on the couch to our right, albeit reluctantly, at the therapist's insistent suggestion. The mother is to the left of screen being addressed by the therapist. The daughter has her back to us in the center of the screen and the therapist is on the right at the foot of the couch on which the father is reclining.

S: Oscar, why don't you just lie down there for a second and . . .

H: [reclining on couch] You know, I can't relax like I used to.

S: That's okay, just lie down.

W: [nervously laughing, swinging back and forth in her swivel chair] That [referring to the husband getting ready to take nurturing], ha ha. [nervously wringing her right hand over her left]

S: Now using this as an example, [to wife] what would you do, how would you. . . ? [to husband] You are not feeling good right now. Let's go even further, let's overdo it. You are about through, you're not feeling good at all. [to both daughter and wife] How would you nurture him? How would the two of you nurture him? [to wife] Now just think if you were yourself, what would you do to help Oscar, and then do it.

W: Well, I would . . .

S: No, no, no, [leans forward and gestures toward husband] do it!

W: Well, if I were nurturing him, I would get close to him. [getting up and kneeling by his right side] I might, ah . . . [places her right hand on his right arm which he then raises up and sort of pulls away as the chatter continues]

S: Just go ahead and talk to him.

W: [patting his arm like it is a puppy as he lifts it]

D: [laughing nervously]

W: . . . and I might . . . [to husband] I'm here. [to therapist] . . . and I'd probably start laughing because I'm laughing the whole time. He knows that.

H: [mumbles] I feel terrible when she does that [puts forearm on forehead palm up].

S: [to husband] Do you feel terrible when she does that [referring to laughing nervously]?

W: [laughing] But I tell him that.

S: [to wife] Let me get out of the way, you are talking to me. [directing her] No, you talk to him.

H: [has returned arm to his side]

W: I know but I do it [referring to laughing] so much. [now looking at him and shaking his arm] I'd just tell him that I'm right here.

D: Talk to him!

W: You lie right here [stroking his arm and abdomen]. I can't help you cause I know it's in your mind [touches his temple with her right forefinger] if you are thinking about it. And that stomach's [stroking stomach] gonna be okay. You can control that [touching temple again] and you can control it best when you think about something else. [looks around to therapist] Now I tell him that and I may just sit here and I'll talk about something else. . . .

S: [interrupting] Oscar, as she is doing that, how are you feeling?

H: Comforted.

S: You do? Or do you feel something different.

W: You always tell me I preach to you.

S: Well, but see, that is not what he is saying now. Listen to what he is saying now [moving in close to wife, husband and couch, and blocking the view of the daughter].

H: Ya, the closeness . . .

S: . . . is comfortable . . . [husband nods] Okay, good.

W: I feel good. [therapist encourages] I guess that what I was trying to say is [to husband] rather than come down with you and make your weakness or weaknesses an irritation, I can just be close to you . . .

S: Okay, that's all we need. Just deal with that thought.

W: . . . instead of just saying "Oh, how horrible" and building up only that . . .

S: Okay, so don't even talk. I guess not even talking is not as important as just your being close. Is that what you are saying?

W: Okay, I can do that.

S: Okay, good [smiling, warm laugh, moves away behind daughter]. [to daughter] Laura, what would you do?

W: [stands and goes away from couch]

S: [to daughter, standing behind and touching the back of her chair] Go ahead with whatever you'd do.

D: Normally, what I would do [unfolds hands from chest into wide arcs] is, I'd ask you what is wrong. What's hurtin' with you [moves hands back to her chest and then face]?

H: [as she speaks he moves his hand from his mouth to his heart and finally puts right hand on stomach] My stomach is hurting me.

D: Has it been hurting [swings hands] through that whole relaxation time [referring to the trance]?

H: Well, [garbled] . . .

D: [leaning closer to hear him] You what?

H: I got very uncomfortable a number of times.

D: Like stomach uncomfortable?

H: [inaudible] Like right now.

D: I see. So you think your stomach's kind of a nervous thing from what has been going on?

S: [moving in close to daughter] But you know, he has already told you what he wants.

D: He told me what he wants from *her*!

S: What can *you do*?

D: The only other thing I would do is rub his back but I don't feel comfortable.

S: [moves to the father's side and puts his arm around him, strokes his arms and neck, speaking to daughter] But can you just come over and give him a [referring to the touching he is now doing], or give him a [referring to the face touching], or what can you do?

Because, see, when you do this [touches shoulder tenderly] it just says, "Everything's gonna be okay." And it gives him something positive here [touches his own heart]. But this is a test . . . it is one of the things that you said you'd like. Both of you [to wife and daughter] come over and say, "Everything's gonna be all right," and touch or whatever in a way you'd feel comfortable with but don't say anything more than maybe one or two short sentences. And just try it and just see how that feels. And just be aware of that feeling and [to father] I'd like some feedback from you about how that feels. Why don't you try it first, Laura [pointing to her], since your mother has already done it [moves away from couch]?

H: [moves right hand out to daughter, palm upward]

D: Look at you. You can't ask for it! [gets up from chair and walks over to father, takes his right hand in hers, and begins to bend over him]

S: Yes, he can. He can ask for it if he wants it.

D: It looks like he is on his death bed [goes to her knees]. I swear it.

S: All right [holds both hands out as if giving away a gift], so, let's saying he is dying.

D: You're dying? [rubs her neck with left hand and rotates neck as if trying to loosen up].

S: You feel like that, so what would you do? If he was on his death bed, what would you do, just do that?

W: What would you do? He doesn't want you to think about his chest pains.

D: Well, how would you like this [falls to embrace him]?

H: [he embraces her back with left arm and rubs her back appreciatively]

S: Okay, good, good. What would you say?

D: I'd tell you I love you.

S: Okay.

D: [sitting up, she and Dad, still stroking each other's arms, exchange some tender but inaudible words] [warm laughter] [stands and takes her seat]

S: [to wife] Okay, now Betty, would you do it this time and not say anything, not . . .

W: [finishing his sentence] . . . not, not give me no program?

S: No program.

W: With no program. [moves to husband] Oscar [gives him a very close neck embrace], I'm right here and I'll always be right here.

S: [slowly] Thaaat's it.

W: [moves back to look at him and talk] And I'll always be right near you, you know that. Always know that [squeezes hand]. Always. Do you feel it? [her face is *right* in his face as if to kiss him]. You are getting a lot of love today [patting his arm, and laughing]!

H: [smiling]
S: Good. That is a lot different really, it really is. There's a lot of feeling
there. It's neat.
W: [kisses husband's cheek] You'd get that all the time. [laughs]
S: Okay, Good. I'm going to run on downstairs now [to the supervision
conference room].

Here they go about saying the brief goodbyes to the therapist as he leaves
to come back to the supervision group room. The father, who did not even
want to come to this session, left wanting to go shopping with the wife and
daughter. That is an added plus to the session that we did not entertain as
a possibility at the beginning of the session.

In this example we see the result of the therapy session, and I think you
can tell a lot about the diagnostic areas we have been covering. For instance,
the roles that are played begin with Dad taking care of others, and intimacy
and touching-related transactions are avoided by all. Each person can trans-
act about the daughter's illness but not about his or her own needs. The
mother and daughter usually act as a team and avoid confronting the obvious
needs in the father and no one talks about or feels sexual desires. The
function of the symptoms may well be to provide some gratification via
nurturing and touching that would otherwise be entirely absent. But we see
some real strength in the way they have incorporated the therapy work of
this session. Also, of course, this was a rehearsal of the assignment for each
person to become ill on a specific day and then to get nurtured by the others
in this manner. When the next session comes, the way they have used all
of this for the intervening week will be used in the same diagnostic way.

We always want to ask how the diagnostic parameters fit together [Illus-
tration 3] with the system dynamics [Illustration 2]. The developmental stage
in this family is the stage of rediscovering the spouse when the last child
leaves home. The family organization here, as briefly summarized in the
preceding paragraph locks in the roles: mother is pleasant, religious, and
superficial; daughter is the "sick one"—everything she says can be talked
about and pulled apart by the parents; father is unquestioned, worried, and
ineffectual. These roles limit the communication: Mother resorts to prayer
when all goes badly; father withdraws in silence and works with his con-
gregation; the daughter can't ask for any healthy needs to be met for fear
they will be seen as a sign of her problem. Father can't ask to be nurtured
because that is inconsistent with his caretaking role and the daughter can't
just go out and nurture Mom or Dad because her behavior is always under
suspicion and is not taken to be what it is intended by the daughter to be.

Now, the communication limits beliefs in an obvious manner. For one
thing, the daughter considers herself the person with the problem; mother

believes prayer—not her own effort—will work; and the father does not *even consider* the possibility of turning to his family for help. Most importantly, the belief and preceding structure limits the unconscious resources they each have: The father will not interpret his experience as a need for touching and he will not find the words to ask for touching and love—he will not find himself crying. Likewise, the mother will not feel comfortable touching—we saw her nervous and awkward even with the coaching and therapy. Finally, the daughter will not feel that her sexual impulses are normal, she will not feel her aggression, and so on.

I think you can see the obvious connection to the interventions and the goals that we can establish to help this family. Please be patient about the explanations of goals, paradoxes, and so on. This entire matter will be put together systematically over the period of the next few days. Likewise, the logic of choosing each intervention and the delivery of each will build systematically. I think in the family interview we do on the last day, you will appreciate how these seemingly disconnected bits represent a great deal you have learned about our elaboration of Erickson's work as it applies to families. You know, I have to repeat, since you missed it: The father began this session *only* to help the daughter—only that—and literally walked out of the room at one point when the daughter began to speak about him getting something from this session! So, this tape is very touching in more ways than one. This was the first time the daughter and father have touched like that in over five years, and this is the first move towards sexual relations between the spouses who have not hugged like this in four years!

SYMPTOM FUNCTION

We need to discuss the symptom function and therapy goals. The function of the symptom can be a touchy matter. The *function* of something depends on the level of analysis. The function of this table leg is to hold the table up—at this level of analysis. The only way I can determine the *function* is to go above the level of the entire *structure* and examine it. I have to look beyond the top and the legs as a unit and examine the way the leg "acts" in the larger system. Well, it acts like a relatively solid object that is placed between the floor and other objects such as lamps and books. It impedes those objects on the table top from falling to the floor since it elevates the table top.

This entire structure of the table with its top and legs and bolts and cross braces has meaning at the next highest level—that of the room. From the vantage point of the entire room we can glean that the *function* of this table is to hold objects off the floor—and be attractive in the conference room decor. Well, from this level of structural observation, I can better understand the structure for any individual part of the system *below* it—those that are subsets are *below*. In other words we can see, when we get outside, that the leg has the *function* of holding up the top and is meta to the entire system of subsets that make up the structure. Now I don't know for certain that all cybernetic theories jive with me on this. But I do know that this is a practical and reasonable way to approach these understandings of structure and function in therapy.

That seems like a simple topic because the concept of a table leg is simple and people are complex. To examine and explain the *function* of the symptom, we need to look at a larger context, including a historical context. We saw another adult with bulimia [case recounted in *The Answer Within*] and it happened to make her feel disgusting. Eating and vomiting and feeling disgusting kept men away from her, but *was* that the *function* of the symptom? No. That was part of the structure of the entire symptom.

The function of the symptom originally *was* to express a willful defiance towards the tyranny that she felt when her family moved for the sixteenth relocation. She was only 13 and had spent plenty of her formative years trying to have *real* friends and even *boyfriends*. Her natural learning was being thwarted by her parents. She had taken a physical slap in the face from her mother when she expressed her anger about the move, and she stormed off to bed and launched a hunger strike. It turned into bulimia—I skip the unpleasant stages. Finally, she achieved a college graduation or two and became very independent, but she did still have bulimia.

Can you see here that assigning a function to a symptom can be very "theoreo-centric?" That's a word I made up to say that your assignment of assumptions about a family can be biased by your pet theory of causation, personality, cybernetics, and so forth. In order to think that the function was that of pushing men away or not being close, I picked on a link (that is, that bulimia helped her avoid men and she had an issue with men) that is a popular "eclectic" theory trap.

So look at it that way and let's get practical again. If you have a person coming in "psychosomatic" and being touched by doctors all the time, then perhaps the function of the symptom is to get attention focused on the body in some kind of a caring way. And if you have a child who everyone is worried about, part of the function of that symptom is that it helps everyone *unite* and have experiences of being useful and helpful. All of that is stimulated by that child's problem. And you can't get rid of that symptom until you find another way to help these children *stabilize that role* of being helpful, having a positive resource, and talking to one another. And they can accomplish a stable state doing *that* regardless of the symptom! Only they don't realize it. They don't need to realize it any more now than they did before—which was not at all! They just need some new ways to accomplish things *now* and do them better.

You are probably aware of the changes in a theory over time and how something that is certain at one time is considered absolutely false at another time. So look at the function in a real mechanical way and psychologically from the gratification that is derived and that includes *the state of consciousness that is stabilized in each member by virtue of interactions with the symptom carrier.* You'll be on much safer ground with the gratification of being able to feel that "We all are doing things together," "We are all working together, finally," and "It's too bad Johnny feels so bad but the rest of us feel good." How can we help them get *that* good feeling and *that* gratification? How do we get them to talk to one another the same amount of time? People can be sick in order to stabilize states of consciousness in everybody else. And the therapist is often induced to accept it that way—by the people who need it otherwise! How can we get the resources or the actual state of consciousness stabilized without the symptom carrier having a symptom?

So if that is the case, then your therapy has to be aimed at helping your clients find the resources to stabilize that state of consciousness for themselves without using the other people. Or help them find a justification for the role that doesn't involve helping the sick person, avoiding the sick person, hating the sick person, arguing with the sick person, or whatever it happens to be. And for that matter, you may be wanting to change the state of consciousness that family members are having anyway.

There are some families where everyone is functioning *perfectly*, except the symptom carrier. In that case, what we are saying applies. In most cases, of course, everyone has problems here and there. And you want to help increase everyone's level of functioning. They are stabilizing the function they've achieved at that point in their family development by having a symptom carrier.

Now we want you to take a look at the interpersonal checklist we have already spoken about. There are 128 adjectives (see Illustrations 8 and 9). You need to read through and check the ones that apply to you in a generally characteristic manner. If the list says "bossy" and you are "bossy," then check it. If you are "firm but just" with your children, check it. But if you just can't be firm in any context, then it is not ever characteristic of you and should be left blank. If it says "cruel and unkind" and you aren't cruel and unkind, don't check "cruel and unkind." If you *are* then *do* check it—and then *don't* come back, please.

What we want to do now that you've completed this checklist is talk about the assessment parameters that Erickson seemed to use and the ones

NAME_____DATE_____

Make a (✔) in the column marked "S" for each adjective which applies to you.

	S					S		
1A	_____	1.	ABLE TO GIVE ORDERS		3O	_____	52.	GENEROUS TO A FAULT
1K	_____	2.	APPRECIATIVE		2O	_____	53.	GIVES FREELY OF SELF
2H	_____	3.	APOLOGETIC		2A	_____	54.	GOOD LEADER
1C	_____	4.	ABLE TO TAKE CARE OF SELF		1J	_____	55.	GRATEFUL
2K	_____	5.	ACCEPTS ADVICE READILY		2D	_____	56.	HARD BOILED WHEN NECESSARY
1G	_____	6.	ABLE TO DOUBT OTHERS		1O	_____	57.	HELPFUL
2M	_____	7.	AFFECTIONATE & UNDERSTANDING		4E	_____	58.	HARD-HEARTED
3P	_____	8.	ACTS IMPORTANT		2G	_____	59.	HARD TO IMPRESS
1H	_____	9.	ABLE TO CRITICIZE SELF		3D	_____	60.	IMPATIENT WITH OTHER'S MISTAKES
2J	_____	10.	ADMIRES & IMITATES OTHERS		2B	_____	61	INDEPENDENT
4L	_____	11.	AGREES WITH EVERYONE		2E	_____	62.	IRRITABLE
4H	_____	12.	ALWAYS ASHAMED OF SELF		3G	_____	63.	JEALOUS
2K	_____	13.	VERY ANXIOUS TO BE APPROVED		2N	_____	64.	KIND & REASSURING
3P	_____	14.	ALWAYS GIVING ADVICE		2A	_____	65.	LIKES RESPONSIBILITY
3F	_____	15.	BITTER		2H	_____	66.	LACKS SELF-CONFIDENCE
2O	_____	16.	BIG HEARTED & UNSELFISH		2C	_____	67.	LIKES TO COMPETE WITH OTHERS
3B	_____	17.	BOASTFUL		3K	_____	68.	LETS OTHERS MAKE DECISIONS
2C	_____	18.	BUSINESSLIKE		3M	_____	69.	LIKES EVERYBODY
3A	_____	19.	BOSSY		3K	_____	70.	LIKES TO BE TAKEN CARE OF
1E	_____	20.	CAN BE FRANK & HONEST		4M	_____	71.	LOVES EVERYBODY
4J	_____	21.	CLINGING VINE		2P	_____	72.	MAKES A GOOD IMPRESSION
1D	_____	22.	CAN BE STRICT IF NECESSARY		3A	_____	73.	MANAGES OTHERS
1N	_____	23.	CONSIDERATE		3I	_____	74	MEEK
4C	_____	24.	COLD AND UNFEELING		2I	_____	75.	MODEST
1F	_____	25.	CAN COMPLAIN IF NECESSARY		3J	_____	76.	HARDLY EVER TALKS BACK
1L	_____	26.	COOPERATIVE		2P	_____	77.	OFTEN ADMIRED
3F	_____	27.	COMPLAINING		3I	_____	78.	OBEYS TOO WILLINGLY
2C	_____	28.	CAN BE INDIFFERENT TO OTHERS		2F	_____	79.	OFTEN GLOOMY
2E	_____	29.	CRITICAL OF OTHERS		3E	_____	80.	OUTSPOKEN
1I	_____	30.	CAN BE OBEDIENT		3O	_____	81.	OVERPROTECTIVE OF OTHERS
4D	_____	31.	CRUEL AND UNKIND		3E	_____	82.	OFTEN UNFRIENDLY
3J	_____	32.	DEPENDENT		3N	_____	83.	OVERSYMPATHETIC
4A	_____	33.	DICTATORIAL		2J	_____	84.	OFTEN HELPED BY OTHERS
4G	_____	34.	DISTRUSTS EVERYBODY		3I	_____	85.	PASSIVE & UNAGGRESSIVE
3A	_____	35.	DOMINATING		3B	_____	86.	PROUD & SELF-SATISFIED
2H	_____	36.	EASILY EMBARRASSED		2L	_____	87.	ALWAYS PLEASANT AND AGREEABLE
2L	_____	37.	EAGER TO GET ALONG WITH OTHERS		3F	_____	88.	RESENTFUL
3K	_____	38.	EASILY FOOLED		2P	_____	89.	RESPECTED BY OTHERS
4B	_____	39.	EGOTISTICAL & CONCEITED		4F	_____	90.	REBELS AGAINST EVERYTHING
2I	_____	40.	EASILY LED		2F	_____	91.	RESENTS BEING BOSSED
2N	_____	41.	ENCOURAGING TO OTHERS		2B	_____	92.	SELF-RELIANT & ASSERTIVE
2O	_____	42.	ENJOYS TAKING CARE OF OTHERS		3D	_____	93.	SARCASTIC
4P	_____	43.	EXPECTS EVERYONE TO ADMIRE HIM		3H	_____	94.	SELF-PUNISHING
2G	_____	44.	FREQUENTLY DISAPPOINTED		2B	_____	95.	SELF-CONFIDENT
2D	_____	45	FIRM BUT JUST		3D	_____	96	SELF-SEEKING
3M	_____	46.	FOND OF EVERYONE		3C	_____	97	SHREWD & CALCULATING
2A	_____	47	FORCEFUL		1B	_____	98	SELF-RESPECTING
1M	_____	48	FRIENDLY		3H	_____	99.	SHY
3N	_____	49.	FORGIVES ANYTHING		3C	_____	100.	SELFISH
3E	_____	50.	FREQUENTLY ANGRY		2F	_____	101	SKEPTICAL
3M	_____	51.	FRIENDLY ALL THE TIME		2M	_____	102.	SOCIABLE & NEIGHBORLY

Please complete the other sheet.

Illustration 8

S

3G	_____	103.	SLOW TO FORGIVE A WRONG
3B	_____	104.	SOMEWHAT SNOBBISH
4I	_____	105.	SPINELESS
2D	_____	106.	STERN BUT FAIR
4O	_____	107.	SPOILS PEOPLE WITH KINDNESS
2E	_____	108.	STRAIGHTFORWARD & DIRECT
3G	_____	109.	STUBBORN
3L	_____	110.	TOO EASILY INFLUENCED BY FRIENDS
3C	_____	111.	THINKS ONLY OF SELF
2N	_____	112.	TENDER AND SOFT-HEARTED
3H	_____	113.	TIMID
3N	_____	114.	TOO LENIENT WITH OTHERS
2G	_____	115.	TOUCHY & EASILY HURT

S

3O	_____	116.	TOO WILLING TO GIVE TO OTHERS
3P	_____	117.	TRIES TO BE TOO SUCCESSFUL
2K	_____	118.	TRUSTING & EAGER TO PLEASE
4N	_____	119.	TRIES TO COMFORT EVERYONE
2I	_____	120.	USUALLY GIVES IN
2J	_____	121.	VERY RESPECTFUL TO AUTHORITY
3L	_____	122.	WANTS EVERYONE'S LOVE
1P	_____	123.	WELL THOUGHT OF
3J	_____	124.	WANTS TO BE LED
3L	_____	125.	WILL CONFIDE IN ANYONE
2M	_____	126.	WARM
2L	_____	127.	WANTS EVERYONE TO LIKE HIM
4K	_____	128.	WILL BELIEVE ANYONE

ADJECTIVE CHECKLIST

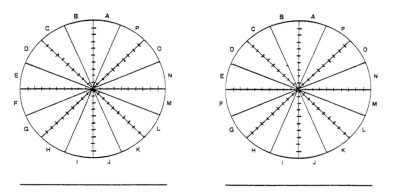

From: Leary, T. THE INTERPERSONAL DIAGNOSIS OF PERSONALITY,
New York: the Norton Press, 1957.

Illustration 9

that we use. Since we will be going over the diagnostic parameters, I want to refer you to one of your handouts. Here is a chart that will be helpful, and it actually contains three previous handouts (Illustration 10). We want to illustrate something with this chart that originally was made by William Matthews,[12] in Boston, a student of ours for several years. What we want to illustrate here is the recursive aspect of the client-therapist system. This little flow chart helps a bit. A family interacting within its ecosystem discovers one or more members who displays a symptom. I guess that you know it could go away "spontaneously," in which case the members develop a new relational pattern, avoid therapy, and return to the ecosystem. But if the symptom continues and the family enters therapy, then the therapist draws some distinctions here. Those distinctions involve the *diagnostic categories* that we just went through and result in some idea of desired therapeutic outcomes.

THERAPEUTIC OUTCOMES

Therapeutic outcomes [Illustration 11] are distinctions from which you draw other distinctions if you are a strategic therapist. One of the things that you are interested in doing as a *strategic therapist* is *initiating each phase of therapy*. Strategic therapy, in the illustration, essentially means that the therapist initiates the next therapeutic goal. In a way anybody that does anything more active than the Freudian analyst's classical approach would be strategic. Even Carl Rogers can be considered strategic. He just wouldn't explain his goal.

Rogers would have a goal in mind. His goal would be to get you to be more congruent or get you to display your feelings more genuinely. And so in order to accomplish that he would say, "Tell me more about that" or "I think those are your feelings and . . . I wonder if you appreciate the importance of holding onto them and being yourself with them now." And *that* is directing the flow of the works. This is obvious and more than just a little bit so!

So really most people are pretty comfortable at this point being strategic in therapy. Erickson and the Palo Alto or MRI group he strongly influenced were major proponents of active therapy. They promoted and helped us all come to realize the importance of selecting certain goals and initiating actions to help our families reach them. The goals that we have here are grouped in six major categories [Illustration 11]. And they correspond a

---

[12]An extensive discussion of this chart is found in Matthews, W. (1985). A cybernetic model of Ericksonian hypnotherapy: One hand draws the other. In S. Lankton (Ed.), *The Ericksonian monographs, number I*. New York: Brunner/Mazel.

little bit to the sheet that we just looked at, as you will see (bottom of Illustration 10):

1. *Changes in emotion or affect.* Let's say you have a sibling who is developing symptomatology and he hasn't grieved for a lost brother sufficiently. He is depressed or remorseful or whatever. So one of your goals would be to help him grieve. That is an affect change.

2. *Changes in behavior.* It is most important to remember that this means *behavior.* You won't even realize that this is important or difficult unless you have paid some dues struggling with a behavior modification approach. Not that the behavior mod approach is a dinosaur or anything. It's just that behavior mod approaches, more than any others, make it *extremely* obvious to you that a behavior is a specific, observable, and carefully described event. That is, "Lift your hands to waist level, elbows at your belt line, turn your hands palm up, and move your chin downward to within about an inch of your chest." This is far more specific than saying, "Assume a gesture of needing help." You will want to assume this degree of specificity when helping build associations to result in a behavior change.

3. *Changes in attitude.* When the concern is a limiting belief, the temporary solution is to help the family suspend the conviction about the belief. This is done by pairing confusion that is caused by an overload of consciousness. The overload is often self-induced when members try to compare and contrast information that conflicts with their expectations. This can be facilitated with homework and many other means. The easiest may be information in a particular kind of story.

4. *Changes in self-image.* These are changes that hold together the first three by means of internal, goal-directed, visual thinking.

5. *Changes in social network or family structure.* These hold together the first three by means of new family structure. This basically means that the group can tolerate, and in fact support, new roles. And the content of those roles draws upon the new behaviors, feelings, and supporting attitudes that were changed by the work towards the first three goals.

6. *Enjoyment and discipline.* Another area of changes that Erickson definitely worked for and which we were unsure of the category for, we have come to call enjoyment and discipline. Erickson was a big proponent of both of those aspects of living: He thought that one should be disciplined and that there is no reason to do it in a way that is less than enjoyable whenever possible.

Now the way we determined the categorization with these outcomes really started in our listening to his stories on our audiotapes over and over. We tried to determine what was different about them and separate them

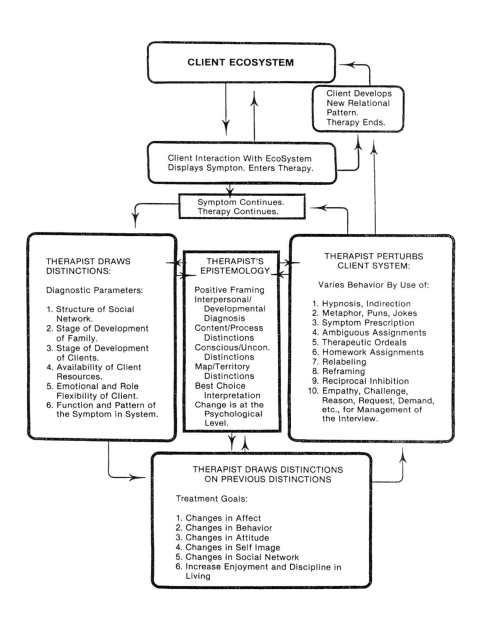

Illustration 10

THERAPEUTIC OUTCOMES

1. Family structure change.
> Goal stated in terms of change in who is in the network, who speaks to whom, what is spoken about, what affect is typical, what subgroups form, what is the time sharing of roles, etc.

2. Age appropriate intimacy or task behavior.
> Goal stated in terms of change in perceptions, experiences, and transactions occuring in approximations of the chronological age-appropriate intimacy situations that could be achieved by each family member.

3. Attitude restructuring.
> Goal stated in terms of the actual changes in perception and belief system (priority of perceptions and the weight given to perceptions). This includes changes in the client's assumptions which may have previously been used to justify, make predictions, or guide each family member to have or maintain the problem.

4. Affect and emotional flexibility.
> Goal stated in terms of each family member's understanding and use of emotions necessary to the contracted therapy goals, including supporting perception of internal physiological components of the emotion.

5. Self-image thinking enhancement.
> Goal stated in terms of improvement in each family member's ability to anticipate using himself or herself in various desirable situations. This includes the ability to imagine, believe that certain new situations would be beneficial to become involved in, and formulate an awareness of one's self as worthwhile.

6. Enjoyment and discipline in living and changing.
> Goal stated in terms of each family member learning to appreciate living even during the process of change and to acquire the necessary and proper amount of discipline to achieve the defined goals.

Illustration 11

from one another. You hear some stories and you cry. And it is clear that he was interested in something like that as the goal he had in mind. So he wanted you to have an affect change. But you don't change your attitude or your behavior.

There are other stories he tells where it is real clear that the point is an attitude, like the one I mentioned about the guy on the hillside and the passersby. That story obviously doesn't give you a feeling, doesn't teach you a new behavior; it questions an attitude. Right? So some of the stories seem to have one effect, whereas others have a different effect. It finally dawned on us one day that there were clearly some things he would do that would make changes in these specific and different areas.

We've mentioned stories that change the structure of the social network, and we have mentioned those stories that have to do with self-image like the tractor and dancing, and so on. There is an example of behavior in terms of communication behavior and I'll read it to you. It is short. Can I borrow a copy of *The Answer Within*.[13] This brings to mind the question: "Is there an *answer within*?!" Since Erickson uses indirection and utilizes existing behavior so people do the thinking, *they* really develop the answer to the problem in their own experience. That is why we called that book *The Answer Within*.

Now there is a metaphor in here that we originally used to illustrate an example of Erickson's multiple embedded metaphors. Right now I just want to show a selected portion about behavior, so I won't read the whole thing and you won't like this example particularly. I'll be reading from pages 112-119 if you care to follow along and I will read it in the voice tone and inflection that I've taken from Erickson so you can get a little more feel for being there in his office. The point here is we have a husband who is letting his soon-to-be ex-wife cause him hurt. He doesn't stand up to her. He doesn't quarrel. He backs down. Since I'm starting in the middle, you won't get the multiple embedded effect of this metaphor. Erickson is doing the talking and is discussing a picture one of his clients painted.

> It is a beautiful picture of a circus. There was a horse. A girl riding a horse. A dog, everything you'd see, or expect to see at a circus. A clown was standing beside the horse. The blonde girl was sitting on the horse wearing a blue jacket. A blue ribbon in the horse's tail was appropriate, same as on the neck of the clown. The same color of blue, different pigment, the same shade as the merry-go-round in the background. The same shade of blue.
> Amil had been my patient and his first wife had kept him and teased him, treated him like the south end of a northbound horse, making a clown out of him. She kept him on a merry-go-round, never knowing if he was going up or down. I don't believe he yet understands what the picture means; it is out of his system. (p. 116)

We know we are talking about a man whose wife treated him like the south end of a northbound horse. Now there is the behavior part of this metaphor moving on through another part of the same metaphor. Here Erickson is about to explicate some ways in which the husband can change his role and conduct with the critical wife. This is stimulating thought and experience about a new role and, hence, a new family structure when only one member of the family is in the office.

[13]Lankton, S., & Lankton, C. (1983). *The answer within: A clinical framework of Ericksonian hypnotherapy* (pp. 112-119). New York: Brunner/Mazel.

At Elouise, I had to discharge some oldtimers who weren't doing their work. And one of them got angry enough to come in my office and say: "You're a dirty bastard." I said, "You are quite mistaken, I'm a dirty bloody bastard of a . . . " "No," he said, "You are a dirty son of a bitch." "I'm a dirty, bloody son of a bitch of a bastard." And he couldn't think of any way to improve on that. [pause] So subsequently, new attendants were encouraged to come to my office and insult me. So I always improved their insults. (p. 118)

Now in Erickson's rendition, that portion about communication behaviors is immediately preceded by this next bit about Amil's wife. And remember that these things are being connected by association with the ideas that he has just stimulated with those specifics about how to quarrel and stand up for oneself, albeit in an unusual way.

And I had Amil's wife do all those nasty things she wanted to do that drove Amil so far up the wall that he divorced her. After the divorce she wrote him acrimonious letters intending to hurt his feelings. He showed me the letters and they were very nastily worded. So I had him underline phrases here and there and put under them in fine writing some other words. And she stopped writing. She couldn't stand to see her writing with those additional words added.

It's like a trick I use or a maneuver or a manipulation, or a trait, one term for it that I've employed. At Elouise, I had to discharge some old timers who weren't doing their work. And one of them got angry. . . . (pp. 117–118)

So you see we have an articulation and a careful mis-speaking so he has to redundantly say those vulgarities—in the context of suggesting that somebody respond to his wife, in the context of another client whose wife treats him like the south end of a northbound horse. So what you have, then, is you don't learn an attitude, you don't learn it is better to do that than not do that, you don't learn a feeling, unless the vulgarity pulls a bad feeling out of you, which would be incidental. But what you learn are a bunch of ways of talking back to somebody who is criticizing you. That part is a behavior metaphor. That makes a different impact than something I hear that makes me cry, and something else I hear that makes me question an attitude.

All the while, by the way, the therapist's epistemology influences his or her selection of these distinctions and delivery at every step. Erickson's work indicates that there was a strong need for "positively framing" the family's behavior. You're not putting it positively because you want to "trick" them but you're positively *conceiving* of it! This is represented by the center of the chart we already looked at right here (Illustration 10).

Like procrastinating, for instance. How many of you would say you procrastinate? You have to write a paper, so instead you clean the house, empty the garbage, wash the windows, and answer the mail. And then you finally get around to doing your paper, but, well, it's time to *do something else now*. So you have procrastinated and not gotten it done. That is the scenario. And you think that is terrible. Well, it may be at times but it also may have a very good function!

There is a purpose for that behavior in my life. I don't criticize myself for it. When I do that, I think I know exactly what I am doing. I am amassing resources of *mastery over my environment*. And when I have enough of those, then I know I can tackle the new job. There is nothing else impinging on my consciousness that is waiting to be done out there that needs to be done. I have a clear slate and I have amassed feelings of success from doing all these little chores that I can do with one hand tied behind my back.

That is a real important step if there is no other way to get those feelings generated. Negatively labeling it "procrastinating" only adds insult to an injury of the preparation process that you *could* see very positively. So I am saying this positive framing is finding a way to interpret human behavior so it seems it is the best choice that people can make at every step, rather than thinking you've offended *the gods of doing it the right way*, or something. There is an interpersonal developmental diagnostic angle to things.

Process and content distinctions are being made between how each person puts things together versus *what* they put together. This is similar to the conscious/unconscious distinctions. This is like the case of the woman to whom Erickson said, "Can you sing in trance?" She said, "Maybe" [while moving right hand to touch cheek]. You need to recognize this [looking out and defocusing] and *this* [while moving right hand to touch cheek] as *unconscious communications*, and maybe as conscious behavior—but secondarily. There are many instances in which the person is completely unaware, at the conscious level, of abundant unconscious communications. We've had people in trance who have their hands levitated to their faces and then *open* their eyes and say the levitation suggestions aren't working.

Map/territory distinctions are next. Consider, especially, the difference between the theory or the family's explanation and the real human beings in front of you. Those are real important distinctions to make.

Best choice is best choice. People make the best choice possible that they have so far learned how to make. That is, if the person can't conceive of anyone in his family (including him, especially) having a college degree, or thinks that he couldn't possibly change, then he doesn't have those choices in the *map of experience*. If he gets the experience, then he can go on to the next step, which is trying to figure out *how* he can change. And you, the therapist, should be noticing if there is, in fact, a map of experience, and should be interpreting failure to get there as a failure of either having the area on the map or having roads to the area. It means that what you are doing is you are teaching people to make changes and choices rather than trying to take them away. It is a good thing to remember here that changes are created at psychological levels. Insight is not very important for learning. Ah-ha.

So from these distinctions, with this attitude in mind, you now go about figuring how to *perturb* the client-system in order to make some changes. It's not that you give a metaphor to somebody and they are cured. It *is* an interactive process.

There (Illustration 10—the box on the right side of page) the bottom one should perhaps be the top or most important one. That is the *delivery*. For interview management, there is the use of empathy or challenge or reason or demand, whatever it is *appropriate* to use. If you have a person in the family who is challenging and cocky and you try to be empathic to him or her, you are going to get social worked! And being challenging back is the most reasonable thing to do. There is an example Erickson gives of the fat woman who visited him and said that she was a plain fat slob and pitifully in need of help.[14] She explained her family history briefly, and it will be self-evident for our purposes.

Greeting her at the door and failing to get her to enter when she was courteously invited in, Erickson realized that rapport would have to be established quickly and he said something rather shocking as she backed up. Now this case has been written up in *Uncommon Therapy, The Answer Within*, and in the *Collected Papers*, but it bears repeating to make these points. When Erickson told this to his students, he said that he had to do some quick rethinking and knew that he couldn't continue to be kind to her. Hence, brutality would be used to convince her of his sincerity. Any other possible approach, any kindness, would be rejected or misinterpreted. She could not possibly believe courteous language. He said:

> You haven't really told me the truth. I am going to say this simply so that you will know about yourself and understand that I know about you. Then you will believe, really believe, what I have to say to you.

---

[14]A more complete discussion of this case can be found in Erickson, M. (1980). Hypnosis: Its renascence as a treatment modality. In E. Rossi (Ed.), *The collected papers of Milton H. Erickson on hypnosis, volume IV: Innovative hypnotherapy* (pp. 66-70). New York: Irvington.

You are *not* a plain, fat, disgusting slob. You are the fattest, homeliest, most disgustingly horrible bucket of lard I have ever seen, and it is appalling to have to look at you. . . . Your nose is just mashed onto your face. Your teeth are crooked. Your lower jaw doesn't fit onto your upper jaw. Your face is too damn spread out. Your forehead is too hideously low. . . . Your feet slop over the edges of your shoes . . . and that dress you are wearing—polka dots, millions and billions of them.

He continued to the effect that now that she knew he wouldn't lie to her, wouldn't she please come in and let him put her in trance, so he could say more uncomplimentary things to her unconscious mind, things that her conscious mind couldn't bear to hear.

And she did, then, and he proceeded to tell her all the things that her conscious mind couldn't bear to hear, namely that she was worthwhile and deserved to improve herself. So what we are saying here is there is the use of the appropriate joining behavior for starters, and as the symptom continues you make further diagnostic distinctions based on that and then further refine your goals and further develop interventions which may include hypnosis, metaphors, puns, jokes, symptom prescription, task assignments, relabeling, reframing, reciprocal inhibition, trance phenomena, and so on, as it shows on the chart.

The important part here that you really need to remember is that this is a recursive system. The family members do something, you do something, and there is an ongoing loop, ongoing diagnosis, ongoing goal setting. And so, finally, the family members develop some new relational patterns that satisfy developmental demands and the symptom is no longer carried. Then the family rejoins the ecosystem *at a higher level of functioning*.

What we want to do first, then, is to figure out something about these goals today. The interventions will wait. If we don't have any goals in mind, it doesn't do much good to have interventions to achieve those goals. So let's look at those goals.

EXAMPLE OF DIAGNOSIS AND OUTCOMES

The best way to determine the goals is to interview the family and observe their pattern of interaction with one another and with you. And another thing that can be done is to back up some of your perceptions with this interpersonal checklist [Illustrations 8 and 9]. Before we look at that, I want to show you a tape to highlight some of the diagnostic interacting you need to do with your clients. You won't see it in its entirety because the treatment portion is not relevant to our immediate learning needs in this context. This is a tape of a woman with extreme back pain.[15] I had met her only moments before and so I had formulated very little, if any, treatment plan before *this* interview. What is special about this, besides the success we had, is the way this displays the interview process which leads to the intervention. As you will see, by observing the unconscious as well as the conscious response from this woman, I get very good information on every one of these diagnostic parameters *without* sounding like I am "making a case" against her. My initial need is to determine to what extent she has learned the pain and to what extent it may be regenerated by psychodynamic processes. All right, let's watch it from the introduction and I'll interrupt it with commentary as we go. I'll tell you what was in my mind as we went along.

> S: [to group] I want to make sure that you realize the things we do here really ought not be recreated with every client in exactly the same way and as a matter of fact, 50 minutes may not be the amount of time Lisa needs. She may need 10 minutes or she may need three days. So keep in mind that our major activity here is to demonstrate some things, and cure is optional in this case. The mass of you should gain some useful knowledge from this and I know you want to hear from Lisa. I also want to thank her for sharing herself, because my major attention goes out here [to the audience]. I want to start by asking Lisa to tell us something about her difficulty and then I'll explain to the group what I'm going to do.
> S: Would you be willing to tell us your age?
> L: Sixty-two. . . .

So, what is her developmental situation? What can we expect to be the social pressures and sanctions at the age of 62? Right—Retirement. What else? How about the adjustment to the youngest child leaving home? Okay.

> S: And married, children?
> L: Married. Four children.
> S: The youngest?
> L: Youngest will be 30 next July [smiles and moves her left hand upward and outward at the wrist].

Did you see that smile and wrist movement—as if to indicate that he was "long gone" and that all is well? I don't need to question her about this

[15]Lankton, S. (1984). The clinical use of trance phenomena for therapy and pain control. Phoenix, AZ: The Milton H. Erickson Foundation, Inc. This videotape was recorded in Phoenix, AZ, on December 5, 1984, at the Second International Congress on Ericksonian Approaches to Hypnosis and Psychotherapy.

because we can see that the unconscious response here, the responses of the face and hand, say "everything is great." Now these could be consciously controlled to falsify information . . . but why would she do that? And besides, she has no reason to suspect that I am searching is these areas. So let's find out if she is adjusting to retirement.

S: And you are still working or are you retired?
L: Semi-retired. I'm retired from the state office of vocational rehabilitation in February this year. And a month later I started a part-time job as mental health counselor at a business school in Tucson. I'm enjoying it greatly.

Well, this is an odd response. For starters, "semi-retired" is not a category one tends to think about as "official." Also, do you see how she put the information in imbalance? She said one thing about what she left and she said three things about the new position. That terminated with the statement, "I'm enjoying it greatly." I wondered why she said that, but it became more clear later.

In this next section many in the group will flinch and look away. But notice that I am in trance watching her and watching those subtle responses.

S: Now, tell me about the pain I heard about.
L: At age 16 I injured my back in three places: lumbar, thoracic, and neck area.
S: How did you do it?
L: I ran down a beach in Hawaii and dove [moves hands from lap and moves hands toward one another] into the water to skim on the top [moves hands from lap to show how she would skim the water]. The wave dissipated [slaps palms together] just as I arrived, so I went in here [pointing to upper chest and neck] and my feet and legs went over my head [moves left hand in a circular motion from behind her head and over her head, twice—illustrating the leg movement] . . . that way [becoming short of breath]. So um . . . [she stiffens her upper lip and takes a deep breath].

Now what did she do here? Did you notice how many looked away? What did you see her do with her face and her lip? Did she do this "So, um . . . [grimace]" as if to indicate, "I always screw up?" Or, did she do this "So, um . . . [smirk]" as if to say, "That'll show 'em?" Or, did she do this, "So, um . . . [heavy exhale]" as if to say "Life is ruined now"? No, what did she do? This is *very* important. Watch it again. She has a stiff upper lip and moves her hands apart and later shrugs as if to say, "Life goes on and you must make the best of it!"

L: At that time . . . what . . . in 1936 [separates hands in a shrug-like motion], they weren't performing the kind of surgery they do now when you mess up [shrugs left shoulder] a part of your back.

So this is her indication of the mood she had about it. It is something about "life is tough and you have to just cope and make the best of it and keep on going." "There is no time to lay around and lick your wounds and moan about it." Now here she is speaking about the worst trauma in her life and what does she do?

S: [to audience] Can you hear all right? [They say no.]
L: Goodness sakes [looking down and lifting up microphone]. Do I repeat?

She has enough consciousness to try to help the people in the room! Remember that the definition of the ego is that it contains mechanisms of perception, motility, and the seat of consciousness. The function of consciousness means the ability of the ego to be aware of stimuli, among other things. Having a lot of it, as it were, is how the term "ego strength" got started. And here we see that she has much ego strength. This is a very *capable* and *strong* person. Her mind is strong enough and capable enough to take care of herself, me, and the group of professional observers. I wonder at this point if I will be able to get her to go into a trance or if her awareness will just subsume my entire effort and keep control. At any rate, her ability to help and do things for herself is a resource, if I use it that way.

S: No, no, that's all right.
L: So, I was wearing a brace most the time but continuing to be active because I like to ski and play tennis. So I wore a brace to do these things. Finally, in 1960, I think approximately, I had to have surgery . . . a [wiggling fingers] laminectomy.
S: And you said there is pain even now as we speak.
L: Oh yea, I have arthritis in all the injured areas.

Well, arthritis fits right into the diagnosis that I have in mind. I expect that arthritis illustrates that she has repeatedly put her sympathetic nervous system in an adrenalin-dominant imbalance. That is, some people try to cathect their skin nervous system, musculo-skeletal system, or their cardiovascular system with adrenalin fluids so they can keep themselves strong. They do that as they avoid flooding their tender organs in the center of the body with cholinergic fluids. This latter situation causes relaxtion and a relinquishing of self-support. Well, that is a rule of thumb that I have noticed and which is, of course, a nonmedical opinion on the subject. But what I do know is that I see people who are intent on being strong getting sometimes one and sometimes the other of these problems. She is having arthritis and that simply supports the contention that she avoids appropriate experiences of weakness *to some degree beyond that which is healthy.* That was a long diversion to underscore what I have in mind at the point where she tells me that she is having arthritis. I figure in one more point in favor of the conclusion that she is avoiding relaxations that might result in her being treated as an invalid. If there are any questions about this, I'll answer them when I continue this later.

S: And you are taking medication?
L: I take both codeine and motrin.

Do you have any idea of what I am getting at here? I am trying to lead into something also diagnostic and extremely relevant. What would happen if she could not conceive of changing? Then her self-hypnosis, the limits of her belief system, would undo any changes I might help her make.

S: And you'd be able to . . . we could use you as a barometer of the success by your report that the pain went away at the end of the session.
L: Absolutely. The codeine helps but . . .
S: But you know it's there . . .
L: I know it is there.

What did that prove? Yes, I found out that she is able to conceive of a change in this session. She could have said, "Well, let's wait and see," or "Nothing has worked so far," or "I don't see how this one session could really help much." But she *did* say, "Absolutely." I can be certain that she *has an attitude in her map of experience that she can change, possibly even quickly.* If the answer was anything other than this one she gave I would have to make, as my first goal, the attitude that says she can change today!

S: Lisa, you mentioned that you use concentration, meditation, biofeedback for yourself.
L: Yes most successfully at night.

So some of the needed and available resources are the ability to do this self-hypnosis and to use the context of nighttime. I will want to also use this context when I do the rehearsals or metaphors with her.

S: Is there anything that this problem keeps you from doing? You said you wore a brace to still be active in sports.

L: I don't wear a brace. I haven't worn a brace for the last few years or so.
S: So, you are not slowing yourself down at all.
L: No! I just want to do more.
S: Well, do we need any more information from you? Does anyone else in your family have any pain problems?

Well, I need to know about her modeling as a woman. Is it that everyone in her family, or every woman in the family tree, has pain that she endures? Is it okay for her to be free of pain or is it a burden that is carried to keep everyone from happiness? Is there anything in the family of origin that might tell me answers to these questions?

L: Not that I know of.
S: Parents?
L: Just a mother . . . and she is *quite* pain free.

Well, here mother is *quite* pain free. That sounds like everyone in this family is expected to be free of illness and sickness. It certainly supports the picture we have seen so far. And again, I don't believe I need more information in order to proceed with some confidence. Well, now I want to see if there is any hostility directed at Hawaii as a defense mechanism, any thought generalization. Or has she just completely repressed or otherwise worked through the trauma of the injury except for the pain? If so, then the learned pain is my primary concern.

S: What were you, a military brat? Why were you in Hawaii in the '30s.
L: It was just a nice place to go.
S: It still is, as a matter of fact.
L: It's changed.
S: Have you been back?
L: Just one quick trip.
S: Did you enjoy it?
L: Yes, it was fun [smiling] to be there with my husband but I have no desire to go back.

Here we see again some further indication of her marriage being enjoyable and they are a "we," together as a couple and not two "I's" who are competing and disagreeing.

S: It was separated from the memories though?
L: Oh yes, but it was just so beautiful [smiles] at that time. After all, two hotels on Waikiki beach . . . in the '30s.

Well, now I have all the information that I want. By the way, what psychological age would you say we have here? How about "adolescence"? After all, the biggest trauma of her life occurred when she was a teenager; she is extremely active and prone to get involved doing more things; she is concerned with her independence, which are all teen issues; and even her dressing reflects that age of person I'd say, especially when taken as part of the larger whole.

I see that this is a strong woman who seems to have a bit of a fear that someone will try to put her in an invalid role. She defends against that by stating that she "is enjoying" whatever it is she is determined not to lose. That is like saying, "I enjoy it so don't you dare take it away from me." So I am sure that this session will be well spent if the major learning is about how she can use trance phenomena such as dissociation, time distortion, negative hallucination, and amnesia to unlearn a hypersensitivity to the pain.

> S: All right, uncross your legs and, ah, I think it is a good idea to place your hands on your hips. You may need to place them where it is most convenient for your back.
> L: Okay. That's good.
> S: I don't know where we are getting the pop. It is out of your microphone cord so . . . yeah, get your hand on top of the cord just in case that is the hand that wants to levitate up to your face.

Here was a harmless presupposition that she accepted. It tells me that she might be willing to accept presuppositions and that I can package suggestions that way to help her use them. As you will see later in the film, she does raise *that* arm.

> S: Usually, when people go into trance it is important that they be comfortable—in this case doubly so. So feel free to move at any point, regardless of how concentrated you think you need to remain in order to get the usefulness out of the trance.

I have presupposed that she will "remain" concentrated. That way I don't have to establish that she is or is not. It saves time and she has not challenged one of my presuppositions. I gave that rather obvious one about her arm levitating up and she accepted it, too.

> S: You said that you had been in trance before but light. So, you'll [looking down] probably be glad for me to be the hypnotist for this trance. Usually people find some spot to stare at and make minor adjustments [jerks neck at shoulders] that are actually out of their

awareness. And, ah, before you go into trance you might want to use your conscious mind to summarize the things you said. Your unconscious is no doubt interested in what is most relevant for you. And you might become aware of the diminishing need to notice the people around you and I hope you will remember to listen to the sound of my voice. That's right. And my words are actually a stimulus for you to do a lot of thinking about things that are important for you. I don't really know very much about you but you know a good deal more, and your unconscious knows more still. So use the trance as a way for your conscious mind to discover something from yourself about yourself.

Here I have continued to presuppose 1) that she would go in a deep trance and 2) that she is diminishing her awareness of the rest of the room. You might note that I looked away when I presupposed that I would put her in a deep trance. I did not want to enter any interpersonal tension that would create a different motivation.

I have discovered that presuppositions work well with her. And, as you can hear, I have concentrated her on *herself* by saying that she knows more about herself and that she will learn from *that* and not from me. This is true. And it leaves clients with the power. In her case, that is especially appropriate. She wants to be in control of her life . . . and she is!

> S: There is really no need to talk, no need to share anymore—no need to pay attention or analyze what I'm doing—no need to keep your eyes open—but you can close them [she closes them, opens them very briefly, and closes them again for the duration of the trance]. And concentrate your attention on something you would like to concentrate your attention on in order to go into trance just as deeply as you think necessary, as you diminish your awareness of the stimulus outside you and more and more we apply the resources you have to the pain.

I have put everything here in the reverse or "no-set." I don't think she would be the kind of person who waits for permissions from a stranger. If I were to say, "You *can* do that and you *can* do that," wouldn't I be a bit presumptuous? This woman does what she wants to do and she does not need a stranger telling her, "It is all right not to pay attention to me," etc. So I got the same information across with the no-set.

This is the first statement of my goal and our contract. It is the learning set. I hope to confuse her normal way of junctioning so that she has to work harder at finding *her* way. In the process she will discover some new trance phenomena to use—those retrieved later in this session.

S: Your unconscious is quite suggestible and it is important that a woman like you know that your conscious mind can be quite an aid, a disability, a liability. You have tried a number of things that your conscious mind thinks are important but I bet that you will really have some doubt about your ability to fail at doing nothing . . . [pause] . . . and I hope that you do . . . [pause] . . . and I wouldn't be surprised . . . [pause] . . . if you do . . . [pause] . . . respond in a way that I would not predict.

You recall that I mentioned my fear that she would not go into trance due to her strong ability to outthink me or be more aware than I was. So, in order to help her get her conscious mind to relinquish control, I used that confusion piece. I have probably caught her attention by saying "a woman like you . . ." and then, immediately following the triple negative, I suggest that her response will be different than I predict.

How could she respond in a way that is different than I predict? She could figure out all the ways I think she might respond and do something different—that seems unlikely. She could just forget about what I might think and do her own responding—that seems more likely. So, I have taken myself out of this equation as much as possible. She won't be competing with me, she won't be trying to comply with my suggestions, and she won't be trying to defeat me or prove anything to a person who has her all figured out, etc. She'll just be responding as she needs to respond *for her.*

S: [pause] . . . While your conscious mind may be paying attention to monitoring your responses, you might be glad to know that your unconscious, taking care of a lot of things, has regulated your breathing, slowed it, and is using lung breathing. Your muscles have relaxed and the left side has relaxed differently than the right side of your body. The people behind me can notice that cheek muscles on the left have relaxed greatly, the eye is relaxed greatly. Your head is turned slightly towards me. Your right ankle can be seen by all to be. . . . Now I wonder which of your hands really needs to discover whether or not it will be the one to raise up to your face. While you are wondering about that I might just mention that I hypnotized a woman in Jackson, Michigan, a long time ago. . . .

Now at this point in the session I begin with metaphors to accomplish my goals. I would like to stop the tape here since my focus at this point is diagnosis and not treatment. Let me skip ahead to the conclusion so you can hear how the woman experienced the entire trance and trance phenomena.

S: Was that deeper than the usual? You said you went lightly and it looked quite deeply to me.

L: Oh, yes! Interesting. Fascinating.

S: How much time do you think went by? How much does it seem like?

L: Not a long . . . I know it was a longer time but it did not seem long.

S: Yes, it's been 45 minutes, basically. It did not seem that long? Can you give a report at this early stage on your experience in your back?

L: It's great. I don't have any pain at this time [holds her hands out as if holding a large ball over her lap]. I really don't [smiles].

S: Is that because of the medication?

L: No, no. Because that never has . . . before it has never. . . .

S: I hope that it returns a little bit so you can get rid of it your own way.

L: [smiles and looks away] What fascinated me was that the two sides of me are . . . so totally different.

S: I told you you are the androgynous woman. A woman of the '80s. Thank you. I think we are concluded now. Thank Lisa, too, for her openness.

Now, I spoke with Lisa recently. It has now been about one-and-a-half years since this session. It was her only treatment. She said that she has completely ceased her medication at night and has cut daytime medication by two-thirds. She has completely retired now or at least taken a permanent leave of absence, if that is the same thing. She said she has listened to the tape over and over and found it helpful, and she has given it to friends who have also found it helpful.

Now to recap. The tape nicely illustrated the ability to gain sufficient diagnostic material in a first session. If a second session was conducted, the results of her reaction to this session would provide further information that would possibly modify the diagnosis, of course.

The goals were primarily these: for behavior, I wanted to teach the exact way to use the trance phenomena and link it to perceptions of her back pain; for attitudes, I wanted her to realize that she could depend on someone to help her and not worry about who would take control; for self-image, I wanted her to conceive of herself in a dream where she would dream of herself having all the opposite problems—like being too weak, too frightened, etc.—and see someone there who she could depend upon. Those were all I accomplished in the session. If I had another appointment it might be to help with two related goals: for emotion, I wanted her to feel dependency needs in a safe way; and for attitude, I would want to help her question the perceived attitude that appears to be, "If I act helpless, someone will place me in a role I don't want to play and curtail my freedom."

Behaviorally, I think I would cover some ways of depending upon others but I don't know which specific behaviors I would pick, not without thinking it through. Finally, this tape should have demonstrated something that is hard to show in a demonstration where the diagnosis is discussed—going straight into the treatment from the interview.

THE INTERPERSONAL CHECKLIST

Now unlike the situation on the taped example, I said that usually we get a description of the problem from the family ahead of time. That will help us decide about their state of mind. There is a story about a man whose girlfriend urged him to come for therapy. He said he *just can't stop* thinking about his ex-wife and wanting to get her back. He knows that is impossible, but he just thinks about it all the time. I don't like the sound of that; he hasn't got it conceptualized to where it sounds like he is going to solve it. The problem may be that his girlfriend is bugging him and he is keeping some distance. She is getting too close. I don't know. But you see how it gives me some idea of what degree of psychological sophistication family members have.

The next question is can we be of help to the family? This man mentioned, "I hear you use hypnosis sometimes, is that right?" He implied that he would come in and we would hypnotize him and remove his ambivalence or something like that. I recommend that you say something to the effect of, "Yes, if the problem merits the use of hypnosis. That is one of the tools that we may use." So it is clear that hypnosis is used according to the therapist's discretion and not the family's.

Oftentimes someone in the family will pursue the use of a technique or present the problem in a way that makes a direct connection to hypnosis: "I have Hodgkin's disease. I understand you use hypnosis." But what do they think we are going to *do* with hypnosis here? So my next concern is how much magic they have invested or how realistic or unrealistic their goals are. I don't want any false promises being promoted. I've got the word magic in the title of one of my books so that sounds like I might be promoting magic.

If we get a letter in the mail, we write them back a letter than says, "The use of hypnosis is often shrouded with various kinds of expectations and misconceptions." If they have a therapist, we ask them to talk over their motivation with their therapist before seeking the use of hypnosis, so as to make sure that something of value that may lie there has been taken care of even before they come. We'll write something like this to them:

We don't want to promote any false hopes or mislead anyone. So what we would like to know is if, in fact, we can be of reasonable help in a reasonable amount of time. To do that, we want you to write us a letter that says something about your problem, your goals, the history of your problem, age, occupation, family situation, and any other historical information you think we need to know regarding your family of origin or your past experiences in order to be of help. This should be a page long at the very least, up to two or three pages—whatever you think is necessary. And we want you to complete and return to us a checklist that is enclosed.

By the time we receive all of this information, we know a good bit about the family before we ever agree to see them.

The only real hassle with this checklist [Illustrations 8 and 9] is that it is extremely sexist in its wording. Carol and I tried to change it but it ended up more cumbersome than before and that was worse than its being sexist. It is written in the third person singular. We tell people, "Pretend you are looking at yourself at a distance and check it the way you see yourself. When you encounter a comment like, 'Wants everyone to like *him*,' just read *her* if that is appropriate."

The copyright on the checklist is 1957 when the only other means of diagnostics were aimed at Freudian work or behavioral work a little bit, but not interpersonal work at all. Before it was published then, the work was really done in the early '50s. So 1947 was Wolpe's work. That was the closest thing to interpersonal there was. Eric Berne hadn't promoted his ideas until the mid-'60s. And Fritz Perls was still doing hypnosis and was in therapy with Karen Horney. So this was real advanced thinking for this time.

Now the way the checklist is supposed to be used is a little more mathematical than we are going to use it. We don't reify this information at all. We have the family members check this thing for themselves and the others in the family as appropriate. They send their checklists back to us. I go over this like *we* are going to do. And *then* I make a determination. We call them back or write them back and say we think it is reasonable to assume we *could be* of help. We set up a time and then we see them.

When we see them in face-to-face interaction it takes on this kind of dimension. We interview the family more to back up our prejudgments and the goals that we have in mind, modify them or throw them out or whatever, and eventually move right into the therapy from that—just like you saw happening in the tape here.

Now you need to know how to score this thing. Any questions: Yes? How many times do clients complete this checklist? Oh, 100%. If a family doesn't want to see us, then they don't need to do all of this. We have never had anyone not do it. I take that back. There was one girl in the not too distant past who had some eating disorder—I don't remember which. She would not send the material in or back. Her father was the one who wanted her to come for therapy anyway.

So Carol encouraged her to do it one more time. She had lost it in the mail or "this'ed" or "that'ed" it. And it was clear she wasn't going to be a person we could work with because she needed to be encouraged and dragged and so on. So Carol suggested that maybe at another time she might be a little bit more interested in seeking help *from us*. We gave her some other people's names who would hold her hand, essentially, a little more. That is the only family or person who hadn't done the checklist since we have been in Florida. We have been in Florida five years.

So everybody gets to do one of these things. Often we will have four graphs representing the spouse's view of self and other and two more representing each parent's view of the child, if it is the child they are concerned with, and then we'll have one more representing the child's view of himself or herself. And sometimes we get other peoples' views too. We have used up to nine graphs in a family.

It is interesting because there will be one child who is *exactly* like Dad, and how interesting that that could happen. It is almost like Dad has been whispering in this kid's ear and the kid has been listening and formulated the exact same view of somebody. But generally speaking, we have husband and wife do it for themselves and husband and wife as seen by the other spouse. Most of the people we see are married couples. We get probably two-thirds or even more with the child being the problem. And that could just be our reputation. You know, you get married couples getting counseling and therapy and they refer others. And if we had gotten the ball rolling with adolescents, perhaps we would have had more of those. There is a lot to do in Florida in our city and stealing cars is not one of them. There is surfing and a lot of outdoor activities. We are not stuck in New York City where it is overcrowded and everybody is getting in trouble. We are a pretty calm and peaceful little community. It is easier for teens to enjoy themselves and define who they are and otherwise stay out of trouble. And a lot of the problems have to do with married couples: "He bought a truck, and he's never home."

Sometimes we see people who haven't done this checklist yet for some reason. They need to be seen and we know we are going to see them anyway, because they are the daughter of a local dignitary and it is a type of courtesy that is extended. And it doesn't matter what the story is if we are *going* to see that family, in which case we will usually ask them to take the first few minutes of the interview and answer this. And the checklist only takes us a few minutes to score. On rare occasions we will put it off until the next session. We had some people come from Saudi Arabia who didn't do this ahead of time because they were coming the next day. So when they flew in and landed, we gave it to them. They brought it in to their subsequent session.

It bears repeating today that *Erickson did not use any checklist.* He would never treat all clients the same, including giving all family members a checklist. We can pick and choose our cases, but he worked with darn near every case who came to him. We don't. But we will put the checklist aside and work with the family without it—maybe never have it for the entire duration of the case. But usually we don't see it being a problem for the sessions. And part of that is due to the fact that the family complete it before they even come for a session.

Now, let's look at how to score this checklist. You've already completed it, checking those adjectives characteristic of you. Look at the items you've checked on here [Illustration 9]. You will notice that there is an alpha and numerical one of each in fact, so if you checked #114, you have a three (3) and an N. The way to score this is find the pie piece that corresponds to the alphabetical character, A through P, counterclockwise. Three (3) is the weight for that N score. So put a three (3) in the N pie piece. 3H means find the H pie piece and put a 3 in it. 2N means find the N pie piece and put a 2 in it. And so on until you have 1's, 2's, 3's and 4's in each of the pie pieces corresponding to each of your check marks. There is a quick way to check here. You can only have one 1 and one 4 in each pie piece. You can have three 2's and three 3's, for a total of 20. So if you have two 4's in the same piece, you goofed. Start over.

So take a couple of moments to score this so you can see how it works. The alphabetical characters refer to the contents of this pie piece. You are going to have a circular bar graph when you are done. Let me show you the final results so you know what you are looking for here [Illustration 12-A and 12-B]. You are going to use the one on the left for your numbers and the one on the right to graph it when you are done. Here is one that is completed. So here you have a bar graph, and zero is at the center. That is very convenient that way because they are related to one another.

Don't graph it yet. Just put in your raw score like we did with Paco [Illustration 12-A]. We'll graph each of yours on the right [Illustration 12-B]. Get your scores first and then we will graph them. Twenty is the most each pie piece should add up to, and it shouldn't be lower than zero. I recommend that you go through it chronologically. It will be easier to not make a mistake. Now don't be copying from your neighbors on this!

The next step is to take your numbers and make them into a graph. This is not that hard. Think of something that you have done well and at which you have excelled. Now there are only two things you have to know about this. First is that the center is zero, and the outside perimeter is 20. So if

ADJECTIVE CHECKLIST

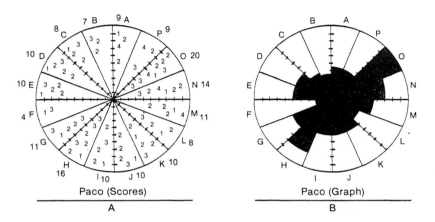

Paco (Scores)   Paco (Graph)

A   B

Illustration 12

you have 20, it is a cinch to find and the center zero. Now the other thing is each of these hatch marks is *two*. Make sure when you do the graph, you go across the pie piece with lines that are parallel to the circumference. You don't want to go point to point. Your line goes *across* the pie piece. Then fill in the graph that you have created.

I want to single out and review some of the graphs. I get to veto it, of course, if it looks bad. You two are living together, sharing resources, decision making, and time together? I would like to use you two. I will cover the graphs by thinking of each individual first and then the operation of the couple. Then you can learn to look at them in the context of a family, having built up your knowledge systematically. So while everyone is finishing up, here are two that we can begin looking at [Illustrations 13 and 14].

First, what about the magnitude of the scores? It will often be the case that the graphs have several pie pieces in the range of 6 to 14. That will give a readable and usable graph. Sometimes that will not be true as it is in our first examples. Why? Well a couple of things come to mind. You don't know what any of it means at this point, probably. Let's take one thing at a time. One thing that you *will* notice first is that some people in the same family mark more than the other people mark.

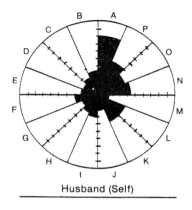

Husband (Self)

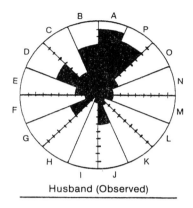

Husband (Observed)

Illustration 13

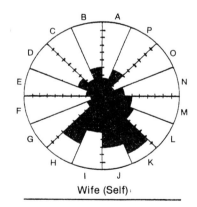

Wife (Self)

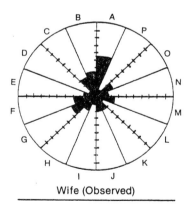

Wife (Observed)

Illustration 14

You will see some graphs that are so tiny that they look like a virus. And you can't make anything of it without an electron microscope. Some will be quite small, or you may get some that are right out to every border with the score of 20. The difference between those then is that with a very small graph you have either a clinically paranoid person or someone who is suspicious of test taking. Or you have something that leads to that paranoid appearance which isn't of that proportion. This would be somebody who is not getting any feedback from the environment and doesn't really know how to think of himself. And by contrast, if it's blown out in every category, you may have a person who is grossly hysterical in her thinking. You know, it may be that she kicked at the dog in the yard yesterday and now she checks "cruel and unkind" because she's kicked the dog. Or a very large graph may represent that the person wants not to be suspicious, but to please. And so s/he marks everything that could be helpful. This may also be part of the hysterical structure or it may just be a person who is starving for some attention, or for a sense that s/he is wanted and helpful.

And then there are those people who do not accept the feedback they get from others and the answers are blown out of proportion in all categories. So someone says, "You are not cruel and unkind because you kicked the dog." And Martha says, "Oh yes, I am." So Martha doesn't accept the feedback. That is another hysterical thinking structure. If it is a really small graph it has a paranoid characteristic, either clinical or just unfortunate. Or if it is blown out to the boundaries it is hysterical, either clinical or just an unfortunate living situation, as I explained.

And now what follows is primarily our experience and interpretation. It is only *based* on Leary's interpretation of observable behavior. Leary would go to a step of mathematical absurdity here. He'd find the mathematical point that best represents the area under the graph. We don't see why he should really do this. He's got adjectives that describe behavior which is already one step removed. And then they are going to be related to one another and that is step two. But to then go to step three in the abstraction process, reduce it to a mathematical point that best represents that graph, is absurdity. That's what Leary would have you do. But when you do that you lose data. So let's leave it at this level. It is quick and easy to do for most families.

The next thing we notice is we need some kind of dimensions on this thing. Splitting the graph along the horizontal axis displays dominant behavior on the top half and submissive behavior on the bottom half. Splitting along the vertical axis shows hostile behavior on the left and friendly behavior on the right. You may think that "hostile" and "friendly" are odd words for this. It is really affiliating and disaffiliating, respectively, that are being referred to. But "hostile" is an easier thing to say quickly.

Now see what we have just at this level of analysis. This man [Illustration 13, left-hand graph] *in the self-report* sees himself primarily dominant and friendly. It means that in an interpersonal situation he is going to prefer to maneuver in a dominant and friendly manner. The theory is that people will have less anxiety if they can do things they know how to do. And what this person knows how to do is use behaviors that are dominant and friendly, primarily.

I want to know where people primarily *aren't* scoring and where they primarily *are* scoring. On this graph there is no place that this individual has eliminated behavior radically. He can be a little bit hostile. He can be a little competitive. He can be a little submissive. Well . . . he avoids intense aggression, that is, he doesn't *see* himself doing that.

Now this woman's self-report here [Illustration 14, left-hand graph], on the other hand, balances pretty much on the hostile/friendly axis. She sees herself as submissive and she is not going to look particularly more friendly than hostile in any typical transaction. She is going to simply look dependent.

So you can start making some judgments now, especially if you know a little bit about the person. I want to elucidate how much correct information and guidance a therapist can get from the graph. I don't mean to make this sound like a parlor game, okay? It is not a horoscope. But there are some logical things you can assume if you have reason to believe that it is accurate for starters—that is if the person is accurately talking about him- or herself.

There might be some question about the issue of accuracy in self-reporting. There will be a question about it if this area H and I is very large. If it is, you can be sure the whole graph is skewed radically in favor of reducing the scores for socially acceptable behaviors. And I will tell you why in just a minute. This woman's graph is possibly skewed due to that factor. This is a bit premature, but look at the graph here [Illustration 14, right-hand graph] that is the husband's view of her. You see that he thinks she is, in fact, dominant in her behavior. It may well be that her view is greatly discounting this dominant portion of her behavior.

There are cultural reasons for this type of thing, too. Why would a young man *not* see himself as friendly for example, as a man did recently in a workshop setting like this? It is positively valued in our culture to be friendly. It is possible he is from a "good" Italian home where you show allegiance to the family and you don't show it socially. It appeared that he didn't trust outside the family very much and often behaved in disaffiliating ways. He didn't have any apparent problems that would lead him for therapy, according to the graph. There is a learning here about how the graph must be interpreted within the context of the culture of the respondent. Still, I wondered, for this person, what was wrong with being friendly and submissive?

I asked him if he was from an Italian family and how he explained the apparent unfriendliness represented there? He said that he was from a Jewish family who expected the children to be very loyal and close to them and essentially to avoid outsiders. He said that in his family you didn't want to ask for help or you would get smothered with help. The cultural norm is sometimes extremely important information and, this reminds me again, you must talk to the people—it does help shed light on the graphs!

Let's look at the words that will help better explain it. These are adjectives now that subdefine these groups of pie pieces [Illustration 15]. I will go counterclockwise. A and P are "managerial." A high score here would be likely for the typical effective manager who can take charge, give orders, delegate authority, and so forth. B and C are "competitive" and represent mildly hostile or disaffiliating behaviors that are very dominant. So, with

ADJECTIVE CHECKLIST

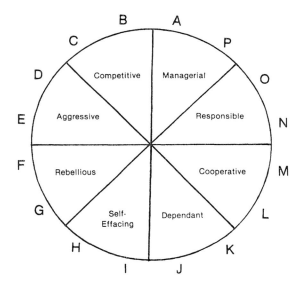

Names assigned to sections

Illustration 15

a high score this is "narcissism." Mohammad Ali would score high here at B and C. He is not grossly disaffiliating, but he has to be better than you. He is pushing you away. And then we have "aggressive" behaviors at D and E. These are aggressive and, if they are extreme, sadistic. Charles Manson comes to mind as someone who would probably score here because he is very hostile and sadistic. The guy with the gun is in control, so we call it somewhat dominant too, you see. So the person scoring here is dominant, right, but primarily hostile.

Now F and G are "rebellious." That would be the other place that Manson would probably score high. Rebellion is disaffiliative behavior that provokes hostile rejection. And in many families where a member is labeled as schizophrenic, he or she will score very high in the rebellious area. We are taking rebellious in the sense that it provokes hostile rejection frequently and even without deliberation. So Manson would score high in both C and D, and E and F. I believe that at his trial he said, "I'm already dead, you can't kill me." That is hostile and submissive. That is the comment he made in the courtroom. I'd take him up on that personally and see if he was right. So you can see that it has provoked hostile rejection from me!

"Self-effacing" is represented by the pie pieces labeled H and I. This is the other hostile submissive grouping. So it is hostile because it is disaffiliative to criticize yourself: "Oh, I am no good, don't talk to me. You don't want to be around me. Go away, I shouldn't have bothered you." These are disaffiliating statements and they are self-effacing. So Van Gogh would score high here. But you have probably had an earful of his problems right?

J and K are "dependent." So a person would occupy this area if he or she were a "wooden leg" player in Transactional Analysis—one who makes excuses to avoid certain things and says, "I can't do it because my father was an alcoholic," "I can't do it because I haven't made up my mind yet," and "Yes, but" players, etc. This provokes friendly dominance. It provokes leadership. And each individual doing this remains dependent. The person's interpersonal movements would be dependency-establishing maneuvers and so he or she would score high on dependence. This would be like Goldie Hawn's typical movie role.

L and M are "cooperative" and O and N are "responsible." These are difficult to discuss with clinical words because they are not something usually seen as a presenting problem. You don't come for therapy because you are too cooperative. So you see them in the clinic when there are other situations that are troublesome and which are caused by the overcooperative stance.

People who score high in the "responsible" category will often have psychosomatic complaints and will not have other family problems. Lisa, a woman we saw on the videotape, would presumably score high there

[Illustration 16]. She would probably score very high on the "responsible" and very high on the "managerial" unless she thinks that it is not proper to be intensely managerial. In that case, the managerial would be a little lower and the responsible would be a little greater. I imagine that is what she would show, and probably some of the cooperative, also.

I would expect to see many women score in this L, M, N, or O area because it is culturally expected of women. And if a woman doesn't then I would wonder why not. That is, how did this unique individual manage to overcome family pressure and cultural pressure? Or was it that the family did not expect that at all? In which case, why was the family being uncommon? Was it a healthy rebellion from sexist cultural norms or was it a perceived inability of the family to comply with the culture's trends? If she did, in fact, seem friendly but did not score that way, or vice versa, is her self-image different from my observation of her? Or is my observation really wrong? Did I miss something or is she different with me than she is out there? That validation of observation is what really makes this checklist helpful.

If I saw this person who we have here [Illustration 12] in the extremely friendly area of L and M, I would wonder—especially since this is a man—whether this guy is really this friendly, or whether he is just putting me on. What am I missing? Is this guy going out and kicking the dog or what? But if he is not, he is really friendly all the time, as far as he sees

ADJECTIVE CHECKLIST

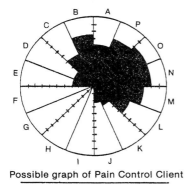

Possible graph of Pain Control Client

Illustration 16

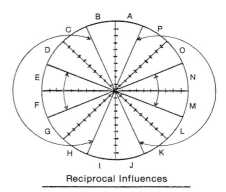

Reciprocal Influences

Illustration 17

himself. If we got on well, I'd know he wasn't just stacking the deck and lying to me.

Question: "Do you ever ask someone to score how they think their spouse or another person would see them?" Yes, always there is an interpersonal aspect to the presenting complaint: "She just always thinks I am trying to get back at her." "I do not." That's an example when I must. We usually ask each family member involved in the complaint to score it the way they see each other. And then we compare the way the husband thinks of himself to the way his wife sees him and vice versa. A lot of times we show the family the results, especially if they are intelligent but unsophisticated in psychology. Engineering people or lawyers or accountants might be examples. It is really handy for them to go, "Holy cats, psychology does have something behind it."

But you are not going just on these checklists, remember. You are going to use your own interpersonal experience and your selective history. For me, this really helps back it up. We don't usually have families with members who try to lie to us on this. We have people who lie to themselves and the world. We've had families bring children diagnosed as schizophrenic who would be the kind of people who would just blow that graph out of proportion in many ways, because they have a totally idiosyncratic sense of reality. But otherwise, people don't seem to lie because they are coming to us voluntarily, we are seeing them voluntarily, and we want to solve a problem together. Sometimes one family member feels coerced into coming, but the scores from others about that person plus our observations fill in the missing portion.

THE DYNAMICS OF A MARRIED COUPLE

The interaction of the couple with the therapist and with one another in the session is *the* major source of information about the system dynamics, of course. However, from the difference between the observed and the self-report of the clients, we can gain some corroborating support. Look now at the left-hand column of Illustrations 13 and 14. I have asked this couple to provide the observations from each spouse of the other spouse's behavior. You will note, at first glance, that the self and observed reports of the husband [Illustration 13, left and right] are very similar. But, even on casual observation, the self and observed reports of the wife [Illustration 14, left and right] are very different. What does this tell us? It says that the husband is not seeing the wife the way she sees herself. Either she is not showing and telling her needs to him or he is not seeing and hearing them when she does.

Now look closer at her view of him [Illustration 13, right side] and you will see that she does not see his dependency and instead sees him more aggressive and competitive—hostile behavior. *If* that is the proper interpretation, then the scenario is this. She does not show her needs to him because she thinks that he is hostile. Why does she do this? Look at her score in H. She has so much self-effacement that she imagines the competitive and aggressive aspects in her husband even when they are not there. Leary, as I recall, pointed out that people with strong scores in self-effacement or rebellion will hold in their own anger and they will project anger onto others. Well, that is what we see here. From the brief talk I had with them and the interaction I witnessed, I would guess that she does not show him the dependency she has. She gets angry that he does not read her mind and she competes with him, argues with him, and tries to take over the house. This is *her* report as well as his, by the way. She thinks she has a problem.

His graph, incidently, makes me wonder about his avoidance of aggressive, competitive, and hostile behaviors. Some goals for this couple would include helping him realize that it is okay to have anger and help him find some ways to show it in this relationship. The same is true for competitiveness. For her the goals would involve learning behaviors about asking for needs to be met and changing her attitude about not asking (for whatever reasons she currently holds). She needs to be comfortable expressing her anger and to become more managerial rather than recreate the drama she had as a little girl involving "playing stupid" and getting criticized by her father. Those are feeling, attitude, and behavior goals. We would want to change the family structure and self-image thinking, as well. One change in structure would be a change in the roles about initiating sexual contact in this family. But I will mention more about that during our coverage of paradoxical symptom prescription. For now the concern is on diagnostic assessment and treatment planning.

What we want to do as therapists is go from here to outcomes that you make in therapy. Examining the major dyad that defines reality in a family—and this is usually the father and mother—is the first important step to me. As we saw in the earlier illustration [Illustration 1], the organizational structure of the family delineates the roles and resources of the members. The couple or the individual who defines reality and is the primary hypnotist in the family is the key piece. I want to see the checklists of the married couple whenever there is a husband and a wife. Then I want to relate the developmental stage and demands upon the family to the graphs.

To do that we need the checklist and a problem that brought the people to therapy, and we want to relate the two. In these volunteered examples we don't have any presenting problem but let's see if I can look at the dynamics of this other couple [Illustration 18] and tell you about a potential one based on their graphs. The husband is on the left, the wife is on the

ADJECTIVE CHECKLIST

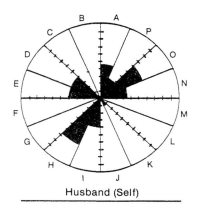

Husband (Self)

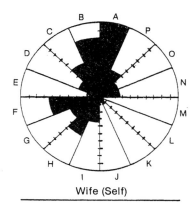

Wife (Self)

Illustration 18

right. We have arrows drawn here [Illustration 17] to illustrate some important relationships. Competitive narcissism pulls hostile and self-efface-ment behaviors. Self-effacement pulls competitive narcissism. This arrow says that aggressive/sadistic behavior pulls rebellious/distrustful behavior. And distrustful/rebellious pulls the aggressive/sadistic. Likewise, managerial pulls dependent and vice versa.

Cooperative and responsible pull one another. Here is an example: If you see a child lost in a grocery store who is crying and looking up into your eyes, managerial behavior is "pulled" out of you. You want to help the child find his parent and you take over as a friendly parent. Whereas, if you sit beside a bag lady who has a strong streak of self-effacement you can try to be Mr. Rogers and say, "Nice weather we have been having until recently."

She will say, "Oh, it is always bad. Every place I go is always bad."

"I am sorry to hear that, are you warm enough?"

"Oh I don't think so but I have all I deserve."

"You know you really deserve as much as you need."

"Oh yes, but you know I might need to change every day and I don't know where I am going to be and I couldn't take it if I had it."

"Well, since you have an attitude here that things are always wrong, maybe you should look at your attitude."

"No it wouldn't do any good, because you can't teach an old dog new tricks."

"Well, have you thought about psychotherapy?"

"I don't know if they can help anyone like me."

"Well they can do remarkable things nowadays, you know. There is Ericksonian hypnosis and things I have heard about."

"It wouldn't help me, I couldn't pay for it. I don't trust a lot of those therapists anyway. I hear that they get involved sexually with their patients."

"Well look, lady, no one would get sexually involved with you. You are disgusting!"

What has happened is that the hypothetical Mr. Rogers had moved from managerial and responsible, friendly behavior, because of the repeated self-effacing behavior, to hostile behavior and become hostile and competitive. So others eventually shape your behavior, and we want to look at that in a marriage.

There is also one other reason for looking into the family of origin. Let's examine this family-of-origin-directed thinking, for just a minute, with this couple system. Here we have a male who does not show very much submissive behavior at all, not much submissive friendly behavior at all. That is very odd considering the degree to which he shows friendly behavior. His graph [Illustration 18] had a lot of scores [as in responsible] and there is less here [in managerial]. So I presume that this person grew up in a family where it was a good idea to be responsible. It wasn't a very good idea to have needs that you show.

Here [in aggressive] is an interesting thing. How does a child learn to be aggressive like that? It is either shaped or it is modeled. It is not liable to be a genetic tendency towards sadism or something. It is not that strong, but how does a child learn that? And isn't it interesting there is self-efface-ment [H and I], too? How does a child learn to be self-critical? That is not genetic, it is learned. There was a person in this fellow's family who oc-cupied this behavior [competitive]. And it is funny that he doesn't have any of it [no scores in competitive], because if it was the male who did it in the family of origin, then why wouldn't he have modeled that behavior if he identified with the male sex figure in the house?

He's got strong self-effacement. A child learns that because of the recip-rocal arrangement with somebody who is competitive. And if he is a male and if it was Dad who was competitive, why didn't he learn it through modeling? That is usually what happens, and then you identify with the aggressor. Even if you didn't want to be that way, you would learn how to do it anyway. That's odd. So somebody was competitive in the family. And my guess is that they were competitive so that any time this person [the man] showed inadequacy or anything that could be interpreted as depend-ency or inadequacy, such as submissive behavior in need of help, those dependency needs were ridiculed by this parent. So this person would stop doing it and learn to be self-effacing instead. So it is like he starts to cry and is told, "That is because you are a baby. It's too bad you are not like me." So he stops his crying and criticizes himself a little bit. And he doesn't identify with this critical parent person.

Now this is either because this person is too difficult to identify with, or another really wild possibility is that this person is not present and didn't really criticize. The criticism was only imagined: "If Dad had been alive, he wouldn't have liked this." So he didn't identify because there was no person there at all and he imagined the criticism and learned his self-effacement that way. That is a possibility. These questions are easily answered if you have the real person to talk to, of course.

And another possibility is that this is a person who didn't identify because of sex identification differences. Maybe it was the mother of the family or bigger sister and not a male who was critical. And why this aggressive portion? This was possibly the result of not having the needs met from time to time. There was an angry outburst and he modeled that. It would be unusual that he would model this from the parent of the opposite sex. So it would make sense that maybe Dad did this angry outburst and the person identified with it. Mom did that critical behavior and he didn't. That is my guess. Or perhaps it is not Dad represented there as angry outbursts, but it is simply the angry outburst from time to time of not getting his needs met when self-effacement didn't make him feel any better either. So when Mom criticizes him for crying, he says, "You are right, I really shouldn't have done that." If he doesn't just stop with the need and finally gets mad and that self-effacement doesn't win Mom's attention either, then he may finally say, "Well to hell with it." So that may be the scenario that leads to the angry outburst. Now, I don't know, but it would be fun to ask.

You can see the logic here when it starts getting specific. You do get some idea of family of origin and you may be surprised how often this will turn out correctly today, even before we speak to the respondent. The more interesting is that the person is left with this map of experience that we see in the graph and is now interacting with it in his current family.

Could you give me some feedback about my accuracy? [Man in audience]: "Yes, in fact my father did die when I was very young. He was an overachiever and I was always trying to live up to his successes. They named a hospital after my father. No one has ever told me that my father was inadequate in any way. So he continues to be a ghost against which I compete. He had two large corporations, for example, and I had to get at least one. I felt that there was never any time for just being a child and that did make me mad from time to time . . . I guess that is the outburst part."

When I said it was the long shot (about the absent male parent) it turned out to the right shot. Thank you for the feedback. It sure helps show the validity of interpretations that can be made. Notice that we go beyond Leary's simple behavioral interpretation and go to the family of origin interpretation. We also add feelings and attitudes in our interpretations. But we stay with the raw data and not the mathematical reification done by Leary.

See, in that case, the way we got the right answer was to ask the question of how a child could have self-critical behavior and not have incorporated the reciprocal behavior of competitiveness. If the parent was there to model from, he would have it. So the other possibility in my mind was he just imagined that a parent would have been critical and that is what you are saying. That is incredible. Thanks for sharing that with us.

Any questions? All right, how could you be high in two complementary areas? That would be due to two factors, as I see it. One is that the child was trained to be, say, self-effacing by a critical parent, and then two, the child models and therefore incorporates the critical behavior, too.

Are there other questions? Okay, a man just mentioned that a number of his clients have a great deal of self-distortion. So are the respondents accurately seeing themselves or is there a halo effect where they distort the content to suit their needs? Well, this graph represents the way they intend to interact and that is important to me; it represents the map of experience. As far as they are concerned, their self-image is represented here, or this is a desired self-image. In that case it is causing stress because they are not really that way. Usually people really try to give us answers that are accurate. At least, this is true for the population that we see.

If H and I are very strong, then you can be sure that they have diminished their degree of managerial or other culturally syntonic behavior because they don't think they are that good. There was a fellow in Australia who anyone here from Southeastern Australia would certainly know. His position in mental health in Australia was prominent. And he was the nicest guy, as most Australian professionals were. This guy was even better still. And he had a strong self-effacement score and he didn't have much managerial score. For a person who's pretty well known for his leadership in psychiatry in two continents, we wondered why. But then we read his actual scores. He didn't check "Makes a good impression on others," "able to give orders," "well thought of," and so on. That was incredible because he was certainly those things, if nothing else. But because of the strong self-criticism, he couldn't say, "I am well thought of." So if you see a strong score here, that is when you know that the person, despite himself, has just biased it grossly to get rid of all the positive characteristics.

If people have scored a strong rebellious score, Leary noticed that they misinterpret and overvalue anger in themselves and others. So if they have a strong rebellion score, their score of the spouse is bound to be skewed, reflecting too much anger in that person that is not there. Those are the only two things I know for sure about misperceptions.

Let's do the same estimation of historical information on the spouse and see if we can make sense of her background or family of origin, too [Illustration 18]. I see a lot of competition behavior, relative to anything else, and that is kind of unusual as a cultural stereotype. That managerial should be a little lower, and responsible should be a little higher to match the cultural stereotype. That is no problem, but if you are going to score real high on the competitive, why not be high elsewhere? Why is it actually somewhat lower? These are some of the questions I would be asking for starters.

And somebody asked what if it is in one and not both? This is a good time to answer that. This person here [Illustration 18, the man] has scored high in the H and low in the I, but these are both self-effacing. So how would you make sense of that? Or she has scored high in the B and low in the C and they are both competitive. So how do you make sense of that? Easy! Any set of two pie pieces is in relationship to major axes, right? This H score, this self-effacement score, is closer to the hostile than it is the submissive. And the I is closer to the submissive than it is to the hostile. And this B is closer to dominant and further from hostile than C is. So in other words, it is possible to be competitive in such a way that you intend for people to see you as trying to compete in order to take over and do things, but not to compete to be hostile. And somehow you can make a distinction and it shows up on the graph: "I don't mind competing if you understand it is to win. It's not to beat you." And this self-effacement is disaffiliating. It is not self-effacement to be dependent: "I don't want to look dependent. I want to get away from you by being self-effacing."

So let's see what else we can tell about this. So why would a person want to win but not beat anybody? One thing I have learned that seems to fit nicely is that I can go on to consider feelings and not just behavior. And I take this way beyond Leary because I also want to know what attitudes are at work, where you can see the implications for attitudes right away. The previous gentleman was saying that he was fighting against a ghost, you see, and that reflected a need for an attitude adjustment after childhood which he may have already acquired by now.

PLANNING INITIAL THERAPY GOALS

We initially form a hypothesis for an understanding of a needed feeling, attitude, and behavior in each case because we want the goals to be formulated in these categories [Illustration 11]. And so it is clear which behavior is the goal because that's what this checklist is all about but what about the attitude and the feeling? And we can stretch it three times further than Leary did with a little speculation. The speculation requires that we attribute feelings to each set of pie pieces: If you are going to be managerial you are going to have to feel confident and powerful, or secure. To be in the submissive area you are going to have to have tender feelings or feelings of sadness and hurt and grief. If you are not showing those, you are not doing the emotional part that goes with the behaviors of being submissive on this checklist. If I need help and I am scared, then I have to be able to show that. And that is a feeling.

So belonging is a feeling that I found fits nicely in the responsible area of N and O. If I feel like I belong to you guys in America here, then I'll do what you guys do in America. I'll wipe my shoes before I come in, wash my hands before I eat, make my bed in the morning (for I don't know what reason). But if I don't really feel like I belong, then, well to heck with it—"What good is it to make my bed anyway, because there is no payoff." So such a person would not score high in the responsible area and would not feel like she is affiliated or belongs. And the feeling of acceptance or belonging in that regard is what I mean here in the responsible pie pieces.

And that responsible score is lower than this managerial score [Illustration 18, the woman]. So I wonder if this person was in a family where the attitude was suggested somehow to her as a child that if she excels and wins she can belong and she is accepted. But otherwise, she is not. In that case she is going to try to do things and get them done and succeed at them, and even take it over and do it first as a way of winning acceptance. Is that true for you?

[Woman in audience]: "I always wanted to just do things myself. Independence was very important to me and I was always willing to compete."

Did you feel like you didn't belong, though?

[Woman]: "No, not at long as I was needed!"

Okay, not until you realized there was more to living than achieving and winning, huh? It could be, then, that this behavior of responsible friendliness in the spouse was attractive because it is lacking here in the wife. A lot of times we see something in our spouses that we think we lack in ourselves.

[to the husband] It is odd that you said you have at least one corporation because your dad had two, which means you are competitive, and yet you don't see yourself as competitive. So this tells me that he is competitive but he doesn't feel comfortable with it. So we need to help him feel comfortable with his feeling of ownership of this talent. We don't have good words for that. It is something like his own personal power. Righteousness is a word that has to do with those feelings, but without the religious meaning to it. But "I am right, damn it, and I don't care if you disagree" is the feeling.

Smug is a word for it. There are not good names for these feelings, but there ought to be a culturally better name, more acceptable than "smug."

But there are feelings like that that this fellow isn't having. So he can compete, but he is apologetic about it. And he feels scared about it—his voice quivers when he talks about it. You could hear that when he spoke, right? So the attitude goal is that it is okay to live up to his own standards and not those of others. The feeling goal is having that kind of smugness or being right or having ownership for his own ideas, so that he might say, "That idea is mine, I would rather do it my own way," and feel good about it. Like his wife can say, "My mother's first word is 'I'd rather do it myself.' " She represents, at least, that capacity that if you do it yourself you are perfectly okay and you can feel good about it. It would be nice if he gets that from her. If there is any of that going on in the marriage, he can get it for himself.

Now he sees himself able to come on and be friendly and affiliate more quickly than she sees herself being able to do and that may be what she liked about him in the marriage contract at the ulterior level. It is as if she said to him, "I'll show you that it is okay to have your own ideas and do things your way and feel good about it." And he says, "If you do, I'll show you how to feel okay about coming on and being friendly and assuming people are going to like you." So they say, "Hey, that sounds like a good deal to me." And she says, "Are you going to criticize yourself?" And he says, "Oh no, I wouldn't do that." But he lied and he does. And that is okay because if she does this [competitive behaviors] in a certain way, then she'll pull that behavior from him. So his self-criticism feeds off her doing things her own way. And he goes, "Damn, that is neat the way you do that, I could never do that." Now it is not pathological, necessarily; it is simply a dynamic that we see. The real question is, "What is the problem?" What I want to do is I want to try to fit the problem into the dynamic I see.

Is there a problem that we can take one step further? Even though she scored 20 in the A piece, we could say that the woman doesn't see herself as a person making decisions and managing the situation. She has to do what she does to the extreme and that reveals her insecurity with it. In addition, she has very little P. She is much easier with the competitive behavior. So the problem that is being identified here by both of them is he says she doesn't make decisions comfortably or perhaps you would say, ". . . doesn't make them well." We don't see her as having a sense of knowing those behaviors easily that are managerial behaviors that blend A and P. And she says, "Well it's not that, it is that I am critical" [competitive response]. Well, that is right. Her strongest thing is to be slightly hostile and dominating, which can be critical. To this he says, "I don't see this" [referring to critical behavior]. And she insists, saying, "I do this" [referring to managerial behavior]. So they agree. He can't rightly say she doesn't manage better than he, can he?

And so that really would be one of the first places to start intervening. It would be to help her fill in this managerial behavior so she could feel more comfortable making decisions and perhaps to teach her to do "as if" decisions. Rather than getting her to change her personality I would just use her personality. I would say, "Some people probably can't even decide what kind of silver to have." And she would say, "Ya, those stupid people." Then I'd say, "Which one do you like the best?" And she will say, "That one, of course." And so I would get her to make decisions from the competitive part of her personality and the critical part of the personality. In contrast to someone else, she would probably be able to do it. But thinking for herself about her needs is not likely to work as well.

So I would paraphrase her as saying "I'm not thinking about my needs very well and I'm not making decisions based on that." So this whole area is missing in the dependency area. But a lot of help she is going to get from him because he is not thinking about his needs very well either. He is thinking about, "If I can do the responsible thing and ask her to make a decision, then we will both be better off." So both of them really need some training in recognizing what their needs are. There would be a lot of feeling goals involved about that. I want to explore whether there is unresolved grief about father because, if there is, that would be a super way to begin having dependency needs surface there. That is the feeling goal for both.

Then for the attitude goal, we would want to find out why, if there is some conscious attitude at all, it is better to just do things and get them done than to worry about what you feel. For example, if she has that attitude, then the attitude goal would involve something about an opposite attitude that it is better to really notice what you feel rather than just get things done. I am sure I can make some points about how crisis centers solve problems that way and get people to have a catharsis for their feelings first and then get them to problem solve for the problem second—which often becomes a much easier problem to solve at the point after the catharsis has occurred.

When we sit down with a family and go over the graph and they can begin to see the logic of their communication difficulties and behavioral deficits, and so on, it is a nice feeling. We all understand each other. Some families hate that, so we don't do it all the time. Other families really need it because they have no psychological savvy at all about things and that really helps them. It can be especially helpful for families headed by attorneys and lawyers or any family where the caretakers think, "What's the problem then? Let's solve it. I asked her what the problem was. She wouldn't tell me so I brought her here for therapy."

Back to you two who I spoke about, do you want to say anything or correct me in any way? I don't want to leave you feeling badly because I said something wrong. She said, "I see us both as competing to do things. He had several years as a pastor and that fits in there somewhere." And she just added that the part about her was very accurate. Again, she has reminded us that the therapist must talk to the family members and in the context of the family and not just look at these graphs. I want to stress that we *teach* it this way, without talking to the family, so we can demonstrate the accuracy it *can* have. This blind interpretation is a training game to help drive home the point that this is a very accurate and helpful tool and that you can look at merely the graph alone and find out some real interesting things. But in real life, there is no need to try to rely on the graph alone!

Now, looking at this couple [Illustration 18], the wife is on the right, and the husband is on the left. And the husband, as we pointed out, leans slightly to the hostile. This man was raised in a family where he suffered a good deal of criticism and somebody else was in control and they didn't encourage him to learn managerial behaviors in an effective way. And then they would criticize him for not having them but didn't really show him how to do things. He probably was expected to achieve and was not really shown how. Or his parents showed him how to be raised to the age of seven but not really how to be a teenager, or man maybe, so he was left to his own devices, which means he would be scared. I see that because we are looking at this [J and K] being very low, and this [A and P] being relatively low, considering the magnitude of this [H and I].

He has managerial behavior that is fragmented. Another thing I have noticed is that if you get a solid block of behavior, then you did that behavior a lot as a child. And you learned all of the nuances of it. It was modeled for you and your behavior was shaped. But if it is fragmented, then nobody shows you how and you learn it the hard way. By fragmented I mean there is a high score in one of the four dominant-friendly pieces and perhaps one more that is almost as high; and these two are not adjacent to each other; and, finally, the other two pie pieces are very low or missing entirely. So you have only a skeleton of that behavior but not a lot of ease with it. So that is what I see here. He can be managerial but he learned it on his own. He learned it the hard way and nobody ever said, "You did a great job." Somebody also did angry outbursts and he modeled a bit of those. He probably learned how to be friendly after he got out of the house and that is why that is sort of fragmented.

Now I would want to talk to him a little bit. I don't know how his interpersonal impact is. If he looks as friendly as this [O and N] indicates, he may look far less submissive than this [H and I] would suggest. So it may reflect his inner reality and not his self-presentation. In other words, he may be more friendly and managerial than he shows, so we can be looking at his residual self-image from childhood more than we are at the man that we have. How am I doing so far? Very close, huh? Okay, thank you, and please feel free to step in and correct me.

As for competing, it is better to not compete because in the family of his childhood someone was going to criticize him for it and laugh at him for it. So competition was avoided here so that he could avoid shame and embarrassment for being competitive. There is a question of how did I know the avoided feelings were of shame and embarrassment. It's a guess, but because he has strong self-effacement, somebody must have criticized him so he learned that self-effacement. And he didn't want to say, "Oh yeah, dammit, I'll show you." He tried that and said, "I don't think I'll do that again." He said he would just "eat it" and so there is probably a lot of anger with which he is not comfortable.

Let's look at the woman's chart. If you score 20 any place you are two-and-a-half standard deviations beyond the mean. You translate this to a standard score, which we haven't done, because you don't have the chart to do that. After that the results are statistically meaningful and have, in fact, been correlated to the MMPI. But I do know that 20 is two-and-a-half standard deviations beyond the mean. So that means not very many people are going to be *that* managerial. And she is. That is pretty managerial. She's pretty rebellious, too. So she comes in and she knows how to solve the problem or take action. She and the others are not even going to bother to talk it over. And if her family or superiors don't get along with that, then she rebels. That is pretty much the name of that game.

There is a little bit more on here. There is some N and some D, but if everything was reduced to a more moderate magnitude of score, you would hardly see these. So I am discounting these almost entirely and saying the whole thing boils down primarily to A and to F, G, and a little H.

When she rebels she is not fully convinced that it is the best thing to do. She is having some self-doubt which we see in H and I. Nobody probably sees that. And he gets mad about it, probably because it would clearly provoke that [D and E] behavior from him to some extent and that is a strong piece from him. And the other thing is that she doesn't have that much of that angry aggressive behavior compared to the magnitude of everything else. So when she gets mad she is uncomfortable—they are both not real comfortable with anger, that's what it comes down to. But he will still do it sometimes and when he does she doesn't know what to do. She may rebel for a while but she is not comfortable and that we should know because of the self-effacement. So that may be when they finally decided to solve the problem. Am I close? They are in agreement with me at this point, so I'll go further.

Well, why does a person develop such a huge amount of managerial behavior as the wife did? A couple of scenarios make sense. Maybe she had to take care of people in the family because somebody was an invalid or there were younger brothers or sisters and the parents copped out or somehow demanded in some effective way that she take care of them. Or the parents were sick or something. Maybe Dad had cancer and her needs came last because she had to run around and help mother run the house.

I don't know why there is so much rebellion. I figure this out by pretending identification sometimes: "I'm real managerial and I'm really rebelling sometimes." I don't quite know. One possibility that would get there is if I have a parent to take care of and get real tired of it now and then and have to rebel. The wife just said this and I'll repeat it for you. She said that she had to care for her mother who was incompetent to do the normal caretaking and home maintenance. That is more or less what I just speculated.

So since that is the case we have a real bind because this [A and P] is the way she would interpersonally maneuver to be comfortable but it embodies feeling a little resentful and pressured at the same time that she's choosing to do it. And so then she would relieve the tension of that by sometimes rebelling and there is just going to be that cyclical quality and there is that conflict within her, regardless.

And to make matters worse, her husband will encourage her to do that [A and P] because she does that better than he does and he does that [M and O] better than she does. That I do know is true. But I don't know about the pull/push thing. [to the wife] Are there any ideas you have about why you are so strong managerially, and yet rebellious too? She said that she is the youngest child and she did a lot of modeling from her siblings and felt that she needed to be where they were and feel what they did. So she tried to keep up and succeeded at it pretty well. That is admirable, yet you [to the husband] were expected to keep up and were not clear on how to do that. She was expected to keep up *and did.* And you both share a bit of the "to heck with 'em" attitude here—you and me against the world. I saw a Ziggy cartoon recently where Ziggy was holding up the world, and it said, "You and me against the world." When you opened it up it said, "Frankly, I think we are going to get squashed." But it seems that there was a real attraction between you two in those two areas. She was expected to make do and succeeded and you were expected to make do and you admired the fact that *she* succeeded. You probably wanted a bit of that. At the same time both of you can say, "Damn, we can defeat them together and that would be fun. Let's do it together." That was at the unconscious level. And the things that attract us at the unconscious level usually become the problems later because we did not see the whole package.

So the problem I would see is, if you [the wife] do get resentful for taking over and taking charge (when in a sense you encourage it by having been so successful at it in the past), then you get resentful because, "Why doesn't he do it?" Is that one of the scenarios? You guys are acting like you don't want me to say a lot more. Please comment, because I could say something with a slight twist on it and it might make you seem bad in the eyes of the group, but you could correct it by saying anything that is more accurate as an interpretation. The man said, and I'll summarize using his exact words, that he was in competition with his dad and it was "too much." He had an older sister but he was not in any competition with her; it was with his dad. He said that whatever he did it was considered "not good enough" and so he gave up. And I want to ask you this: Did you give up and also feel that you didn't know how to do things that you wanted to know how to do? "Yes." Did Dad have angry outbursts? He said that was how Dad solved problems.

So now what would be the next step? We would look at the couple's dynamics and attempt to understand them within the context of the family's presenting problem. We don't have a problem here really. We would want to assume that we have a family therapy situation on our hands. And by the way, *every* couple's graphs are going to show system dynamics. You don't need family therapy because you show dynamics. That is just the way we are as people. There is logic and there is psycho-logic. And this is the psychological part in systemwide dynamics. If you were in the office wanting therapy, then I would want to find out what the presenting problem was and I'd want to put it in this dynamic and it probably would fit. If it didn't, that would be odd.

It *could* not fit. There could be something like you were mugged on the subway—the trauma of that is with you and you need therapy for it. And that would have zilch to do with the family dynamics at this level of the couple. Except, in each case, you would find the dynamics have shaped the response people make to the event. In this family the husband would have wanted to handle the mugging better than anyone else the police had ever seen.

There has just been a question raised about my implying that the graph of today looks like the graph that would have existed in the family of origin. And the question is whether I am saying that. Yes, in many ways this is probably going to be true. And that is odd, too. It is as if there have been no interventions that created major changes since childhood. But many persons will have worked to improve areas where some deficits existed and to diminish areas where too much culturally dystonic behavior existed. However, unless there have been many years since they really *left* home, the graphs will still reflect the major foundation of behavior that was shaped and delimited in their original family. That is why we can see many correct interpretations made in workshops such as this.

With this man, the N and O were probably learned after childhood and the A and P, as well. I say that because those areas are culturally desirable and yet they are not, in his mind, strongly and solidly learned. However, the friendliness he actually shows is likely to be more intense or frequent than you actually see it displayed here in self-report because he will have a tendency to discount how much others tell him or show him that *they think* he is friendly. That is because the foundation here is that "Men in authority don't think I can do it." So consciously he will probably fight all day against that attitude on the job and perhaps he should actually have scored higher there. But he has reduced the feedback he needs to see himself correctly by misunderstanding those authority figures he runs into now.

And, you see, he would not have learned communications to figure it all out. He couldn't have said, "Dad, time out for just a minute now. We can get back to competition in a minute, but I just want to find out if I'm doing better or not." He never would have learned the transactions to figure that out. Here again, make sure this graph is looked at in contrast to really talking to the person. I think that attitude probably does apply here [referring to low scores in C and B], sir, to your graph [Illustration 18]. You will come to moments where you think that people aren't giving you credit and don't think you can do it. Because that is going to be a feeling that you have used a lot, it will be in your map of experience, and all roads are going to lead to that at different times. It would be called a "game payoff" in T.A.[16] for those of you familiar with that material.

This woman's question concerned whether or not the graph changes with situational incidents. The answer is no, not very much. The score reflects the consistent aspects, of course. I checked this out over several years. A married couple in therapy would call me up and say they just had a terrible fight. I would say, "Stop by the office and pick up some checklists to fill out tonight." And I would tell them to bring them with them in the morning for the session. And there wasn't much change with the situation: Perhaps two points varied in a pie piece or two. But that would be all. That was good. It meant to me that there is some reliability in here. You will see changes in the graph when there have been successful therapy interventions.

On the other hand, I've noticed that *major changes* in circumstances, like getting a divorce, *will* temporarily shift the picture and it will go back later.

---

[16]Berne, E. (1972). *What do you say after you say hello? The psychology of human destiny* (p. 23). New York: Grove Press.

Let's say this couple was getting a divorce. If you saw him getting a divorce you might see the graph shifting so that the H and I are all of a sudden gone. His self-doubt seems as if it is suddenly gone. Situational involvements will stabilize a state of consciousness. Another way to put it is, "I had to stop having those doubts to get that divorce." And so if he had a doubt, he suppressed it and when he filled out the questionnaire it didn't show up on there at all. He said, "That's not me, I used to be full of doubt, but now I am going to get this divorce." So he is not going to have that doubt. So he has temporarily used the situation to load and pattern and build resources of a more positive kind. That situational improvement can become a real problem, as I mentioned earlier. People in a family can all appear healthy *except* the identified patient, due to the ability of people to stabilize a state of consciousness and pull resources into the foreground by sort of using the induced problems of another as a springboard. That is, if someone helps you with your difficulty, he or she temporarily has you as a stimulus for eliciting helping behavior.

So I see that as a problem in interpretation: transient shifts because of huge life changes, like the divorce, but as far as arguments and quarrels and so on, those don't change the graph significantly given the way I'm suggesting we use it. And following therapy you should see change in this graph. We should see the man's graph increased in A and P, N and O, and B and C and reduced a lot here in H and I. He would also indicate an increased ability to show his dependency feelings [J, K, L, M] and he wouldn't have to criticize himself for it. He should be more capable of seeing himself as dominant in both competitive and friendly ways, basically the way he and probably his wife would want him to move. It should reflect that kind of a change. His graph should then start looking more like this [Illustration 19].

His wife's graph [Illustration 20] might look more reasonable if A and P were reduced. This should be a little bit more reduced in H and this might be higher in L, M, N, and O. And the rebellion here in F would probably have been reduced a little bit too. We'll use this couple as an example and say they did come for marital therapy. We touched on this earlier but should review and elaborate in greater detail what we would be setting as goals for the initial therapy plan now that we've examined this couple's dynamics a little more thoroughly. What would be the goals in the requisite three areas of attitude, behavior, and affect change?

What attitude would we have to work on? What would be the attitude goal for either one of them? For the husband, it is okay to show himself to others. Ways to brag and boast would be a behavioral manifestation of that goal. And that would be a separate behavioral goal that was approached with separate interventions.

ADJECTIVE CHECKLIST

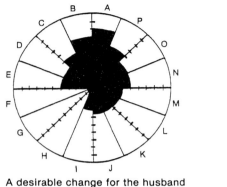

A desirable change for the husband

A desirable change for the wife

Illustration 19   **Illustration 20**

For her, we want to reduce the rebellion, but we don't want to take choices away. I would want to help her reduce the strong need to be managerial and that would coincide with his increasing ability to express himself, as I said a moment ago. And the attitude here would be that she doesn't need to prove herself to her peers. If there is any residual aspect to trying to prove herself to her brothers and sisters—that she can keep up and be one of the gang—she doesn't need to do that. That will help him from being reflexively pulled into self-criticism when she is competitive. After all, she doesn't mean anything by it that he should take personally.

What about goals for emotional flexibility or affect change? [The answer was, "How about a feeling of affiliation?"] Yes, and especially whenever we have a situation like this. And affiliation would have to do with both feelings and behavior in this area N and O. A feeling of belonging.

As for an attitude, "It is okay to ask for help" would be useful for both of them, I suspect. Notice the low scores, relatively, in the J and K pie pieces. Behaviorally, for the husband, the teachings would include how to praise and reinforce other people, and those would have to be specific behaviors that were taught—not just sentences or suggestions about how he could or should reinforce! That behavioral change would go along with increasing his managerial behavior. And as that increases for him, his wife will be increasingly able to ask for and accept help and, in general, develop this dependency behavior we see lacking entirely on her graph.

And I guess since the husband had a father who said, "You are not doing anything right," then he has need for some attitude change that says instead, "You can be the kind of man that you are and that is all right." And for the wife's comparable situation we have, as I said, the attitude that, "You don't need to prove yourself to your peers." There was a lot of rebellion and a little bit of self-doubt that arose from that opposite attitude that she holds. It would be a real good idea, then, to help her learn behaviors that have to do with taking care of herself. She says she did take care of herself a lot but that statement really tells me that she didn't model how to care for herself in a loving and nurturing way. She did it without guidance and without feedback. She did it without reinforcement. And she did it without any help. So you would be reducing any strain on having done those behaviors. For a quick understanding, consider how many street-people have, in fact, been taking care of themselves for years, too. But did they learn to *care* for themselves and groom themselves and love themselves, or did they learn only to "fend" for themselves? There is a big difference.

I'm thinking of something I learned to do by myself as an example of the importance of feedback. I learned to play guitar by myself. And when people who *really* knew how to play guitar sat down with me and said, "You are doing that right," it was great to know that I was. As far as my performance went, it was the same both before and after. But my internal state of anxiety was reduced because of that feedback that helped reinforce what I had done the hard way. And the reduction of anxiety made the whole playing more enjoyable.

All right, let's finish this now. What we should have accomplished is explaining that we want to use the interpersonal checklist, even with only a self-report, as something that is adjunct to a personal interview to give us added help in determining not just the *behavioral* things that go with it, but the *attitude* and *affect* things that might go and give us some sense of the current structure of the *social network* and the *stage of development of the family*. It even gives a little bit of an idea of the *family of origin tendencies* that have been carried on. We use it with all clients at the beginning of therapy. Occasionally, we administer it again during the course of therapy, but more frequently use it as a postmeasure to confirm changes after therapy has ended.

DEVELOPMENTAL DEMANDS AND SYMPTOMS

There's one thing I want to add here about role attribution in families, developmental trends, and systemwide change goals that will wrap this diagnostic material together more tightly and create a segue to the interventions we'll shortly be detailing. For example, in the couple we've just been speaking about, the woman said she was the one in the family who was from a "long line of doers." That was the role that the family allowed her to play. This is an attributed role and it does an aggregate of things. It pulls certain resources because she comes to believe that this *is* her, and it also delimits certain communications that she will make because of the imposed sanctions by the self and the family. For one thing, she won't fail to *do*. If something needs to be fixed, she'll do it, by golly. And it wouldn't be likely that she would say "I can't" or "I need help to make it" or "I don't know how." I have mentioned only three sentences, but really what I am speaking about are hundreds of thousands of communications that could be delimited in that role attribution. Then, eventually, experiences that would apply to a congruent expression of those lacking communications would be repressed or suppressed or both.

If there was a therapy problem here, that kind of role attribution would be the thing this graph helps us understand. What we are concerned with in the Ericksonian approach, which brings us back to one of the first comments at this workshop, is that Erickson's approach is not interested in trying to directly produce a removal of the symptom or the family's presenting problem. Rather, he'd use indirect suggestion aimed at retrieval of the resources needed for the whole family to make more adequate—in fact, creative—adjustments to developmental demands. It might be enough to make adequate adjustments to the demands, but as change agents we should really help the family make an adequate and a creative adjustment. Erickson would not settle for adequate if he could get a creative adjustment or change out of the family.

Before we think about how to stimulate that kind of creative adjustment in families, we should make a comment about the extent to which the demands of life concern us when families change. This is going to be framed as linear, when, in fact, development is probably more of a spiral than a straight line. One humorous way of looking at that is "You get to foul it up later on if you fouled it up the first time around."

As the family system moves through those developmental stages, each individual in the family, as well as the couple or any subsystem, will be affected differently [see Illustration 21]. If it is the couple, for example, they have courtship, and then they have some kind of commitment stage. They may then have marriage or some decision amounting to, "We are not going to get married, we are going to conquer the world together instead." Then they will encounter decisions on childbearing. If they don't personally have a value for that, their parents do or the culture does . . . and biology certainly does! So they definitely have developmental demands that are going to impinge and decisions that have to be made, and on and on and on. Now at each of those stages, Erickson would put things rather simply. He'd

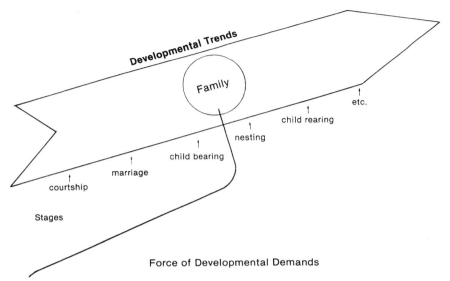

Successful movement through each stage is marked by a disorganization and reorganization of family structure. This change is intended to accomplish the retrieval or learning of necessary **trans-actions** and necessary **experiences** which are needed to negotiate the present stage and prepare for the next stage.

Illustration 21

say you have two kinds of things you want to help the family develop: It is necessary to have the ability for the experiences and the transactions to negotiate each of those stages.

Let's examine this couple's graph in light of that. The wife was our focus. If a role was prescribed for her that she was able to play and from that certain communications are available, that means *certain* transactions are available and certain ones aren't. Then, consonant with the belief system that develops at some point with the formation of the conscious mind in the child, certain unconscious resources are available and certain ones aren't. So, certain experiences are available and certain transactions are available and some aren't.

So if it should happen that in the course of the developmental thrust that is going on in her life, the experiences and transactions are called for and she hasn't been practicing them for decades, then she has a problem and she develops a symptom of some kind that shows us a manifestation of that higher level of family disorder. The higher level I'm speaking about is the organization of her family of origin and/or current family that could only allow her to play a certain role and not others, to the extent that she now, say, is not seeing herself comfortable or versatile with friendly dependency.

She may not appear to be the symptom carrier who brings the family to the office. She may subtly distort reality and, essentially, hypnotize a child into having a symptom. She could do this by blocking transactions and experiences the child needs to meet developmental demands (all of this outside of her awareness, of course). And we would notice the attributions of certain roles for the child or the ascription of certain traits in the child and the focus of awareness on those traits, and so forth. Presumably, we might find that some kind of behaviors and experiences would not show up on the checklist. And the family is at stage X that is calling for experiences and transactions to be generated that aren't available in the map of experiences. At a certain point in one's ongoing activities a symptom can develop through one of two ways—to simplify it: either because there is an overuse of actions and experiences that are available or because there is a developmental demand for experiences and transactions that are lacking.

Say you have a family with a child abuser or potential child abuser whose behavior or state of consciousness is typified by a certain degree of muscular tension, a certain kind of critical internal dialogue aimed at other people, a certain tone of voice, a forcefulness in speaking, a certain breathing pattern, a selection of vocabulary words. To give you a picture of this, he is a person walking around like Steve McGarritt from Hawaii Five-O all the time. He learned to do this in his socialization, of course, and the organization of his family called for him to be this kind of frightened and macho man. But the point is what happens in this current family you have in the office.

When a problem has to be solved, he uses the waking state in which problem solving has most often occurred for him. That is the way his interpersonal grid looks to him and it represents his sense of his usual self most of the time. That represents transactions that he favors and it is only because he knows how to do things that way. But he will try to solve a family problem being, as I put it, Steve McGarritt. He'll try to use those tense behaviors, and when those don't work he'll do it even more. So he will overuse behaviors that will strain his out-of-balance system even more. It is out of balance if and when reality requires experiences and transactions that are not there in that group of behaviors. As he strains those more and more, that is one way a symptom can develop in his personal system or in the family system of which he is a part. Finally, he has a coronary because he has produced more and more adrenalin responses for longer and longer periods until eventually the cardiovascular system says, "Hey, I've had enough." (I hope you are following me with all these imaginary referents.)

The other huge category of symptoms that could develop would be the flip version of that scenario—the denial and repression of experiences over and over and over that demand some kind of logical release or closure for a healthy balance. This is like the suppression of tearing for decades. It's not the tearing from five years old that has built up into pressure. It is the learned *mechanism* to suppress the use of that part of the healthy organism that demands some kind of logical release for closure or balance. To repeat, it is not the tearing from five years old that has built up into pressure but it is the *habitual use of the mechanism to suppress* the healthy function that is the problem. The coronary is a way that registers in an individual, but you'll see that the symptom might just as well register in the family as a marital "communication problem" or a "teenage son" problem, and so on.

Some of us are fortunate enough to have a social system that we can talk into having problems for us, so to speak. The child abuser's unconscious, to anthropomorphize, might say, "I can get my child to be afraid of going to school so that I can use my Steve McGarritt behavior more easily." Steve McGarritt can get his son to be a delinquent so that he can coach him into going straight. Then he can use his normal, healthy waking state behaviors (of being a coach) and keep himself in balance. Then the impulses to go and break a window are being manifested by the child. And so he gets to disown them rather than suppress them in himself without help. He gets to suppress them with the help of somebody else whom he can call "bad" and whom he can cure.

A question was just raised, "When there are communications and behaviors someone avoids identifying with, are they reflected in the person's shadow, as in Jung?" That could be so, I think. Only the shadow knows! So would that be the case? There is a real strong likelihood that it would. In the sense that the concept of the shadow, as I understand it, refers to organized experience that you disown, it may be there. But there is another thing that a lacking on the checklist could show and that is disorganized behavior that you don't even have a chance to disown because it just wasn't learned, as in the case of a retarded person. If you were able to get this checklist filled out, it might only show behavior in dependency. You couldn't say that a managerial part was his or her shadow because s/he never organized the conscious or unconscious mind enough to be managerial and then disown it.

Now back to symptoms that develop and what we do about them in family therapy. Indirect suggestion is one of the interventions we rely upon heavily, but to repeat, *it should usually be aimed at the system's needs and resources and not at the symptom.* Now let's say that a family developed school phobia in one of the children. Rather than using direct suggestions like "You will be relaxed when you go to school," you would use indirect suggestions aimed at the client's system to help the husband give support to his wife and help his wife ask for someone to listen to her anger and scare. And those resources would be developed everywhere else in the system where resources were needed rather than directed at removing the school phobia symptom. That is in the family context.

In the individual context, you might say the person has anxiety attacks driving to work. So rather than direct suggestions to the tune of "You drive to work and be the most relaxed person in the universe," the indirect suggestions would be regarding, perhaps, the ability of the individual to grieve over the death of his father. This is certainly making a potential scenario and a long story short—if you follow my logic here. But it would be in a totally different area, because we'd be seeing a person who was not able to use all of his resources, and would therefore be misusing the resources he has because other areas have not been developed or have been denied for some conflict-related reason.

The value of this checklist then, is to show us the undeveloped areas that may be needed. There is an efficacy to working to develop those undeveloped areas that are needed for current and future demands: Why buy a hammer if you don't need one? And also this is useful to see the overdeveloped areas that are being overused in development. And then it directly shows behavior, and I have demonstrated that you can use it to infer something about the map of experience gained in the family of origin. And you can infer affects that may be needed, and because of that you can infer attitudes that are present. So, Leary would hate me for these liberties I'm taking, because he hates this graph in the first place now that he is on to cosmic matters.

We don't like giving tests to people. It's just that this one is so easy to score and interpret that it is worth the effort and time. It is not the Ericksonian way to give a battery of tests or to give the same one test to every client. Please remember that when thinking of Dr. Erickson's work. However, we find this test to be so useful that we give it to most individuals and families before we even see them and it helps us determine the prospects of being a genuine help to them. Then, after the people take the checklist, we discuss it with them. We are making some therapeutic distinctions here and doing some diagnosis. Following that, we arrive at treatment goals. Following that, we do interventions to meet those goals. I can see this checklist at its most useful purpose working with the whole family. In my mind I go straight to a family and have everyone presented with it so that I can look at their opinion of one another and their roles. Do it for the entire family; do it for the way the parents see one another and themselves, and the way the child sees himself and the parents, and the way the parents see the child.

For the hypothetical individual with anxiety attacks driving to work, let's say his wife's view of him was that he was extremely aggressive and competitive. Why might that be so? Why would a wife so want to have a competitive macho male on her hands that she would deny all of his cooperation behaviors which are real? Or, is it true that he is competitive and aggressive, and in fact he denies it and intends to see himself as extremely friendly instead of hostile? And that is real interesting because you will find those distortions account for a good deal of arguments in a marriage.

When we have four graphs for the couple, as we did for the first couple we looked at here [Illustration 13 and 14], we can see this other aspect that I am talking about. Let's say this husband has some desire to see his wife in a way that is entirely different than she is. Well, they are going to have a lot of conflicts about that. So that discrepancy relates once again to their internal state and what each has brought from their family of origin. So administer it for not just their perception of others but their self-perceptions. Then you can compare that way they see each other.

Let's reiterate here that this is *our* tool for *our* assessment before we see people. We use it to know that we can help a family. It gives us some idea for the first session and we can get started right into therapy. So usually it's only in the highly verbal, intellectual, or analytical families that we find this is really handy tool to talk over with them. That way they go, "Wow, this psychotherapy, there is something to it." The only people who are turned away, generally, are families with members who need the kind of therapist who is going to be there and be a substitute set of parents for a while. In those cases, I will not be able to do my best. I am going to be the most useful to people who have some verbal facilities. It is, of course, useful if they are not hallucinating: If when I say "blue," they hear "red elephants," then we are not going to work together very well in conventional therapy settings. Let's turn our attention now to some more active interventions and speak about less conventional therapy.

CHAPTER THREE

Perturbing Family Organization: Strategic Task Assignments

SKILL-BUILDING ASSIGNMENTS

I want to read you part of the definition of perturb.

per-turb vt [fr. *per-* intensive prefix + *turbare* to throw into disorder, disturb, make turbid] **3a:** to cause (a planet or other celestial body) to deviate from a theoretically regular orbital motion usually as a result of interposed or otherwise extraordinary gravitational pull **3b:** to disturb or interfere with or modify the usual or expected motion or course or arrangement of (as atoms) [interaction between the hydrogen atom perturbed by a passing ion.]

The way I have most successfully *begun* work with schizophrenic folks who are not real flaming, actively psychotic is to use assignments to perturb their social order and roles. For instance, I would drag them out to local art fairs and see them for three hours straight, and two days later for three more hours. I would give them assignments they had to do every night for three weeks. I was just in their hair all the time, making changes. Otherwise you tell someone to do something that they do successfully but they have six days to muck it up before they see you again. That is six days of their bad hypnosis versus one or two hours of me doing it the other way around.

So Greg, for example, couldn't read for one thing, and he wanted to be an ambassador. This was certainly unreasonable, so I took it on. I did think that he might have what it would take to perhaps become a president, however. In fact, as part of this introduction and request for therapy, he sent us a shopping bag puffed way up with a target on it, and instructions to hit it with a pencil and split it open. When we did, money came pouring out. He had 500 crisp, new one-dollar bills twisted tight so they puffed open. We put them back in the bag and went to his house and sat him down and said, "Look, if you want therapy, this is not how it goes. We get to choose when and how much you pay." We looked around his house that day. He had books on the stove in boxes. So you could be thinking, "Ah, food for thought." And he had all of his bills piled up in the soap dish in the bathroom by the mirror. His house was in shambles. He really didn't even have some of the basic skills for living. He was very badly off.

He worked at a hospital and he was aggressively nursing the delusion that the doctors were killing people more or less for experimentation. It's a good thing the movie called *Coma* was something that he hadn't seen. I took the case because I could communicate with him well, for one thing, and he *needed* help, for the other. He had potential. And he really wanted me to do the therapy.

I saw him every week for over two years. I saw him twice a week for three hours for many sessions. One of the things I did in the trance and gave him amnesia for every time was reading. I had him actually read Dick and Jane books—just baby books. There was one called the *Greatest Word Book*. It had pictures of everything. Everything in the world is pictured in there, like safety pins, buttons, tunnels, fire engines, cats, owls, and so forth. We would go through this and see the pictures and read the words, and he would close his eyes and see the word and open his eyes and see the word, and hear it pronounced in his head, and then come out of trance and *not* know that he spent three hours reading that book like a toddler. So we did that kind of thing on a *long* series of the weekly sessions.

The other series of the sessions was spent with interpersonal skills. It took a little time but I would give him written instructions on cards. I had computer cards that I had gotten from someone which fit perfectly in a sturdy travel agency envelope. And I cut a slot in the top so he could read the date on the top of the card and the time. And at that date and that time he was to pull that card out and read it. And he would know when the next one was to be read but he didn't know what it said. And then there would be a typed description of exactly what he was to do.

For example, one day he was to go to a restaurant and order two desserts and write a report on which one was the best. He wrote a great report on the way they tasted. He said at the bottom, "By the way, I didn't know how to pay the bill so I just left the money on the table." He was distracted by the task of deciding whether or not he was going to pass the test of accurately describing the best dessert. But really what happened is I got him in there to learn to negotiate going to a restaurant.

He didn't date. His description of the woman he wanted to meet was unreal. He certainly had some high criteria and he didn't have much to offer. So he had a lot of things to learn before we were even ready to begin getting him socializing. One thing along the line of women in his life was his grandmother who was the person he thought loved him and when she died, he felt things had gone downhill since. To give you an idea of the sequence of these assignments, one was to sit at lunchtime alone some place and make a list of all the people he knew who had died. Then the next day he was to take that list and write down things he learned from each of them or he was to think about those people and make sure that he didn't miss any of them.

There were a couple of other things he was to do along the line of reflecting about that, but they were small. The final thing was that at midnight on Thursday night, the local theater was showing a movie called *Harold and Maude* about a boy who was obsessed with dying. Harold was obsessed in order to get attention from his superficial mother and he met an old woman who was about to die. She was just the most exciting person you could imagine and she showed him a lot about living. To make matters worse, she decided she was going to do herself in on her eightieth birthday. She had done what she wanted to do and she was ready to check out. He didn't want her to die, of course, because he had really used her to stimulate his enjoyment of life. There was a moment of decision at the end: Would he go back to his morose lifestyle, or had he learned the real lesson from her, which was to start living? He decided to start living. So Greg had to see that movie. He called us up at 11:30 and said, "I have to go to work early tomorrow. Do I have to do this assignment?" I said, "Oh yeah, those are mandatory." So he went. So here we have a situation of a couple of days' preparation just to get him to be involved in the movie.

Then one day he showed up when the Ann Arbor art show was in town. There was one statue of a warrior we had seen that had been made by an incredible person, who really had an interesting philosophy. He would watch you and not reflect his insecurities in his face when he spoke about what his statues meant to him. And the little statue of the warrior had a mask over the face with eye holes in it only. I thought that was an interesting relationship. It so happened that the client, Greg, had a Don Juan "warrior" fantasy and we knew that seeing that statue and talking to that guy would stimulate his thinking in some particularly relevant ways.

I also wanted him to see the booth where they were selling halter tops. In every art fair there is at least one buckskin halter top booth staffed by a group of women who could be talked into modeling them. So I went the day before the session and I checked out with the warrior sculptor that he was going to be there if I brought someone around who I thought would benefit from meeting him. Would he be willing to tell him his philosophy? He said he would. Then I went to the halter top booth, and I said, "I am going to come by tomorrow with a guy who I want to play a little trick on, with your help. He is real shy around women and he is from out of town. So I would like you to model these different tops for him . . . and really make him look at them, okay?" They agreed. So I left.

Then Greg showed up at the appointed time and I said, "Oh my goodness, do we have an appointment today? I forgot I have to go down to the printer. Why don't you get in the car and we will go together." He agreed. And, what do you know, the Ann Arbor art fair was there and we couldn't get to the printer without parking on the far side and walking through the art fair. So we stopped at the warrior booth and listened to that man's philosophy. When we saw the warrior, Greg talked to the sculptor and I disappeared for a while. (Later, back at the office, we would be using another two hours, with me telling him all about the meaning of that thing—that warrior—in the trance. I told him a lot of interesting things about the warrior, especially about how the warrior adorned himself with features that displayed his status to others.)

After talking to the sculptor, we passed by the booth where the halter tops were. I said, "Oh, that reminds me, I want to buy one of these for Carol but I just don't have any time." And he would do anything for Carol. He would have walked across Lake Michigan for Carol, so would he pick out a halter top for her. I told him that I knew he had good taste so I could go to the printer. Then I left. And those women modeled their halter tops and made him look at their breasts for an hour, which desensitized him a lot about being able to look at women.

I was doing little things along each step of the way to use these experiences in keeping with his treatment plan. What we want to talk about now are some nuances of those different kinds of tasks. So maybe I should use this moment, as pregnant as it is here, to have you take a look at the skill-building homework paradigm [Illustration 22]. We are right in the middle of that now, so take a look at how everything we have been talking about comes together as a meaningful gestalt that I think you will be able to remember and use right away.

We have Greg unable to do what he needs to do in his mid-thirties and what he should have been doing in his teens and early twenties. That was courtship tasks. He can't come up with the experiences of being comfortable around women. He has incredibly high standards about what woman would be appropriate to "get." Greg is living alone. His parents live far away and he hasn't spoken with them for a long time. He was raised by his grand-

SKILL-BUIDING HOMEWORK PARADIGM

1. Identify the client's developmental tasks.

2. Isolate or identify some of the missing experiences and transactions the client(s) need(s) to improve adjustment in that developmental stage (and/or begin the next stage).

3. Think of some context where those skills are learned or find an activity that is a component part or metaphor for the needed skill.

4. Employ some aspect of the client's life that is a talent, resource, skill, value, belief, etc. to motivate and engage the client(s) into the activity.

5. Appealing to a strength or resource, assign (with challenge, curiosity, humor, suggestion, command, logic, etc.) use of that resource in the identified activity/context.

6. Be sure to distract the conscious mind from the notion that the strategic homework intervention connects to the conceptualized family developmental task (con/unc dissociation, distraction, interrupted proximity of associations, irrelevance of chosen context, etc.).

7. Client(s) will gain needed skill without threat. Skill applies to important parts of future development and the client will be able to handle the developmental task and decide about involvement in family development independently of any percieved therapy bias. (Client(s) is/are left with the power).

8. If necessary arrange for the clients to use the skill in the proper developmental context (by using multiple metaphors, suggestions, commands, activities, assignments, etc. as appropriate).

Illustration 22

mother who was dead. He is working at a hospital where he has probably alienated himself from everybody by talking about and writing letters to the Board of Directors about the doctors' practices, and his other adult skills were terrible, as in the case of his misspellings. For example, he spelled "got" "gought." So here he is moving through what should have been late courtship stage of his life. It wouldn't be too late to get it handled accurately—he might just be a late bloomer. But he is on the verge of missing it. Does he have the experiences? No, he can't stand and look at a woman and say, "Hi." He can't look at her and spell "got." He can't write a note and say "I *got* these roses for you." He can't have the experience of being comfortable around women, partly because his expectations of them were so out of line with reality. And he doesn't have the transactions to socialize, or small talk, or go to the restaurant, and so on. So I wanted to help him get those skills, as well as the basic skill of focusing his eyes and imagining the letters with his eyes closed, and being able to read.

By the way, I should tell you the end of the story. He has just finished his second master's degree. One is an MBA and the other is in Administration and Policy. And you have to work hard for those degrees. You have to be able to read and write and get along with other folks in small groups. So we succeeded.

Now look at the paradigm we have for the strategic homework paradigm. That is the nice name for simple homework. It is not really difficult to pull this off, providing you follow some logic in the area of handling the conscious mind of the family members. To meet the first step on the handout [Illustration 22], I identified some developmental tasks for Greg. The developmental task was that of courtship and being able to socialize with peers of both sexes.

The next step is to isolate some specific behaviors or missing experiences or transactions that are needed. So one isolated one is being able to order in a restaurant and pay a bill. No problem there. That is real specific. Next, think of a context where the skills were learned. Well, that is easy, the restaurant. A lot of times you can find interesting substitutes.

Then, you want to employ some aspect of the client's talents, resources, skills, values, beliefs, or something, so that you can motivate him to do the activity. In this case Greg thought he was trying to pass the test of being a man of good taste since he wanted to be an ambassador and ambassadors have to know about taste.

The next portion of the paradigm reads, "Appealing to a strength or resource with challenge, curiosity, humor, suggestion, command, logic, etc., and you heard the one example where Greg called up and asked if he had to go to the movie. And I said these assignments aren't optional, they are mandatory. I just plain demanded. So whatever way works with each family member or group of members will be different, of course. Some people you have to tease into an assignment. With others you make it logical. With other groups you say you bet they couldn't. Each family is unique and what you do ought to really be different for each one.

So next, be sure to distract the conscious minds. Evaluating the desserts was a distraction, and Greg didn't have the slightest idea that the real task was to pick up the skill of going and ordering and paying the bill. And then the client will gain the needed resources without threat.

Now the last step suggests that the homework learning be related to the client in metaphor during subsequent sessions. I'll give you an example of that for Greg, using a modification of a story Dr. Erickson told me about his own child. The metaphor, whether delivered in trance or out of trance, would begin innocently about my son's first date.

When he went on his first date, he went to the malt shop with his girlfriend, Katrina, and sat down with her and his malt . . . and had mucus membrane stimulation. Then he went to the roller rink with her and engaged in rhythmical physical activity. And then he went back to the malt shop and had a hamburger with all the relishes and a wonderful dessert and more mucus membrane stimulation. The conscious mind wouldn't even be able to fully describe how interesting that dessert was. But you learn something of importance when your conscious mind is distracted. You might not be able to say what you do learn while you are a young man having a dessert in a restaurant. When something is learned, your unconscious knows it can be applied later. And when he came back he told me had been to the roller rink and to the malt shop, but I knew what he had really been doing. He had been engaging in rhythmical physical activity and mucus membrane stimulation with that girl.

You are interested in metaphor, which is the topic of the day. That is a metaphor using suggestion to focus Greg's attention back on what he might have learned having dessert and the idea of applying it somewhere with some kind of learning about being with a woman. As you will see, the learning I'm speaking of is at the unconscious level. So that is the last step.

Now let's look at the halter top incident. You have a developmental demand of the courtship stage with one small isolated experience. The hard part for you as therapist will come if you don't isolate the experiences you can teach. The hard part will be if you want to thrust your clients into a situation where they are out dating.

One experience about dating for a man is to be able to look at a woman's chest and not act embarrassed. That is an experience. Can he be comfortable recognizing his sexuality which is stimulated by visual input from another person? That is certainly a part of what should be learned during adolescence. What context could we do this in that would be totally nonthreatening? I wouldn't want to take him to a dance. Nowadays, perhaps I could get him into an exercise class that is coed. But that wouldn't really guarantee very much involvement. But then I hit upon the halter top booth. Who would ever think that I was trying to get him to learn about sexuality?—We are going to the printer and buying a gift. That is all. So I appeal to some resource, which for this man was to do something for Carol.

And that really helped to distract his conscious mind. So now his conscious mind was distracted into making a choice for Carol's benefit. It was to have nothing to do with him. In that context he learned the skill without threat, the skill of being able to examine that there were more kinds of attractive women in the world than that cosmetic image he had on a pedestal. And he could talk to them and experience them, be experienced by them, and not have to turn away from them. That was what I wanted him to learn. He was distracted, he learned a skill, and then we came back to the office and what followed from there metaphorically, in or out of trance, would be a discussion on using those skills later.

There is another related story which again involves Erickson. It is a modification on his story of a fellow he took to shop for his wife. He had never bought any gifts for his wife or daughter at all and had never bought a Christmas tree and so on. And Erickson had the sales person lift up her skirt and show the edge of her black lace panties and to show her black lace bra. His intention was very similar to the one I had in the Greg case (that is how I got the idea, of course)—to have the client learn to be comfortable with sexuality and related communications, because later the assignment for Erickson's client was to have his wife model those pieces of lingerie that he bought her. You can hear a pin drop when you talk about this stuff, can't you?!

Yes, there is a question, and that is to again speak about how the assignment was related to Greg's developmental task. His problem involves adjusting creatively to the demands of courtship that are being compounded by his thinking that the only suitable woman for him is this playboy image of a woman on a pedestal who has a Ph.D. in physics, and who also will show her emotions, take care of him, have a career, and think he is a good guy when he has nothing to offer. Those are the women he thought he could accept. So one of the skills that I thought he needed to practice was to actually observe a real human being. And he couldn't do that because he was very uncomfortable with his sexuality. He couldn't hold hands, kiss, look at a woman, sit down in the cafeteria next to a woman, or anything. So his ability to be comfortable while being in the presence of a woman he was looking at was a huge isolated portion of courtship.

Another thing I should mention, this guy wasn't going to date anybody until he had a master's degree. He wasn't going to get married or date until he had that degree. Then he felt he would have something to offer these women. There is a step on the illustration [Step 4, Illustration 22] that refers to employing a client's talents. Now most everyone has the talent of standing up and talking and shopping. Pretty much everyone can do that. But those skills could be considered as "talent" if you stretch it a bit. At other times that step might become real important. Maybe you have someone who is good at tying flies for fishing, and so you use that talent to be the basis for getting him to a cub scout meeting as a speaker, let's say. But in Greg's case the talent step doesn't have much emphasis. And it is subsumed under the category of normal living skills that Greg had.

There is another question concerning this case and it is, "Would you do something similar if the client was, say, 50 pounds overweight and thought he had to lose the weight before getting involved in dating?" Well, that would be a different client, who I don't know, but Greg's belief system was an irrational paranoid delusion system. And he had nothing to offer until he had a master's degree. And it is a little bit different than a person who is just uncomfortable with something and using an excuse. So I wouldn't say that you need to apply the same logic. Every individual is different and if you apply these principles in principle to the family, then you should be able to come up with a treatment that works.

So we have the homework assignment and you know some of the outcomes you are after. We have done our diagnosis. We have some kind of outcomes in mind—goals that we have stated in terms of emotion, behavior, and attitude. And one of the things that we have got for those goals is a homework assignment that will help acquire some portion of the goal. There is another kind of related assignment we want to look at now that is usually much more interesting, as well as baffling.

AMBIGUOUS FUNCTION ASSIGNMENTS IN FAMILY THERAPY

This is ambiguous function assignment. Look at the illustration [Illustration 23] in the handouts. This is another kind of assignment. I talked about Erickson rolling the wheelchair on a man's foot. The homework assignment for building skill that we have just discussed will actually retrieve specific outcomes. And you can more or less know ahead of time which ones you are going to get. You put a quarter in the Pacman machine and you get Pacman. But this kind of assignment is called ambiguous function. And we are *not* talking necessarily about retrieving something that the *family* doesn't know. But you are going to disrupt the normal belief system for the family, for sure.

You will want to assign ambiguous function assignments to the family members who are central in the dramas and to the structure of the problems in the family. You may assign one to the father who is withdrawn from supporting his wife and from spending time with his children, for instance. Now, I'll give you examples and exercises so you will understand an ambiguous function assignment and the place it has among other interventions. I don't believe you will have seen anything like it.

One thing we want to remember when we use this is the step in the strategic homework paradigm about curiosity or challenge or demand or something. We had a woman come from Michigan, recently, who had gone through three or four years of therapy and was still real depressed. For several years she had been seeing someone from the school of social work who is a very good therapist, and she had made some real changes. I guess she had been a real wallflower and even that is putting it too aggressively. She was real attractive, however. Everyone in the workshop was caught up

Ambiguous Function Assignments

1. Stimulate the client's (or clients') thought.
     a. Use indirect suggestion.
     b. Use dramatic hold.

2. Deliver with compelling expectancy.

3. Imply value in activity.

4. Assign specific task (time, place, act) but do not reveal its purpose.

5. Make use of an actual physical object.

6. Make sure the client is involved in active behavior.

7. Place binds on the client's performance of the task.

8. Maintain "therapeutic leverage" while utilizing client's responses.

     a. Empathize and reinforce each learning.
     b. Identify and accelerate the client's motivation.
     c. Do not accept the client's initial thinking as complete.
     d. Continue expectancy and imply the existence of more information.
     e. Challenge or stimulate the client to do the continued thinking.
     f. Continue the above until therapeutic receptivity is maximized.

Reasons

disrupts habitual conscious sets
client will think deeply re: self
client gives diagnostic information to therapist
feeling and thoughts both elicited
client attributes special "magic" to therapist
client finds some refreshment and excitation about learning
special rapport is created
client focuses on any self motivation
becomes aware of therapy as active
becomes aware of therapy as something they do
makes it meaningful
stimulates a sense of curiosity
increases sense of therapy's importance

Indications

after rapport and credibility are established
after resources are built by previous work or for diagnostic purposes
with clients who have organized conscious minds (not with psychotics)
when client manipulates or controls therapy
when client's beliefs about therapy or therapist limit progress
when client has seen many other therapists without success

Illustration 23

on that when they saw her. Now you would really think that someone who spent that much time trying to look attractive would have more assertiveness. So she must have been in a real bind trying to make herself attractive and then be that shy. She was 37 and single.

We asked her to go to the beach that night after her first therapy session or go to the top of the Holiday Inn on the beach. It has windows all around it and you can look at the beach. It had to be at sundown. We knew what time sundown was because we did our homework. She was to go there at 5:30. Sundown was to be at 5:40. And she was to take two spoons and she was to take a little ring. And I handed her a little bone ring that had golden leaf all around it that we purchased for $9.75. It was an investment into her future.

She was to take that ring and those two spoons. She could go to the beach or she could go to the top of the Holiday Inn. I made a big deal about it. I really preferred the top of the Holiday Inn. You get a nice view of all the water around. And you can sit on the "sun side" of the lounge. I told her that I didn't know if the sun was going down over the water or over the beach. And if it goes down over the water the only way you can really watch the sundown is from the Holiday Inn.

So you might want to go up there and double-check that the sun is going to go down in the right place. If not, the beach won't work and, on the other hand, people could prefer the beach. And if the sun is going down on the water it is going to be beautiful on the beach, too. But then it would be a little chillier. I think I would prefer the Holiday Inn, but you can do the beach. The beach would be okay, Barbara, if you want to use the beach.

So we placed a bind on her performance. She wasn't thinking, "I'm not going to do this." She was thinking, "I wonder if I want the beach or the Holiday Inn." Also, you notice that there is a physical object involved, which is very useful from the standpoint that projection goes into it rather than clients trying to make meaning out of it. And they don't have to hold everything in their imagination. So it helps to solidify the imagination a little bit and externalize some of the mental stimulation that is going on. So we have a bind on performance and we have a physical object that the person can use. In this case it was two spoons and a ring. Now you want to know what we had in mind for this assignment to accomplish, don't you? So did she. This type of assignment will stimulate the client's curiosity and thought process in some way. It can be done with the entire family as well and in a lot of ways.

If I want to stimulate your thought right now, for example, so that you would pay attention to this exercise—not that you would not pay attention, of course—I could say,

> There is an exercise I want to share with you. And a lot of times you are in school and you think you are learning one thing and you learn something else. I remember in a class on logic once, it was in my geometry class. My teacher, Mr. Rouse, wrote a pamphlet on logic and somehow got that through his teaching objectives and lesson plans so that we could learn about logic—in the name of geometry. I don't know if I really kept a lot of that with me consciously. You never know if you keep consciously with you something that you learned, unless you use it verbatim. But in my group of esteemed books that I never will lose track of, there is a little booklet entitled *Logic* by Rouse. And it sits up there on the garage shelf at home with my other important books and notebooks I have gathered. And I'm not going to lose it. The unconscious learns something different and the learning is symbolized by that booklet.
>
> And your conscious can really think about that a lot while you are standing there looking at something you collected years ago. What could you really learn while paying attention in class to one thing and maybe your unconscious learned something else?
>
> And that physical object is a way of remembering it. It doesn't matter if your glass is half empty or half full. What matters is whether you like the taste of water. Now let me show you. . . .

Now, is your curiosity stimulated by this, or what?! So I told Barbara, "This is what we want you to do, Barbara. Go to the beach or Holiday Inn at sundown. You get there at 5:30. You have plenty of time to decide where you want to be. Take two spoons and this ring." Of course, I demonstrated holding the ring between the two spoons: "And *watch the sun go down* through the vortex. And don't push the rings together hard. Hold them apart so the spoons are supporting the ring but are not touching each other. It will be very difficult because you are going to be concentrating on several things at once. And I know you are going to have a lot of thoughts about why we have sent you to do this. And when you come back tomorrow, we want you to tell us why you think we've had you do this. Any questions? Okay, goodbye." She went. But first I said, "Don't try to solve it now. You must have been a very good student in school and gotten straight As." She said, "I did." I said, ". . . because you did all the homework assignments, right?" She said "Oh, I did." And I said "Don't do this one until 5:30."

Now the assignment had been given, including a specific time, place, and act, but what the purpose is has been elaborately avoided. Even if you think you have one, you don't tell the clients. Basically you are saying "I don't want to reveal to you what the purpose is. I want you to come back and tell me why you think I have had you do this and what you have learned from it."

We also want to make sure the client is involved in active behavior; that is, the task can't be lying in bed at night and, while counting sheep, skip number 97 or something. You want them really actively doing something. Their body must be involved here.

Let me tell you a couple of examples from Erickson's work that baffled us and which led to this formulation. And the reason I went back to see him is because he did this kind of thing with many of us. I'll take you back to his home: Often, he would take people around the house and show them little trinkets. For example, the fertility statue: "Hold this for just a minute." Of course, you would tend to think that he had some learning in mind for you. "How many Milton's are there in the room?" You would guess incorrectly, of course . . . soon you would find the little Milton doll that was there . . . after exhausting all sorts of semi-profound ideas that you may have generated. Now, please forgive the apparent sexism in this statement by Erickson, "Did you know women are two-faced?" And then you would discover that the face on the doll he has handed you will flip over from a smile to a frown with your thumb. Meanwhile, he continued, "Remember that, you are going to need to know that."

One evening he said to me, "The rock over there by the door, go pick it up." "You want me to pick up the rock by the door?" "Yes, move it." It was about the size of a coffee urn. I thought there was some reason for that, perhaps he wanted the door closed or open or something. So I went over and tried to pick it up. It was too heavy. As I fell forward he said, "Remember that next time you start to suck your thumb." I haven't sucked my thumb since! I don't even know what he meant! One thing that happens is that such things take on lots of personal meaning. It was like a zen master with a Koan.

As we've said repeatedly, Erickson was not usually concerned with trying to directly produce a removal of the symptom or the family's presenting problem. But rather he'd use indirect suggestion aimed at retrieval of the resources needed for the whole family to make more adequate, and in fact creative, adjustments to developmental demands. In conjunction, he often gave forceful directives regarding certain assignments that clients were to carry out. While this blend of directives and indirect suggestion is sometimes debated, more amazing to us, after examining his cases, is the creativity behind the assignments and the outcomes the assignments achieved. While it might seem that Erickson was more creative than others could become, it often seemed, also, that his pre-understanding of the way things would turn out was uncanny.

The idea of these ambiguous function assignments helps make possible what seems like an impossible intervention. We think you can begin to see from the outline provided here that some of his apparent genius with pre-understanding can be explained within this structure. Regardless of the specific outcome of any given assignment, it can be interpreted as having gone perfectly according to therapeutic plan and by using it the therapist will have helped the clients become actively involved in their own therapy.

On my (S.L.) third visit with him, Erickson, as usual, asked each trainee, "What do you want? . . . What do you want? . . . What do you want? . . . What do you want? . . ." And each answered, as usual, "I want to learn how you do metaphors; I want to learn about induction," etc. I told him I wanted, "to know about posthypnotic suggestion and how to disrupt it in therapy." I further noted that, in my opinion, it was posthypnotic suggestion that created and transmitted pathology in families. Learning ways to disrupt it and help replace it was going to be a real contribution to family therapists. But then he asked me my reason for coming that day, and from then on, he asked, "What is your excuse for coming this time?"

He continued speaking to me and implied that what followed was a pre-condition for my returning. It went like this:

Sunrise or sunset are very good times to be in the desert . . . or climbing Squaw Peak. Some people prefer sunrise . . . [pause] midnight is another very good time. But you may go at sunrise. I prefer it at sunset but you might prefer it in the sunlit afternoon.

Do you know what a boojum tree is? It's a real tree . . . "B, double-o, g" . . . no, "b, double-o," no, . . . yes, that's right, "b, double-o, j - u - m—boojum." It grows in the Baja peninsula north of Squaw Peak. And it can be found in a strip of southern California, and in the botanical gardens, but don't find it there first. Go north of Squaw Peak . . . you'll find the boojum tree. And when you do your conscious mind will recognize that it is a tree and your unconscious mind won't believe it. So go into a trance and look at it again and your unconscious mind will recognize that it is a tree. And your conscious mind will say, "I don't believe it, I don't believe it, I don't believe it, I don't believe it . . . [pause] . . . I don't believe it." And look around for the creeping devils. They'll be there. All right.

And whenever he said, "All right," it seemed to mean "I'm done talking with you now" and in this case it also seemed to mean "now, go and do it." I left that afternoon and went directly to Squaw Peak, (wanting to do my homework right away). I parked the car and walked around in the desert, north of Squaw Peak. I suspected that I would be in for an unforgettable learning experience that suddenly would bring into the foreground a part of myself or my memories of events, etc., that he referred to as "the creeping devils." Actually, I saw a lot of barrel cactus and sequoia, prickly pear, century plants, and dirt and rocks. And all of a sudden . . . reality was real boring.

It was apparent to me even then how much of my own expectation I had projected onto the assignment. I was actually rather bored with the reality of the desert because I had made up an imaginary scenario. But the richness of my imagination was far more worrisome than the things I saw. And I wondered, "Maybe this is what he wants me to learn."

When I went back the next day the first thing he did was turn to me and say, "Did you find the boojum tree?" I said, "Yes." In fact, I handed him a book about boojum trees—a scientist had more or less lived with the trees and taken their skin temperature for years! This botanist wrote a book about it and I gave it to Dr. Erickson. He thanked me very warmly. And he continued, "And you saw the creeping devils?" I said, "Yes," and was a little reluctant to speak. And then he said, and apparently with much meaning, "Remember that. . . .!"

And a long pause followed. During this pause he held my gaze and smiled. I was shaking my head up and down. I was on the verge of speaking but couldn't find the words . . . the right words to ask, "Remember what, exactly?" "There will always be creeping devils!" he concluded, before I spoke.

So I remembered that! Ambiguity like that will have a lot of personal meaning for years. Now what was or is the point here? What did he want me to get out of this? What did I get? I won't tell you what it has meant to me. What it meant has changed over the months and years that followed. Perhaps you can begin to realize how much I took from it when you know that at that time I walked about in the desert for two hours searching myself for an honest answer to what the creeping devils in myself or my past might be (and spent several hours prior to that and after that doing the same). Throughout the entire incident I dragged myself through a series of unpleasant emotions. Since I got no answer from Erickson, I have added to my learnings, or the personal meanings I took from the incident, the fact that Erickson may have had some intention that I would do that type of searching . . . and what did that say about me?

Components of Ambiguous Function Assignments

We'll say more about how the therapist responds to what occurs from the homework, but first let's make sure we clearly summarize the elements that we see as necessary in designing the assignment. No need for any extra ambiguity! The most important guideline is, of course, that the activity be safe, ethical, and possible to accomplish. Beyond that there is no further logic necessary to the symbolism or the "appropriateness of the task. The task ought to be specific but the purpose behind it ought to be ambiguous. It often involves creativity on the therapist's part and needs to include these components.

1. Stimulate the client's (or clients') thought about what the assignment will bring, what they will learn, and how it will reveal a therapeutic learning. Use indirect suggestion, metaphor, drama, and contagious delivery to hold interest. The most important aspect is that the clients expect that they have to return to therapy and explain what was learned and speculate why the therapist may have intended for them to have this (unstated) learning.
2. Deliver with compelling expectancy. The seriousness with which you regard the assignment will necessarily be communicated with your voice tone, facial expression, and other nonverbal delivery.
3. Be sure to imply that there is or will be value in the activity. This is somewhat related to the previous one, and, of course, with both of them, you have to really believe that there will be value in the activity before you can deliver the assignment with compelling expectancy and imply that there will be value for the client in doing it. That's why we'll have you do the exercise so you can personally experience the kind of valuable associations and ideas your clients are likely to have. Then, with a personal conviction about its worth, you'll have no trouble being congruent as you use metaphor and indirect suggestion to imply something about that worth to your clients. For example, "The more you wonder what you can learn, the more you are going to enjoy discovering exactly what it will be. But, of course, you can't know what you are going to learn until after you have learned it. . . ."
4. Assign a *specific* task (time, place, act) but *do not reveal its purpose.* These acts may be such things as brushing the teeth for a week with the nondominant hand, or carrying a carpenter's hammer on your person all week, or holding two spoons back to back with your spouse and watching the sun set through the vortex of the spoons, or changing the location of all hanging pictures in your house every other day for a week, etc.
5. Make use of an actual physical object such as the spoons, the pictures, or the hammer.
6. Make sure the client is involved in active behavior and not merely fantasy work.
7. Place binds of comparable alternatives on the client's performance of the task. That is, tell the client to consider whether the activity would best fit in on Monday, Wednesday, and Friday or if it would be better to do the task on Tuesday, Thursday, and Saturday? Or

engage a debate about whether the client might learn more if s/he picks the everday silverware vs. the sterling silver, etc. This will focus her/his conscious attention onto the insignificant choice between the comparable alternatives and away from whether or not to do the assignment at all.

Responding to the Family or the Clients after the Assignment

The most important aspect may be the way therapists use the responses that clients return with after the assignment. Briefly, therapists should be certain that all responses are accepted and accelerated. We call this maintaining "therapeutic leverage" which we accomplish by utilizing client responses. For example, we would empathize and reinforce each learning, identify and accelerate the client's motivation, not accept the client's initial thinking as complete, and continue emphasizing our expectancy so as to imply the existence of more information. In this manner we challenge or stimulate clients to continue thinking until therapeutic receptivity is maximized.

You may wonder, "What if the client doesn't do the assignment?" What if I hadn't gone to Squaw Peak? I know what would have happened if I hadn't gone. I would have a different story to tell you that might have been as astounding for me as what did happen. Erickson would probably have responded in a way that would have made it seem like not having gone was exactly the proper thing. And my thinking about it would have been stimulated to search out the meaning from the ambiguous input he gave me. Most important, then, is the thought process that is stimulated in the active family member or members and the reactions that are certain to be highly individualized and creative. I guess I should tell you that I found Erickson's assignment to me so stimulating that on all subsequent visits I continued to tell him that I wanted, "to know about posthypnotic suggestion and how to disrupt it in therapy!"

Here is what I want you to do for this exercise. I want you to do step one through seven [Illustration 23], except you won't do it in physical reality in this learning exercise. You will do it in imagination and it will still work out just as well for the exercise.

So, first of all, think of something that is a task, that is possible for a client to do. Make sure it is possible and of course ethical and safe. Then I want you to explain this to your client—your partner. Making sure to keep in mind steps one through seven: you are creating some practice to get them curious, go into it with expectancy, find some value in it, tell them the exact time, place and activity they are supposed to do, that it involves an object and puts binds on their performance. Then you tell Sally what she is to do during the next week, pretending that you have been seeing her in therapy for some time though you are not to discuss anything about what the problem might have been, just that you have an established therapeutic relationship. Then you switch roles, and Sally, pretending the same established therapeutic relationship as your therapist, tells you the assignment she has designed for you. Then you both sit quietly and simultaneously in your own imagination, really thinking about going through the steps of the activity. If it involves you going to a department store and standing like a mannequin for five minutes, let's say, then imagine when you do it, imagine step by step just like you are doing it: when you go, where you park, walking in, feeling nervous, etc.

So explain the task to each other one at a time. Both of you have told tasks to one another one at a time. And then imagine doing the task, both of you simultaneously. This will take about six or seven minutes of time in imagining, I suspect. And then when you are done you will be ready for step eight.

So now, time has passed and, if finished with the assignment thus far, we are back on the therapist's office and Sally has finished her assignment. Now you are going to do step eight, one at a time. This is what you do. Sally comes in and says, "Well I did it, I went downtown and stood in the department store like a fool for five minutes. I don't know what you wanted me to get out of it." You say, "Ah ha, you did do it, followed my directions, that is good, when did you go?" and so on. "Well, what were you thinking was my purpose in having you go?" And I'll continue this scenario so you can see how it will work. Sally might then say, "Well I was thinking maybe I shouldn't be so embarrassed about doing things like this. There probably is nothing wrong with it and I am no weirder than anyone else. That is what you had in mind, that it is okay for me to come out of the closet a little bit with this silly behavior, and I don't need to be so uptight. I bet that was it."

Step eight, as you know, is to first emphasize and reinforce each learning: "That is *wonderful* learning, that is really *important*. I don't know any other way that could have been driven home, other than this, and I am really glad this learning was important to you." And, "Have you any thought of any way you might use this learning later?" "Yes, I guess I have." And listen to it.

And then accelerate the client's motivation. "I'm glad you got that out of it, Sally. But that is really frosting on the cake. That is not what I intended for you to learn. Think just a little more about what it might have been." So don't throw out the first one, but you don't want her to stop. Why should you stop? The hoop is rolling, so keep rolling it. Don't accept the initial thinking as complete. Continue to imply the existence of more information: "There is something else there. I want you to go for it." Find out how to get the client to do more thinking. If she is doing it for you, ask her to find out what she might have done for herself. If she is going in great detail, maybe ask her to look at a single detail for a moment.

Whatever they think they have just achieved, get them to add something more, so you keep the momentum going. Use the principle we discussed yesterday: If you want to achieve a goal, make the current behavior count as a success and imply the next goal contingent on that success. Now how long do you do this? Continue the above routine until therapeutic receptivity is maximized. All right, now do step eight.

Those of you in the therapist role for starters, did you like it as a therapist role? What did you get from the client? What happened from your point of view as therapist? What happened in the client role? What was your experience? Did everyone like it, yes? It was puzzling and thought-provoking, right? How many of you as clients learned something about yourselves? The therapist sort of intimated that he or she knew the thing that you learned ahead of time. So what does that do to your opinion of the therapist? Then what about your opinion of therapy? The assignment encourages your involvement in therapy. It is sort of an accomplishment that you achieved. It disrupts the belief system about what to expect in therapy.

Rationale for Using Ambiguous Function Assignments

The reasons for using ambiguous function assignments are that they accomplish several atypical outcomes (to varying degrees) depending upon the particular families or individuals. For therapists the most important feature will be added diagnostic information provided by the members as a result of their projections onto the activity. Ambiguous function assignments provide a method by which clients give diagnostic information about roles, motivation, and secret fears in their families. It seems to help make therapy more meaningful, increases the sense of its overall importance, and stimulates clients to take more responsibility for what happens in therapy.

A sense of curiosity is stimulated as habitual conscious sets are disrupted. As a result, both feeling and thoughts are elicited and clients seem to begin thinking more deeply about themselves. Clients find some refreshment and excitation about learning and, hence, focus on any self-motivation. Interestingly, an additional byproduct is that clients often attribute special "magic" to the therapist even though they increasingly frame therapy as active and as something they do themselves. As a result a special rapport is created. These are many of the goals that you have reported as a result of your exercise experience.

You do the other homework assignment that we had, because you want to gain a specific skill of some kind and you know ahead of time what your aim is. Here the *content* is not the goal, the *process* is the goal. And what the process does, then, is disrupt these things and that would give you an indication for whom it is best and what kind is best done.

We teach a lot of structures for doing therapy, but we don't feel bound and constrained. There are huge structures, within which exists a wide latitude. We feel confidence that there are logical boundaries, and we are not flying by the seat of the pants. And within that latitude, with metaphors, for example, it is amazing how frequently something comes up that I have never said before. I had no idea why I particularly said it this time and families comment on the high degree of coincidence that specific detail has applied to them. And something about that is proof of the process.

The structure that we are going to use for metaphor gives you guidelines that are boundaries and you program your conscious mind to be in those boundaries. Just like in karate, you are swinging and kicking, you observe the wall. You don't hit the wall. Your mind knows the limit. You are on the mat. And that defines it. I don't know if that is a good enough example. You know how you can tell yourself, "I'll wake up at 7:55 this morning. And I will get up at 7:55 on Sunday morning." And sure enough you wake up at 7:54 and a half. Have you had that experience? Well, that is the same difference. We're programming, we are telling ourselves to use the set of limits within which we are free to associate, and beyond which we are not allowed to go.

When you write a computer program, almost the first thing that you have to tell it is what format the data needs to be in, and then when to stop reading. And that is what we are doing. That is especially what we are doing with metaphors. Did a lot of you have that sense of syncronicity? For the rest of you, best of luck.

Indications for Using Ambiguous Function Assignments

So when to do this? At the bottom of the page [Illustration 23] are some indications. There are some situations in which the ambiguous function assignments are best used. We use this intervention with any family or clients where the outcomes just discussed are desired after rapport and credibility are established, resources are built by previous work, and with families whose members have organized conscious minds (not with psychotics). There is also benefit to using the assignment early in therapy, primarily for its diagnostic assistance. It will be especially desirable to use this type of assignment with families who manipulate or control therapy or who hold beliefs about therapy or therapist that limit therapeutic progress. This is often apparent, for instance, in families who have seen many other therapists without success.

It is generally *not* a good idea to do it before the client believes you. So it needs to be done after rapport and credibility have been established. If I am trying to get you to presume that I already know you and I haven't had but 15 minutes of contact with you, that is pushing my luck. Maybe I can do it much faster than some can because many families come ready to think I have some credibility.

Erickson could get you to climb Squaw Peak, because this man had some reputation that preceded him. But if the client is off the street or sent by the Department of Social Services under threat of police action, and you try to get Joe to do it after you've seen him for 15 minutes, then you will be likely to lose rather than gain from this type of assignment. But if you have the credibility and the rapport from previous contacts, you can do it.

Lloyd Demcoe, in Jackson, Michigan, where I once worked, is a man who is sightless and an incredibly good therapist. He is perhaps best at two things. He is good at confronting people and at telling them what they are doing, *and he is blind.* And that really blows their mind. So, you see, he gains credibility so quickly in a session that he can get away with stuff like this right away. He has that extra feature of his handicap that keeps him apparently better than people who are not handicapped.

Do this type of assignment after the resources have been built by previous work for the things you want, unless you are using it purely for diagnostic purposes. If I want the family to come up with some positive interpretation in the event, the session should have dealt with experiences that will pull positive experiences into the foreground. If you do this with a fellow who is pathologically depressed about life, he is going to come back and give you pathologically depressed projections. So if you want positive things, make sure you have aimed at stimulating curiosity and resources have been built.

Now, a few other things about this. First of all, don't do it with people who don't have any organized conscious mind. You are trying to disrupt an organized conscious mind, and you don't need to disrupt it if it is not there.

That brings us to the best use for it and that is with the family who controls and manipulates therapy and from whom you need to get control back. Another version of that is for the family who is a bit more passive and whose belief system says therapy is not going to work, you are not going anywhere, and they know the score. And that is limiting progress. And then there is another version of that. Those are the clients who have seen everyone in town without success. So they have already got it in mind what is going to happen. And that disruption of the belief system about therapy is probably the largest proportional gain from ambiguous function assignments. It is surely the pattern that gains credibility for the effective therapist, as it did in the life of Erickson.

Let me give you one example of doing it with the family. It's obvious here, but it will help you realize how it disrupts the family on expectations of everything. One task was given by a psychologist friend of ours, Cheryl Malone, to a couple who were arguing about the management of their three children. Accidentally, the number three pops into this. The couple were to leave the session and go to a nursery, buy a plant to put outside, and decide on the plant without speaking. They were to go home and decide where to plant it without speaking. Then they were to plant it—put it in and pat it down.

And Cheryl told them that when they had agreed without speaking that it was done, they were to dig it up and find another location "and agree upon that location without speaking. Bury it again, pat it down firmly so it can rest there comfortably. Without speaking, decide that it is done. And dig it up a third time. And find the third and final location to plant the thing without speaking." And so, of course, if you want your spouse to put it over in the corner you better not put it elsewhere for your first shot because it is going to get dug up from there. That ought to present a unique challenge to the couple and she doesn't want you to speak about it. Cheryl wanted to see them at eight o'clock the next morning. And then they could tell her the result.

You see how that forces them in a way in that particular incident. Perhaps you could make a case to put this intervention in the category of skill-building assignments. Except for ambiguous purpose, you won't have anything in mind to gain. I suppose you could think it through and say that you want them to spend time with each other with no arguing. But if that was the only goal and you asked them to do all that, you are expending too much effort. That is weak; you are reaching. That is one example.

Another kind of ambiguous function assignment involves having the family members doing little tasks of some sort, such as in this example.

What we want you to do with your son tonight is to get a quarter and get some blue paint, and we want you to paint the back of the quarter. And on the other side of the quarter, we want you to put some glue and glue a string. And then when your son comes home from school we want you to call him in. Put this in a little jewelry box if you have one. And make a big "to do" over it. Give him this quarter with a string attached. We don't want 50 cents and we don't want a dollar—a quarter.

There is some special meaning here and it will dawn on you when you think about the value of a quarter. And we want you to do it with blue paint, not red, or anything else. Blue. You know how they say, "Don't it make my brown eyes blue." Well, that has special meaning. I don't want you to conclude too soon why blue. And give it to your son when he comes home from school. And then we want you to ask him . . . put it this way to him. Say this is something you want to give him, and find out what he would do with it, what he could make of it.

Tell him to examine it carefully and not to tell you too soon. After dinner, he is to tell you what he wants to do with it. Present it with a little bit of curiosity to his mind. And I don't want to tell you why I have done this. You take full credit for it. Don't tell him that we put you up to it, because we want you to get the full credit. And then come back to the session and tell us how it worked.

You can do that two days before therapy or one day before therapy. Make sure there is at least 24 hours before the therapy.

So you see how we get the whole family involved in doing that kind of a thing. And then they come back and tell you some wild things. It is as though you are hot potato-ing an ambiguous assignment. And their son thinks that they are magic now that they preach the value of their relationship with their son.

Of course, you knew that was going to happen. So the parents have increased their sense of, "Wow, this therapy can help us turn our children around." The whole thing has a little bit more magnitude when you have had the assignment done to people within the family, and it also disrupts if you have the family do it to the external world as a unit. So there are a lot of ways you can play with it. And I think you will especially see how you can keep the power in the therapy, how Erickson did a number of those very creative and amazing interventions.

Let me give you one more example to illustrate what I said about stopping when you have maximized the therapeutic readiness of the client. The case I'll be telling you about concerns a woman who was from another country and came to the United States for therapy with Carol. Her father was dying and that was her reason for the trip. And she wanted to piggy back some therapy on it. In addition to her father dying, she had a million concerns.

Maybe that is being too conservative. She was afraid of everything. She was obsessed about her fears of every little thing. It was almost like she grew up excluding the safety that you get from internalized parenting. In fact, it was exactly that way. But that was neither here nor there because the assignment Carol used with her really has less to do with the diagnosis than it does to the process of motivating her. The woman was trying to manipulate for more and more sessions. She had more and more concerns.

Well, we had to get control of the therapy. We designed the task, using some barbell weights we have and the half-mile block around our office. Carol called her the morning of the appointment and said, "When you come for therapy, wear comfortable clothes and walking shoes and be prepared to change." So the woman showed up with all of those things. Carol met her at the door with two barbell weights that weighed 14 pounds each.

She could carry one or both of them. She should think that over. Some people like to do all the work at once. Others want to spread it out. She was to walk around the circular block that is exactly a half-mile in circumference. So she would walk around the half-mile circle carrying one or both of these weights, and when she came back she was to report what she had decided was the reason Carol had sent her walking around with these weights. And if she had really understood it and learned it, then that would be it and the therapy would begin that day.

So the woman took one of the weights and walked around. She came back and said "Well, you let me carry this because I make a burden on myself carrying around my problems with me, and I'm going to weigh myself down. Right?" "Well that is a real good learning, isn't it?" She said, "Yes." "It was so obvious, of course, but that isn't what we really had in mind. You really don't have to walk around the block to learn that, so would you like to carry the other one around this time with you? And maybe you can get it this time."

She carried both weights around the second time. And she came back with a similar kind of thing. The third time she came back with, "Why do I have to get your answer instead of my answers?" Carol said, "Well, I was asking myself that very question, but for now the answer is because I am the therapist. So hit the road." So she went around, carrying one weight again. And she came around the fourth time, and then the fifth time. Now she was getting a little bit tired of this activity. She was coming up with new and useful things each time but there still seemed to be something more she should get out of it. So Carol suggested that perhaps she needed the final clue. That was to walk around the block carrying a glass egg, about half the size of the coffee urn, a little bigger than the water pitcher. It is a glass egg filled with sand dollars we've collected over the years. It is real fragile and practically weightless compared to the 14-pound weights she has been carrying around. "Carry that around the block. I think that will be a better clue for you now, added to what you have already been thinking about," Carol added.

So now all of her associations to weight were worthless. She came back from one time around the block with the glass egg. And Carol always asks me to do this role play here: "You do hysterical women so well, Stephen." So she comes back to the door with the glass egg, crying, "You had me carry this . . . [sobbing] . . . because it's delicate. I wanted to break it one time . . . [sobbing] . . . but you know, it's . . . a . . . it . . . is like valuable, you know. And you trusted me with it . . . [sobbing] . . . like I trusted myself with you, and you carry that part of me around more delicately than I do . . . [sobbing]. . . ."

The woman behaved like that. And now we have a woman who is ready for therapy. She has allowed access to the part of her that she realizes is of value, to the part that she defends and keeps away, and she'll never get that part taken care of with all of her manipulations, her infantile gratification. What we really need is to *get it*, to reach to that, to have that ego state affected. And so we helped her break through those kinds of restrictions of her own obsessing about what we had in mind. I'll leave you with that.

CHAPTER FOUR

Developing Emotion, Behavior, and Belief: Metaphor Protocols

METAPHOR

Now let's go to metaphor, because the best way we have of retrieving resources is indirect suggestion and metaphor. And we will do them separately starting with metaphor. [We will explain the addition of indirect suggestion in Chapter 6.] Now when the woman comes in that way [see previous page], Carol says, "Fine! You are absolutely right, sit down and let's begin our session." And the session in this case, as in most cases, was telling metaphors.

Erickson's primary way of retrieving resources would be in action either with the homework assignment of one kind or another, or with metaphors and indirect suggestion. By contrast, Fritz Perls' way of retrieving resources would be to have you enact something he suggested from fantasy. Similarly, Moreno would do the acting out. There's nothing wrong with that way. It's just that I'm trying to point out how therapies tend to do that. Satir does it with indirect suggestions and fantasy play or sculpting.

Another device that you've all used is the focusing of attention with, "Stay with that, and have that feeling more deeply." That is handy. But it works best for feelings; it doesn't work so well for experiences that are a little bit more subtle. You can't grab onto them like you can a feeling. Haley and Minuchin tend to rely more upon the situation caused by changing the balance in the family order. They create what Dan Overlade calls the

153

"Resolution Seeking Set"[17] by changing the balance of the family. The need for a closure that is thus created will stimulate new arrangements of resources. But we would rather promote the use of metaphor and indirect suggestions to do that since we have more precision and control in the therapy with these interventions.

So metaphor is really a handy tool to add to the other ones, not to diminish any of your choices already. You have a whole bunch of handouts on metaphor. Let's look at one of them real quick before we have a demonstration or two. We'll be starting with the definition of metaphor, which is important here [Illustration 24].

We are talking about a story with dramatic hold that captures attention. It really needs to capture attention and in a noncondescending way. We don't tell animal stories to people who are adults because we would have to anthropomorphize these animals and that really is going to sound silly. It is hard to hold the attention on the story because part of the attention goes to, "Does this guy think I'm a child or something?" So you want to eliminate that.

We also have another little rule for ourselves. It is "Don't use yourself as a major protagonist in your metaphors." You'll wonder if this is true for Erickson. I'll have to tell you why it is. Erickson told stories and he was the character in the story a lot of the time. But he didn't usually become the major character to have the learning in the story. So if I'm a person who got in a hassle with my father and figured out a way to get out of it, I don't tell it that way. I tell it as if it were somebody I knew. Maybe I use them in the story as if they talked with me and shared the ideas this way to me as the observer. But we would say, don't make yourself the main character. Your transference and countertransference problems are going to be out of control. You are going to be telling stories where you are always smarter than the woman, or you are always ripped off by the authority, or whatever it is. And your client will get hooked to that and that will be a factor that ruins your therapy.

DEFINITION OF THERAPEUTIC METAPHOR

A STORY WITH DRAMATIC DEVICES THAT CAPTURES ATTENTION AND PROVIDES AN *ALTERED FRAMEWORK THROUGH WHICH THE CLIENT(S) CAN ENTERTAIN NOVEL EXPERIENCE.*

Illustration 24

---

[17]Overlade, D. (1984). The pervasion of the resolution seeking set. In J. K. Zeig (Ed.), *Ericksonian psychotherapy, vol. 1: Structures* (pp. 282-292). New York: Brunner/Mazel.

I think it was in North Carolina that somebody told me he had been in marriage counseling and the therapist was telling stories of how he had pulled one up on his wife, and he had been right and the wife was wrong. So the couple stopped seeing the therapist after the third time. They realized this man's investment in proving hè was smarter than his wife was more important to him than the therapy.

Now we have to have a couple of ideas. For one thing, we use an altered framework. We have to learn how to construct an altered framework, which the client can use to entertain novel experience. We have to know how to retrieve the experience when we want that framework. So we will take those two steps one at a time. And metaphor needs to capture attention with drama. So we want to know how to add drama to a framework that guarantees a certain experience. So we will take those three pieces one at a time.

The next thing you have on here [Illustration 25] is the story line. That appeals to the conscious mind, that has the drama in it, that is where you see the train and you see the car, and you see the train, and you see the car, and you see the intersection. And you see the train, the car, the train, the car—you want to know what is going to happen, consciously. That is the story line and you want to consciously know what happened. That is all the conscious mind gets out of it really—a resolution of what captured curiosity.

If it is a mystery or suspense story, there is information not known and it stimulates curiosity. What is really learned therapeutically, at the unconscious level, are the experiences that arise during the telling of the story. And the association of those becomes your unconscious learning. And that is what you really get out of it.

For example, did you see *The Alien*? *The Alien* was a scary movie. As

CHANGE IN METAPHOR

Change does not result from the story line or story outcome.

Change results from the retrieving and linking of experience.
   Experience is retrieved by detailing, imagery, or symbols.
   Experience is linked by proximity, suggestions or binds.

Illustration 25

you may recall the movie deals with how an unarmed crew aboard a freightship in deep space reacts to the life form they have picked up. The life form is the alien, of course. It is extremely lethal and it is in a mean mood. The movie is the drama of the crew's ordeal and victory. There is one scene where the creature drops in for dinner unexpectedly. Boy, was that scary! Someone was sitting in his chair, if you know what I mean. The creature jumped out of a man's chest (and the crew thought he was all recovered, too). So, you know that it is an unpleasant creature . . . rude and it has no table manners!

It eats people and you can't destroy it. You cut through it and the blood drips through seven decks of the metal spaceship. So you have a tough creature and it changes form from time to time. When the creature is killed in the end, by the heroine, your conscious mind has a resolution of this story. The monster is dead. She forced it off the spaceship with a spear gun. It is gone, probably. If that were all there was to it, then you should walk out going, "Hey, good prevails and do I feel great." But you don't; you feel paranoid when you walk out because your unconscious mind has been exposed to all the other retrieved experiences along the way: suspicion, urgency, danger, and helplessness.

You can't trust anybody on the spaceship because they all hate each other. So there is suspicion and hatred and jealousy. The science officer is a robot. It turns out he is an android and not to be trusted. The computer that runs the whole show has been programmed by the company, and the prime directive that they find out near the end is that the crew is expendable. So wonderful—the company doesn't care if you die. So this suspicion is retrieved. There is this other sense of urgency and danger. The creature jumps on the guy's chest. You can't kill it. It kills your friends in the most unpredictable ways. So you are really helpless. You are helpless and you are prepared for a surprising sense of your inadequacy or helplessness.

And then there is this sense of urgency. And the urgency is created by, for example, in the ending near the final climactic moment, having red lights blinking on and off in the ship. The ship is going to explode; they intend to self-destruct the ship and all aboard and kill the creature. The woman is running down the aisle like crazy; sirens are going beep beep beep, the lights are blinking red, red, red, and the ship is saying, "This ship will self-destruct in 14 seconds. Have a nice day." Then, "The ship will self-destruct in 10 seconds." The lights are blinking, the heroine is running down the hall, and the creature is somewhere, as well. So you haven't forgotten your helplessness and the sense of suspicion. And it is urgent now.

And then, finally, she kills the creature. But to remind you of some of the helplessness from time to time, the final scene is the heroine getting into an ejection pod to get off the ship, where it will blow up without her and the creature will be blown up. But the creature is in the pod with her. She takes her clothes off, and here she is in her panties and tee shirt, to put on her spacesuit, and there is the creature. So what could be worse than to be in your panties and a tee shirt? By the way, she escapes by forcefully ejecting the creature from the pod.

So you see you get these experiences retrieved and you're not allowed to forget them either. So you have suspicion, helplessness, urgency, all combined and that creates paranoia. So when I walked out of the movie theater, I was paranoid and I actually turned around and said, "What am I turning around to look for? I'm feeling paranoid here." I looked over my shoulder. What a movie. So the point is, if you want your client to feel paranoid, take them to see the movie *Alien*. And the other point is it doesn't really matter what happens at the conscious level obviously; what really matters is what you've retrieved and linked together unconsciously.

So what we want to do with our stories is we want to have a construction protocol that will allow us to tell a story line that has moments of ideas that are going to become the resources we want to retrieve. We will show you our construction protocol or formula shortly, but for now we just want to say some introductory remarks. We are going to retrieve them by using indirect suggestions and binds to elaborate upon these introduced ideas.

With that in mind you see how easy it is to have a story having nothing to do with the client's conscious life and yet the outcome at the therapeutic level having everything to do with it. And that is why I could leave Erickson's office, as all of us did, in a way thinking every story applied to me, but on the other hand not having the slightest idea how. How did that story about the bamboo and the butterfly wings apply to me? I can't tell from the content. How did the story taking the guy to shop for underwear apply to me? I can shop for underwear. I like to shop for underwear. Also, I do buy gifts and I do give of myself to my wife and children . . . that can't apply to me in content. How does the story of the obese woman apply to me? I'm not obese; I'm not a woman. I'm not addicted and so forth. So I, and others, walk out wondering. But in this workshop we want to demonstrate how you can create therapeutic outcomes with metaphors in family therapy—in any therapy modality, really. And these metaphors will give you a great deal of confidence about the effect you are creating, yet they will have, at most, only a hint of the isomorphic construction method you may have heard about.

So here I take exception with the beginner's protocol, with the construction strategy I shared in *Practical Magic*.[18] It was late 1978 when I wrote

---

[18]Lankton, S. (1980). *Practical magic: A translation of basic neurolinguistic programming into clinical psychotherapy*. Cupertino, CA: Meta Publications.

that. Back then we were trying to convince people that metaphor worked. I had it backwards. You don't make an isomorphic story that is parallel to the problem; the client does that unconsciously. The client makes an iso-morphic connection of identification to your story. So that is fine, but that is not the way to solve the problem of construction. That is not the way to present and create your metaphor. That isomorphic method will require running it all through your conscious mind, before you take it back to the client and worse, the parallel matching to the client's problem will lead the client right through the memories of the problem and, of course, may retrieve all of the associated bad feelings. What we want to do is be as far from a match with the problem as we can be and achieve our outcomes with some specific rules that apply to the movement of images within metaphors and the related experiential effect these will have on listeners.

We'll be going beyond the notion of story line and detailing with sug-gestions very shortly. So watch how we do that now. This is a tape of a paranoid young man who came from Mexico when he was 15. I want you to see this in action first, so don't worry that you can't construct metaphors. Here is the client you are about to see. This fellow is single and is dating. His girlfriend is critical of him. He feels such anxiety that his palms sweat, his heart palpitates, his breathing is shallow, and he has to go home and sleep. And that is the only way out of it. He goes home from the job at two o'clock several times a week and takes a nap, which is going to get him fired. The anxiety comes because he thinks anyone watching him talk to a man will know that he is homosexual. So he talks to a man at his job and then he starts thinking they all think he is homosexual.

And his hands get sweaty, his heart beats, and he has to get out of there. He thinks he has a psychiatric problem, so he is seeing a psychiatrist who has asked if we'd see him. His peer group has been constantly critical because, perhaps, of his coming in with shyness. Kids often find someone to pick on and keep it up, and they picked on him a lot. Now he imagines his peers are doing what the peers of his family of origin did. So he has that imagined stress coming in. He has no other support group, really, except for the people at work who tell him he is doing a good job. But this preoc-cupation with this fantasized-other stops him from getting support from them. And here is what he thinks of himself. He thinks of himself as an extremely responsible person. Sometimes he can get angry and lash out, as he tried to do with us during the intake interview, when we chose him to be a candidate for this session.

What are we going to do for therapy then? You are going to see this all again on the tape but it won't hurt to underscore some of the logic twice. Look at the checklist graph and you may recall you have seen this one earlier [Illustration 26]. You'd want to reduce the man's need to affiliate by

ADJECTIVE CHECKLIST

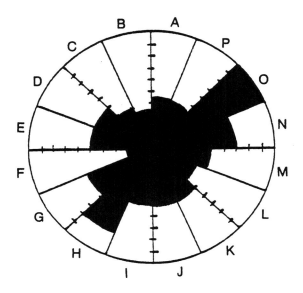

Paco (Self)
Illustration 26

acting in an extremely helpful and friendly way. How could you do that? What feeling must he not have that you can help him get? If you were without some feeling, then you'd try real hard to get people to accept you. What feeling would you be without? Feeling of acceptance of some kind. So some feeling of belonging or acceptance, if he could feel that more strongly, should reduce his need to prove it all the time.

How could we reduce his self-critical comments? You don't want to ever take choices away from somebody, but if you give him a feeling of acceptance, then he doesn't need to do those behaviors. We would behaviorally teach him some ways to interrupt those thoughts. That is the best way. So we're not taking his self-criticism away by blocking it; we're simply teaching him some new choices.

And what sort of attitude? The attitude is sometimes so obvious that you miss it. What is the most obvious attitude he is entertaining with this problem? "I'm not okay because other people evaluate me in some way." So the attitude that we would want to teach is that it doesn't matter how people evaluate you as you can ignore that and be an okay person. And that is it.

This is an example of a first session here. And some of those goals will carry over and be repeated in the second sessions and so on, because they are learnings that we all could do with being reinforced: feelings of belonging, reduced self-criticism, and an attitude that we know from talking to him that he thinks his peers' evaluation of him is the most important thing. So those are the three goals.

Now we want to teach these experiences to him in such a way that he will accept and not be threatened by them and that is why we use metaphor. He knows verbally, "I shouldn't do this." So the value of metaphor in this case is going to be that we can tell a story to him that will allow the feeling of belonging to sneak up on him. He will have the experience before his conscious mind figures out where we are headed. He will have gotten the answer from within. So we won't have to argue about it—he got it from himself. So remember this during the videotape. You'll see us go through the same thing I have just explained to you.

The context in this taping would help a person be a little more paranoid. He is in front of 400-500 professionals who are capable of deciding that he is crazy or homosexual, with the eventual psychiatric stamp of disapproval. There is obviously something about the delivery of information in the story context that will give you a different outcome. That is what these protocols are to explain.

For attitude, then, we are going to oppose the perceptions of two different protagonists and hear and contrast the outcome. For emotion, we are going to create a relationship and create a change in the relationship to focus on the body and response.

Now, the protocol then can happen, the story can be very long, and there can be three protocols in it. The easiest thing is to have one story, one protocol. That is what happens in this first metaphor about Alan and Dick. The second easiest thing is to have one story and two protocols. That is what happens for the story of Wolfgang. There is one protocol on emotion in the first part of the story, and one protocol on self-image thinking in the second half. Do you see the difference between the word *protocol* and the word *metaphor*?

GOALS IN A CLIENT DEMONSTRATION

Here are the therapy goals we designed for this client demonstration that follows. We will review specific goals and the interventions used to achieve them with this individual, prior to looking at the same process with a family. He was a paranoid young man who had acute anxiety attacks. And you can see that from his graph. He is self-critical, unless he can be seen as extremely responsible. So if anybody challenges his being "mister nice guy," which they will from time to time, then he is going to be self-critical and have an anxiety attack. This session will illustrate the use of the checklist to formulate goal selection. That, in turn, will lead to the selection and delivery of the interventions.

We will use hypnosis and metaphor, but be aware that we want to teach systematically. Ericksonian interventions are complex and often layered. We can overlay our diagnostic orientation with strategic goals and overlay that with interventions of metaphor that are themselves vehicles for carrying trance phenomena, interspersed messages, and so forth—and all of this is planned and purposeful. So to help convey everything accurately and precisely and to help ensure that you leave here with some skills in observation and intervention, we'll start by providing you with the interventions in the context of hypnosis, since hypnosis acts as a microscope for close examination and also slows things down for closer examination. We will be able to observe the delivery of metaphors to meet the goals and hopefully you will be able to observe the changes in the client. *And* these changes are, or ought to be, directly related to the person we see and the checklist we will discuss. [Stephen is represented as upper case in this transcript and Carol is represented as lower case).[19]

NOW WE HAVE A CLIENT WHO WILL BE JOINING US SHORTLY. THE FIRST THING I WANT TO DO IS HAVE SOME UNDERSTANDING OF WHAT WE'RE GOING TO DO WITH MULTIPLE EMBEDDED METAPHOR TECHNIQUE AS *HYP-NOTHERAPY*. WE DON'T DO HYPNOSIS TO REMOVE SYMPTOMS. WE DO HYPNOTHERAPY. WE'RE GOING TO TELL A SERIES OF STORIES AND IN ORDER TO UNDERSTAND OUR GOALS YOU NEED TO UNDERSTAND THE CLIENT. WITHIN THREE OR FOUR MINUTES WE CAN AT LEAST GIVE YOU A GENERAL IDEA IF WE REFER TO THE CHART FOR JUST A MINUTE.

WE HAVE ASKED OUR CLIENT TO TAKE THE INTERPERSONAL CHECKLIST AS AN ADJUNCT TO OUR INTERVIEW TO GIVE US MORE INFORMATION. YOU CAN SEE [Illustration 26] THAT THE STRONGEST PIECE IS THE BLUE IN THE "O" PIE PIECE, WHICH IS RESPONSIBLE BEHAVIOR. AND, IN FACT, HE SCORED AS HIGH AS YOU CAN POSSIBLY SCORE AND THAT'S TWO AND A HALF STANDARD DEVIATIONS BEYOND THE MEAN. NOT VERY MANY PEOPLE ARE GOING TO USE THE INTERPERSONAL BEHAVIOR OF FRIENDLY DOMINANCE TO MANAGE THEIR ANXIETY AS MUCH AS THIS GENTLEMAN WILL.

---

[19]Lankton, S. and Lankton, C. (1984). Use of multiple embedded metaphor for psychological reassociation. Phoenix: The Milton H. Erickson Foundation, Inc. This videotape was recorded at the Los Angeles Seminar on Ericksonian Approaches to Psychotherapy, December 2, 1984.

It means that he feels he has very little choice about whether or not he uses that maneuver. It's not a choice; it feels necessary for him to manage his interactions in that way.

HE TRIES TO BE A NICE GUY IS WHAT IT COMES DOWN TO. THAT'S HIS FIRST INTERPERSONAL MOVE. NOW THE NEXT ONE IS SELF-EFFACEMENT—THE NEXT LARGEST PIE PIECE. SO IN THE "H" AREA THERE, YOU NOTICE THAT HE WOULD INTEND TO COME ON TO SOCIAL SITUATIONS AND NOT BE TERRIBLY DOMINANT, BUT BE FRIENDLY DOMINANT. SO IT'S VERY, VERY FRIENDLY. IF THAT'S NOT RESPONDED TO IN A WAY THAT CONTINUES TO SUPPORT HIM DOING THAT, HE FLIPS TO SELF-EFFACEMENT, EXTREME SELF-CRITICISM AND ANXIETY. HE SOMETIMES COVERS THE ANXIETY WITH THE AGGRESSIVE AND REBELLIOUS PIECES WHICH ARE THE NEXT LARGEST. AND HE GETS AN-GRY AND PUSHES PEOPLE AWAY SO THEY DON'T SEE HOW VERY FRIGHTENED HE IS. HIS SYMPTOM FOR COMING TO THERAPY IS EXTREME ANXIETY ATTACKS THAT HE HAS, ESPECIALLY AT WORK. HE SAID IT'S ALL RIGHT FOR US TO SHARE THIS INFORMATION WITH YOU. HE'S VERY AFRAID TO BE IN FRONT OF PEOPLE. HE GETS VERY ANXIOUS IN FRONT OF PEOPLE. SO I DIDN'T WANT TO HAVE HIM GO THROUGH THE DIFFICULTY OF TRYING TO EXPLAIN HIS PROBLEM. HE'D BE CURED IF HE COULD DO IT.

Let's say generally, first, he's a 25-year-old single male. He's originally from Mexico and came to the United States when he was fifteen.

HE CAME ON HIS OWN. HE WAS RAISED PRIMARILY BY HIS MATERNAL GRANDMOTHER [Illustration 27]. HE DIDN'T KNOW HIS FATHER. HIS GRAND-MOTHER WAS THE ONE HE FELT CLOSEST TO, WHO HE IDENTIFIED WITH. HIS MOTHER WAS VERY CRITICAL. YOU MIGHT SAY HE'S REALLY NOT A VERY WANTED CHILD. HIS FATHER WASN'T THERE, HIS MOTHER WASN'T THERE. AND HE GOT THE MESSAGE AND LEFT THE WHOLE COUNTRY AT THE AGE OF 15. HE'S AFRAID THAT PEOPLE SEEING HIM INTERACT WITH A MALE WILL THINK HE'S A HOMOSEXUAL. AND THAT'S THE PRESENTING PROBLEM THAT HE BROUGHT TO HIS PSYCHIATRIST WHO'S A PARTICIPANT IN THIS GROUP.

He is presently in a dating, cohabiting relationship with a woman and he enjoys her company. However, any criticism on her part towards him results in a great deal of anxiety.

RECENTLY HE STARTED THE JOB THAT HE HAS AND IT REQUIRES THAT HE INTERACT MORE FREQUENTLY AND CLOSELY TO PEOPLE. AND SO PANIC ATTACKS HAVE DRIVEN HIM TO THERAPY BECAUSE OF THE RECENT JOB AC-QUISITION. SO WITH THAT IN MIND, I WANT TO REFER YOU BACK TO THE MULTIPLE EMBEDDED METAPHOR CHART, WHICH WILL BE SIMILAR TO YOUR HANDOUT [Illustration 28], EXCEPT THAT WE HAVE THE ANSWERS TO THE QUESTIONS IN THERE. THIS [Illustration 29] WILL BE A GUIDE THAT YOU CAN FOLLOW TO MAKE SENSE OF WHAT WE'RE GOING TO DO. WE HAVE DECIDED UPON SEVERAL GOALS HERE. THE BOXES REPRESENT PHASES OF THE TREAT-

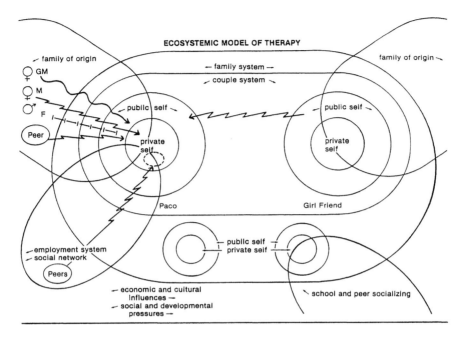

Illustration 27

MENT THAT WE'RE GOING TO GO THROUGH OR, ROUGHLY SPEAKING, GOALS THAT WE INTEND TO ADDRESS.

It begins with induction in the top level box and induction is followed by a series of metaphors, each of which will begin and then be suspended prior to its eventual completion on the way back out.

DURING THE INDUCTION PHASE WE INTEND TO DO THE THINGS YOU WOULD NORMALLY WANT TO INCLUDE DURING INDUCTION, INCLUDING CONFUSION IF APPROPRIATE. I DON'T KNOW THAT WE'LL NEED ANY. PARADOXICALLY . . . WELL, HE'S GOING TO ATTEND VERY CAREFULLY AND NOTE THE PLACES WE'VE MADE MISTAKES IN OUR INTERVENTION. HE HAS A CLEAR AND DRIVING VIGILANCE OF OTHER PEOPLE AND WHAT THEY THINK. WITH SUCH A DELUSIONAL SYSTEM ABOUT THAT, I WOULD SAY YOU COULD SEE PARANOID FEATURES HERE. WE'RE GOING TO ASK HIM TO BE PARANOID AND TO DO THIS VERY CAREFULLY SO THAT HE CAN FIND OUT WHERE WE'VE GOOFED UP, BECAUSE THAT'S WHAT HE'S GOING TO DO ANYWAY. WE MIGHT AS WELL ASK HIM TO DO THAT AS A THERAPEUTIC DIRECTIVE. AND SECOND, WE ARE GOING TO UTILIZE HIS MAJOR PERSONALITY ELEMENTS YOU JUST SAW, THAT IS, WE'RE GOING TO ASK HIM TO DO

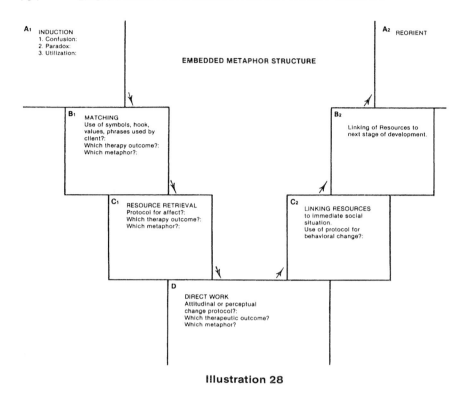

Illustration 28

THE RESPONSIBLE THING BY GOING INTO TRANCE—TRY TO BE FRIENDLY, TAKE THIS ENTIRE MATTER AS A VERY FRIENDLY SITUATION, AND WE REALLY APPRECIATE HOW RESPONSIBLE HE'S BEING, EVEN IF HE'S DOING IT WITH DOUBT. AND THAT COULD BE SELF-DOUBT OR DOUBT AIMED AT US, DEPENDING ON WHICH WAY HE FLIPS THAT. THEN WE BEGIN OUR METAPHOR SERIES. AND BASICALLY OUR GOALS ARE IN B1 AND B2 [Illustration 28]. THIS IS AN ATTITUDE METAPHOR THAT WE'LL SUSPEND, DESIGNED TO CHALLENGE OR QUESTION THE ATTITUDE ON HOW ONE IS AFFECTED BY PEER CRITICISM.

Currently his primary attitude about criticism seems to be that it must affect a person. And we want to give an attitude restructuring story that will challenge that attitude and help build another one that will be conducive to his not being automatically affected.

ONE WAY IT CANNOT AFFECT HIM IS IF HE USES NEGATIVE HALLUCINATION TO BECOME LESS SENSITIVE TO SOCIAL CUES. AND THAT'S WHAT ONE OF THE PROTAGONISTS IN THIS STORY IS GOING TO DO. DICK AND ALAN WILL

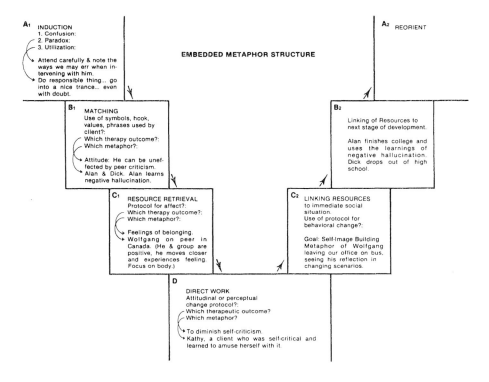

Illustration 29

BE THE KEY CHARACTERS HERE. ALAN BASICALLY LEARNS TO USE NEGATIVE HALLUCINATION SO HE CAN BE ALONE. THAT WILL HELP YOU KEEP TRACK OF THE NAMES. DICK CONTINUES TO GET PICKED ON AND EVENTUALLY DROPS OUT OF SCHOOL. ALAN FINISHES COLLEGE USING NEGATIVE HAL-LUCINATION. SO THESE ARE JUST SYNTHESIZED FROM REAL CHARACTERS WE KNOW IN REAL LIFE.

THE SECOND METAPHOR, C1 AND C2 [Illustration 28], HAS TWO MAJOR GOALS. THE FIRST MAJOR GOAL IS THE FEELING OF BELONGING. IF A PERSON FEELS THAT HE BELONGS, HE DOESN'T HAVE TO KEEP BEING THE NICEST PERSON IN THE WORLD TO INGRATIATE PEOPLE SO HE CAN BELONG. IF YOU'VE GROWN UP IN A FAMILY WHERE YOUR FATHER AND MOTHER MAKE YOU THINK YOU'RE WANTED, YOU HAVE A FEELING OF BELONGING, PRE-SUMABLY. SO I'D SAY THAT WE HAVE A MAJOR EMOTIONAL BUILDING HERE IN SENSITIZING HIM TO SOME OF THE COMPONENTS TO KNOW HE CAN FEEL THE FEELING OF BELONGING. THAT SHOULD REDUCE HIS NEED TO USE THAT EXAGGERATED RESPONSIBLE BEHAVIOR.

The tag name to listen for here is "Wolfgang." He is the protagonist who will be having an experience in an English-speaking country—Canada, in this case. He's originally from Germany. So we'll be able to appeal to the idea of getting the sense of belonging even when you're in a different country.

GENERALLY, WE WOULDN'T HAVE OUR METAPHOR HAVE THAT KIND OF ISOMORPHISM AT THIS POINT, BUT IN THIS CASE IT WILL ELIMINATE THE CRITICISM OF "YEAH, BUT, I'M IN A REAL NEW COUNTRY." AT THE END OF THAT C1 PART OF THE STORY, AFTER THE BELONGING GOAL HAS BEEN REACHED, WE'LL GO ON TO THE DIRECT WORK PHASE AT D. BUT WE'LL PICK UP THAT METAPHOR C2 AND LINK THOSE RESOURCES, ESPECIALLY THE FEEL-ING OF BELONGING, TO HIS IMMEDIATE SOCIAL SITUATIONS USING SELF-IMAGE THINKING. AS THE STORY GOES, WOLFGANG DRIVES HOME IN TRANCE FROM OUR OFFICE AND SEES HIS REFLECTION IN A WINDOW AND LEARNS SOMETHING WATCHING HIS REFLECTIONS.

NOW FOR THE DIRECT WORK AT THE VORTEX OF THE MULTIPLE EMBEDDED METAPHOR, WE WILL WORK SPECIFICALLY ON HIS SYMPTOM AS MUCH AS POSSIBLE. WE THINK THE MAJOR WAY FOR HIM TO DIMINISH HIS ANXIETY IS, IN ADDITION TO FEELING CALM, OF COURSE, TO DIMINISH THAT SELF-CRITICISM. SO WE'RE GOING TO GIVE HIM A NUMBER OF CHOICES ON HOW TO BEHAVIORALLY DIMINISH INTERNAL SELF-CRITICISM.

The direct work will also be accomplished in the context of metaphor. It's a completely separate story, told without being suspended. This time the protagonist is "Cathy." That will help you keep track. Go ahead and bring him in.

[to Client] FIRST OF ALL, WE BOTH WANT TO EXPRESS OUR APPRECIATION PUBLICLY FOR YOU COMING HERE AND DOING THIS UNDER SUCH UNUSUAL CIRCUMSTANCES. WE REALLY HAVE NOTHING MORE TO DO, EXCEPT GET RIGHT INTO IT. SO, IS THAT ALL RIGHT WITH YOU? DO YOU HAVE ANY QUESTIONS?

(*Client*: No.)

IT MIGHT BE MORE COMFORTABLE FOR YOU TO BEGIN BY CLOSING YOUR EYES . . . especially since the lights are so bright. One of the first things people often do in going into trance is just to take a moment to make sure they're as comfortable as they can be normally. So you might want to adjust your posture or find that you're more comfortable with your hands in one position or another, perhaps flat on your thighs. You can experiment and enjoy experimenting to find the way that is most comfortable for you.

SOONER OR LATER YOU BEGIN TO DIMINISH YOUR AWARENESS OF STIM-ULI OUTSIDE OF YOURSELF. AND IT MIGHT BE NICE TO HAVE SOME IDEAS. YOU HYPNOTIZE YOURSELF USING OUR WORDS AS A STIMULUS TO FIND

IDEAS THAT YOU'D LIKE TO THINK ABOUT. MAYBE IT WOULD BE A PLEASANT PLACE YOU GO TO, MAYBE YOU'D REMEMBER US MENTIONING THAT WE LIVE ON THE BEACH.

And you can really think about anything you'd like to in response to our words. And enjoy having your own thoughts.

SOONER OR LATER SOMETHING THAT'S REALLY IMPORTANT AND USEFUL FOR YOU COMES TO MIND. I DON'T KNOW HOW YOU FIRST BEGIN TO NOTICE SOMETHING LIKE THAT. YOU MIGHT REMEMBER THE SMELL OF THE OCEAN IF YOU, IN FACT, THOUGHT ABOUT WALKING ON THE BEACH . . . or the smell of freshly cut grass. There are a good many pleasant smells you can enjoy remembering again. IF IT DOESN'T BEGIN WITH A SMELL IT MIGHT BEGIN WITH A VISION OF HAVING BEEN IN A CIRCUMSTANCE.

And that little fluttering of your eyelids is a convenient way for your body to allow you to become familiar with yourself at another level. And it's not a level you're completely unfamiliar with because everyone goes into trance in a variety of ways, places, and times.

YOU MAY FEEL MORE AND MORE RELAXED. MAYBE YOU REMEMBER A TIME YOU WERE IN TRANCE WITH THE DOCTOR YOU'VE WORKED WITH. MAYBE YOU REMEMBER HIS VOICE. THERE'S REALLY NO WRONG WAY THAT YOU CAN PROCEED WITH THIS. AND YOU REALLY NEED TO KNOW THAT YOU'RE IN CONTROL OF YOUR TRANCE EXPERIENCE. YOU CAN AROUSE YOURSELF AT ANY MOMENT.

You can allow yourself to go deeper at any moment. It really doesn't matter what depth of trance you reach. Your conscious might be interested in one depth of trance, consider one depth of trance appropriate. But your unconscious mind automatically goes about creating that depth of trance that's relevant for you, just for you.

I DON'T KNOW WHETHER OR NOT YOU'VE EVER NOTICED THAT YOUR HAND CAN LEVITATE WHEN YOU'RE IN TRANCE. IT WOULD BE NICE TO BE ABLE TO HAVE SOMETHING TO FOCUS YOUR AWARENESS ON. AND I KNOW THAT YOUR HANDS ARE BOTH CAPABLE OF FLOATING UP TO YOUR FACE. PROBABLY ONLY ONE OF THEM WILL THINK ABOUT BEGINNING THAT. A SLOW JERKY MOVEMENT IN YOUR RIGHT HAND IS A WAY FOR YOUR CON-SCIOUS MIND TO REALIZE THAT YOUR UNCONSCIOUS IS CAPABLE OF RE-SPONDING RATHER QUICKLY TO A STIMULUS. HOW QUICKLY COULD YOU RESPOND TO A STIMULUS OF NOT NOTICING SOMETHING IN YOUR BODY SOMEWHERE. YOU PROBABLY HAVEN'T NOTICED YOUR ANKLES, BUT YOU COULDN'T JUST SAY HOW YOU STOP NOTICING SOMETHING.

There's another small jerky movement in that right hand AND A LITTLE ROTATION IN THE ELBOW AND WRIST. MAYBE IT WILL FLOAT HALF WAY TO YOUR FACE OR IT WILL GO ALL THE WAY. And how does a hand begin to leave a thigh? Does it move upward first from the wrist? Or does a finger first begin to move? Maybe the elbow lifts the wrist which in turn lifts the fingers.

I'D LIKE TO ALLOW YOU TO CONTINUE UNCONSCIOUSLY TO RESPOND TO WHAT CAROL IS MENTIONING WHILE I GIVE YOUR CONSCIOUS MIND SOMETHING TO THINK ABOUT AS WELL. YOU MIGHT BE INTERESTED IN KNOWING THAT NOT NOTICING SOMETHING CAN PLAY A MAJOR ROLE IN A FUNNY WAY IN COLLEGE. TWO OF OUR CLIENTS WERE HIGH SCHOOL STUDENTS, ALAN AND DICK.

And your conscious mind listening to my words and also hearing about people Steve mentions can cause you to wonder just how you're going to benefit and what you're going to learn, how to apply those things we speak about to yourself. And all the while you're still able to notice those sensations that change in your hand.

BOTH ALAN AND DICK HAD HAD SOME DESIRE WHEN THEY WERE AROUND THEIR FRIENDS, IN GYM CLASS ESPECIALLY. THEY WISHED THEIR FRIENDS WOULD SAY NICE THINGS.

Is it a lightness or is it a tingling?

THEY'D LIKE TO HEAR A LITTLE PRAISE NOW AND THEN. IT WAS FOR DIF-FERENT REASONS RELATED TO THE LACK OF THAT THAT BROUGHT THEM IN. DICK WAS GOING TO DROP OUT OF SCHOOL. ALAN WAS DETERMINED TO SOLVE THE PROBLEM SOMEHOW.

Dick had tried everything he could think of. It didn't matter that the things he thought of weren't very good ideas. He was sincere and he was eager to get along, and so he tried to get along with the people that picked on him by shrugging it off and picking on them, fighting with them.

THERE'S A SLOW, GRADUAL MOVEMENT WITH THAT RIGHT HAND, AND ALSO WITH YOUR LEFT. YOUR THUMB OF YOUR RIGHT HAND IS RAISED UP OFF YOUR PANTS, PROBABLY WILL TAKE YOUR FINGER WITH IT, TOO. AND YOUR INDEX FINGER MOVED GRADUALLY WHEN YOU HEARD THAT. AND ALAN, DETERMINED TO SOLVE THE PROBLEM, AND YOUR CONSCIOUS MIND NEVER REALLY KNOWS HOW YOU ARE DETERMINED TO SOLVE A PROBLEM. MAYBE IT'S BECAUSE OF SOME VERY DEEP POSITIVE CHILDHOOD EXPERIENCE THAT YOU INTENDED TO SURVIVE, YOU INTENDED TO MAKE EVERYTHING WORK IN YOUR LIFE. I DOUBT THAT ALAN COULD HAVE REALLY ALLOWED THE CONSCIOUS MIND TO FOCUS ON THAT FEELING, THAT INTENT TO SOLVE A PROBLEM. BUT HE WAS ONLY A HIGH SCHOOL STUDENT.

AND YOU DON'T HAVE TO KNOW HOW YOU ARE GOING TO SOLVE A PROBLEM. IT'S INTERESTING TO DISCOVER AFTERWARDS SOMETHING YOU DIDN'T EVEN REALIZE, LIKE THE SENSATION CHANGING IN A HAND. NOW THE PALM IS ABOUT TO LIFT THE BASE OF THE THUMB OFF THE HAND. I

HOPE YOUR CONSCIOUS MIND IS DELIGHTED TO FIND OUT HOW YOUR UNCONSCIOUS WILL SURPRISE YOU IN LIFTING THE HAND UP TO THE FACE.

And many people only realize as adults that they did, in fact, learn something in high school. It usually wasn't what was being taught in the history books.

ALAN CAME TO OUR OFFICE AND CONVINCED US THAT HE WANTED TO SOLVE THAT PROBLEM. DICK, ON THE OTHER HAND, REQUIRED A LITTLE BIT MORE WORK. SO WE PROCEEDED TO EXPLAIN TO ALAN A LOT OF THINGS THAT EVERYBODY ALREADY KNOWS. EVERYONE KNOWS HOW YOU CAN HAVE A MOSQUITO BITE ON YOUR HAND, AND DECIDE THAT YOU'RE NOT GOING TO FEEL IT ANYMORE. THE FEELING GOES AWAY. YOU MIGHT HAVE TO THINK THE THOUGHT A COUPLE OF TIMES. AND IT DOESN'T MATTER IF YOU INITIATE THE THOUGHT, "THIS ISN'T GOING TO ITCH," OR IF YOU FIND YOURSELF HEARING THE THOUGHT, OR IF YOU WRITE IT DOWN SEV- ERAL TIMES. MAYBE YOU PRACTICE IT. SOONER OR LATER EVERY CHILD LEARNS HOW TO IGNORE A MOSQUITO BITE.

And you may find that you consciously forget to notice the sensations of lightness that your unconscious created in your hand. It doesn't prevent you from allowing your unconscious to continue the progression. YOUR HAND IS STILL GRADUALLY MOVING BACK TOWARD YOUR WRIST. SIXTY-FOURTH OF AN INCH, THIRTY-SECOND OF AN INCH, JUST AN INDICATION OF HOW VERY SYSTEMATICALLY AND GRADUALLY YOUR UNCONSCIOUS CAN WORK ON A SUGGESTION FOR YOUR OWN BENEFIT. I HOPE THE THINGS WE SAY WILL BE TAKEN BY YOU FOR YOUR OWN BENEFIT. AND YOU'LL DO THE RESPONSIBLE FRIENDLY THING OF HELPING THE THERAPY WORK FOR YOU IN A WAY THAT'S USEFUL, EVEN IF YOU HAVE SOME DOUBT.

A responsible person will doubt those suggestions and the feasibility of responding to them. And in doubting and evaluating the suggestion you make certain that you respond appropriately, in a way that fits you. THERE GOES THAT HAND MOVING ANOTHER THIRTY-SECOND OF AN INCH, IN- CLUDING PAYING A GOOD DEAL OF ATTENTION TO THE ERRORS WE MAKE IN OUR INTERVENTION. AND TAKE ONLY THOSE SUGGESTIONS THAT FIT FOR YOU AS A PERSON AND WORK FOR YOU. MOLD OUR WORDS SO THAT THEY WILL WORK IN YOUR BEHALF.

And while we've been talking to you, you may be aware of the other thing we reminded Alan about and how it is that every child learns at some point that you can become so involved in your own thoughts, so engrossed in something that's interesting to you, that you completely forget to even listen or be aware of something else that another person is saying to you. You don't even hear.

IF YOUR CONSCIOUS MIND SHOULD FORGET TO LISTEN TO US, YOUR

UNCONSCIOUS CAN STILL RESPOND IN A WAY THAT'S USEFUL FOR YOU AS A PERSON. SO, ALAN REMEMBERED A TIME HE'D LEARNED TO NOT NOTICE POISON IVY ITCHING. HE REMEMBERED A TIME HE PLAYED BASEBALL AND FORGOT ABOUT THAT ARM THAT WAS HURT. AND IN THE TRANCE, MEM-ORIZE ALL THOSE EXPERIENCES LIKE THAT SO THAT WE COULD ASK ALAN TO BRING THEM INTO THE FOREGROUND AND APPLY THEM TO THE SITU-ATION THAT WAS USEFUL FOR HIM AS A PERSON. AND I'LL TELL YOU A LOT OF OTHER THINGS THAT YOU COULDN'T JUST SAY HOW YOU IGNORED, LIKE YOU IGNORED YOUR EARLOBES.

You probably haven't thought about the comfort in your left ankle or in your toe. YOU HAVEN'T THOUGHT ABOUT A JOKE YOU HEARD RECENTLY. THERE'S A LOT OF THINGS A PERSON CANNOT NOTICE, EVEN THOUGH THEY ARE A PART OF THEM. And it's very pleasurable to be able to not notice and enjoy forgetting that there was something you weren't noticing. And how many times in a supermarket does a person have the experience of looking and looking for a certain item. And you've exhausted your ability to search for that item. And finally asking for help, you find that the item was right there in front of you the entire time. ALAN SAID HE HAS THAT SAME EXPE-RIENCE WITH THE ANSWERS TO THE TEST.

But your conscious mind can't believe it. BUT YOU ALSO CAN'T BELIEVE THAT THAT'S A VERY USEFUL LEARNING, AND THAT ALAN COULD USE THAT IN A WAY YOU WOULDN'T EXPECT. AND I'D LIKE TO MAKE THE SAME POINT AGAIN IN A DIFFERENT WAY.

WOLFGANG WAS A FRIEND OF OURS WHO'D COME TO FIND OUT THAT YOU COULD DRIVE ALL THE WAY FROM THE WEST SIDE OF CANADA TO THE WEST SIDE OF FLORIDA IN MERELY A SHORT AFTERNOON. BUT NOT IN THE NORMAL WAY. Your conscious mind couldn't understand, wouldn't expect it. It's nice to be surprised by things you didn't expect.

WOLFGANG HAD MADE HIS ENTRANCE INTO ENGLISH-SPEAKING COUN-TRIES WHEN HE FIRST WENT TO CANADA ON VACATION AS A YOUNG ADULT. NOW WOLFGANG WAS LIKED AND LOVED BY ALMOST EVERYONE WHO KNEW HIM AND WE HAD A VERY WARM FEELING ABOUT HIM RIGHT AWAY. He'd studied English in Germany and never really realized he was going to be taking a vacation across Canada and speaking English and speaking French.

IN VANCOUVER, THE PEOPLE GATHERED AROUND A PIER SINGING SONGS AT NIGHT. AND THEY WERE A VERY PLEASANT SIGHT. And a very pleasant sound, that sound of soft music just wafting above the sounds of the waves lapping very gently to the shore, into which the pier extended.

THOSE CANADIAN YOUNG MEN AND WOMEN HAD TO HAVE FAIRLY PLEASANT PERSONALITIES TO BE OUT THERE SINGING SONGS ALL NIGHT WITH ONE ANOTHER. SOME OF THEM DIDN'T KNOW ONE ANOTHER. And it was a very charming sound. And he was charmed by the softness of the music at the distance he was when he first noticed it.

YOUR HAND IS STILL WONDERING ABOUT WHETHER OR NOT THAT THUMB IS GOING TO . . . AND HE COULDN'T IMAGINE THE EXPERIENCE HE HAD IN LISTENING TO THAT GROUP AROUND THE PIER. HE WAS OFF ABOUT FOUR OR FIVE HUNDRED YARDS SITTING UNDER THE TREES. But the softness and the gentleness of the music compelled him to move, slowly at first, effortlessly, closer and closer.

YOU CAN TELL SOMETIMES, EVERY CHILD CAN TELL, WHO'S A PERSON THEY CAN TRUST, AND WHO'S A PERSON THEY FEEL GOOD ABOUT. EVERY-ONE KNEW THAT ABOUT WOLFGANG WHENEVER THEY MET HIM. One look at that face. BUT THE CANADIANS IN VANCOUVER ON THE PIER THAT NIGHT HADN'T HAD AN OPPORTUNITY TO KNOW THAT YET. They hadn't had an opportunity to discover the goodness of the thoughts that he thought. They hadn't seen his face, the smile lines, and the interest that his eyes reflected.

AND THERE WAS THE LAPPING, GENTLE LAPPING OF THE WAVES. IT WAS A VERY PLEASANT NIGHT, A MOONLIT SKY, HARDLY A CLOUD. The soft glittering moonlit reflections on that water's surface. THE MOON WAS AL-MOST LIKE THE WARMTH OF THE SUNLIGHT CONSIDERING THE STILLNESS OF THE NIGHT EXCEPT FOR THE STIRRING OF THE GROUP IN FRONT THAT WAS SINGING THOSE SONGS IN HARMONY. And they were singing in Eng-lish, now and then in French. GRADUALLY WOLFGANG DECIDED HE MIGHT JUST JOIN THE GROUP. AND BEFORE YOUR CONSCIOUS MIND REALLY KNOWS THAT YOU'VE DECIDED TO ACT UPON AN EXPERIENCE, YOU FIND THAT YOUR UNCONSCIOUS ALREADY HAS TAKEN YOU THERE. AND THERE HE WAS SITTING ON THE PIER ELBOW TO ELBOW WITH TOTAL STRANGERS. He decided a comfortable way to begin joining that group would be to simply hum along the melodies that he recognized.

NOW I'VE GIVEN SUGGESTIONS THAT YOUR HAND MIGHT THINK ABOUT RISING TO YOUR FACE AND IT DID. MAYBE IT WILL COMPLETE THAT IDEA AND GO AHEAD AND RAISE UP TO YOUR FACE OR HALFWAY. AND YOUR CONSCIOUS MIND CAN NOTICE THE MOVEMENT OF YOUR HAND WHEN THOSE THOUGHTS COME THROUGH YOUR UNCONSCIOUS. SO YOU RE-ALIZE YOUR HAND DIDN'T YET RISE UP TOTALLY. NEITHER DID YOUR LEFT HAND. AND SO YOU REALIZE CONSCIOUSLY THAT THE SUGGESTIONS THAT YOU RECEIVE WILL BE TAKEN BY YOU IN A PERSONAL WAY.

And yet you can't deny the sensations and twitches. And you should be very pleased that you allowed your unconscious to make those movements your way, responsibly responding, to our words and your thoughts, your own ideas. AND THAT IF YOUR HAND DOESN'T RISE UP TO YOUR FACE, THAT'S ALL RIGHT, THAT'S OK. BUT YOUR UNCONSCIOUS IS SO SMART ABOUT SOME PROCESS OF HYPNOSIS THAT YOU ALREADY SHOULD NOT

RESPOND TO QUESTIONS EXCEPT FOR IN A WAY THAT IS MEANINGFUL TO YOU. AND MAYBE YOUR RIGHT HAND WOULD FIND MEANING IN MOVING UP TO YOUR FACE. MAYBE YOUR LEFT HAND WOULD. MAYBE IT WOULDN'T. SO YOU HAVE TO WAIT AND FIND OUT. LIKEWISE YOU CAN BE SURE, LISTENING TO THE IDEAS, THAT WHAT YOU MAKE OUT OF THE STORIES BEING TOLD WILL BE THE PROPER RESPONSE.

And so it seemed very proper for him to hum along, blending his ability to make a comfortable sound, a pleasurable sound, a charming sound, with the charming sounds that appealed to him so much. THEY WERE SINGING IN ENGLISH AND HE WAS HUMMING IN GERMAN. I DON'T KNOW IF YOU'VE EVER HEARD SOMEONE HUM IN GERMAN OR NOT. IT SOUNDS JUST LIKE HUMMING IN ENGLISH. BUT I KNOW THAT HE WAS THINKING THOUGHTS IN GERMAN AND SINGING THE GERMAN WORDS AND THEN SLOWLY HE DECIDED HE'D SING THE GERMAN WORDS ALONG WITH THE GROUP. THE GROUP WAS FEELING NICE AND WARM, ELBOW TO ELBOW. Softly at first in joining and it's nice to be able to listen and hear more than one voice, more than one set of words that can be understood. And he began softly singing and more loudly singing. And the louder he sang, the better he felt. And of course the louder he sang, the more he contributed to that melody, that group product, that sense of joy that all of the singers shared in common.

And he really never thought that not only would his voice not distract but that it would add something very special. And he was quite surprised when the American and Canadian singers turned to him and smiled their greeting AND ASKED HIM TO SING A SONG THAT WAS FROM HIS COUNTRY, IN HIS LANGUAGE. SOME OF THEM SANG ALONG TO THE SONG, SOME HUMMED. SOME OF THEM HUMMED IN ENGLISH. SOME OF THEM WERE SINGING ALONG, SOME OF THEM WERE SINGING IN ENGLISH. Some of them just hummed in German. SOME OF THEM WERE JUST BEING QUIET, ROCKING BACK AND FORTH AND BACK AND FORTH. AND THAT'S WHEN IT OCCURRED TO HIM. THAT'S WHEN SOMETHING THAT YOU'VE HEARD ALL OF YOUR LIFE, THAT MUSIC WILL UNITE PEOPLE FROM DIFFERENT CULTURES, REALLY MADE SOME SENSE TO HIM. AND HE HAD THAT FEELING THAT IT WAS QUITE STRANGE REALLY THAT HE COULD BE THERE SOMEPLACE AND WITH A TOTAL GROUP OF STRANGERS FEELING SO COMFORTABLE. IT WAS UPLIFTING.

[Here the client adjusted his posture. He straightened and appeared taller. Several tears flowed over his face, and his cheeks and forehead lost the small tension that they had. In a word, the client appeared to be experiencing a pleasant feeling.]

And it was a feeling that warmed his heart. Now how do you begin to notice a warm heart? Maybe you notice a warm heart by noticing the warm moisture of a tear. IT MADE HIM FEEL A LITTLE TALLER. IT MADE HIM PROUD TO BE A CITIZEN OF THE WORLD. A TEAR OF COMPASSION TO REALIZE THAT

PEOPLE FEEL THAT LOVE AND YOU FEEL IT BACK, EVEN THOUGH YOU DIDN'T KNOW THEM. AND YOUR CONSCIOUS MIND DOESN'T EVEN NEED TO EXPLAIN THE EXPERIENCE IN ORDER TO KNOW THAT YOU HAVE THE EXPERIENCE. AND IT'S A WONDERFUL FEELING. EVERYONE IS ENTITLED TO KNOW AND TO HAVE IT.

The more warm tears follow, the more your heart pumps that warm blood through all of your extremities, feeling it in your fingertips and your toes. YOU'RE HAVING A LEARNING WHEN YOU HAVE THAT FEELING. AND IT'S A LEARNING EVERY MAN AND EVERY WOMAN COMES TO KNOW AS THEY MATURE. AND IT WAS QUITE A MATURING INCIDENT THAT NIGHT FOR WOLFGANG AS HE SAT THERE. IT REALLY STAYED WITH HIM A LONG TIME AND BROUGHT HIM A FEELING, A PLEASANT CALM FOR YEARS TO COME. SO THAT'S WHY HE TOLD US ABOUT THAT WHEN HE WAS IN TRANCE IN OUR OFFICE THAT DAY IN PENSACOLA. YOU'RE ENTITLED TO ENJOY AN EXPERIENCE, A LEARNING.

You're entitled to memorize an experience that you enjoy. You might want to take a moment to do that. And your conscious mind could participate as you memorize that experience, while your unconscious mind goes about the subtle process of storing that experience away, memorizing all of the sensations or all of the thoughts. YOU MIGHT HAVE NOTICED THAT YOUR CONSCIOUS MIND WAS SURPRISED AT YOUR UNCONSCIOUS LEARNING. I WONDER IF IT'S THE SAME EXPERIENCE YOU'LL HAVE REGARDING THE UPLIFTING OF YOUR ARM. And so you can enjoy that warmth.

[Client opens his eyes and stares into the audience.]

NOW YOU CAN KEEP YOUR EYES OPEN AND REMAIN IN TRANCE, OR YOU CAN CLOSE YOUR EYES AND GO BACK INTO A DIFFERENT STATE OF TRANCE. It's nice to know that you can open your eyes at any time and reassure yourself that all is well outside. It allows you to look even more deeply below the surface.

[Client closes eyes again.]

A CERTAIN STIMULUS THAT STRIKES THE MIND, BEING PAIRED WITH ANOTHER STIMULUS IN THE BODY, BECOMES A LEARNING LIKE A PIGEON THAT'S HUNGRY AND SEES A RED LIGHT AND LEARNS TO SALIVATE WHEN THE RED LIGHT IS SEEN. THE HUMAN BEING THAT SEES A CERTAIN STIMULUS WHILE FEELING THE FEELING OF LOVE AND COMPASSION THAT WOLFGANG FELT CAN'T HELP BUT HAVE A NEW UNDERSTANDING OF PEOPLES IN DIFFERENT LANDS AS HE TRAVELS. And that new understanding might be symbolized by a feeling of warmth and love. Or maybe you'll just be aware of it by your ability to feel very good.

NOW CATHY WAS SOMEONE WE HAD WORKED WITH WHO REALLY HAD SOME CURIOUS WAYS OF COMPLIMENTING PEOPLE WHEN SHE WAS DONE WITH THERAPY. IT WAS REALLY USING A SKILL IN A WAY THAT SHE NEVER

EXPECTED TO USE. AND WE CALLED IT THE "LUCY/SNOOPY INTERVENTION." WHEN CATHY FIRST CAME TO SEE US SHE HAD A LOT OF SELF-CRITICAL THOUGHTS. AND WE TRIED TO HAVE HER AMUSE HERSELF WITH THOSE THOUGHTS. And it never occurred to Cathy that she could actually improve on those criticisms that she heard about herself.

SHE TRIED A VARIETY OF WAYS IN THE TRANCE. SHE'D REMEMBER THE FEELING SHE HAD THAT WAS PLEASANT. AND WHILE KEEPING THAT IN MIND, SHE'D TRY LIKE CRAZY TO REMEMBER A SELF-CRITICAL COMMENT SHE USED TO SAY TO HERSELF. And it wasn't very difficult to do that. You could very readily remember it. AND THEN SHE'D TAKE THE FIRST WORD AND THE LAST WORD OF THE COMMENT AND CHANGE THEM AROUND AND SAY THAT SENTENCE TO HERSELF. THEY HAD ALL THE SAME WORDS. THAT SHOULD SATISFY THAT SELF-CRITICAL PART OF HER, SHE THOUGHT. AND IT WAS VERY AMUSING TO HEAR THE COMMENT WITH THE FIRST AND LAST WORD SWITCHED.

And as soon as she'd think of one sentence and succeed at switching the first and the last word, we'd suggest that she go to another one, find another sentence that had been used by herself to criticize and doubt her abilities, her work. SHE REMEMBERED THINKING, "THAT WAS A STUPID THING TO DO," AND SHE SWITCHED THE WORDS THAT AND DO, AND ENDED UP WITH "DO WAS A STUPID THING TO THAT."

And that really was a stupid thing to do and yet it caused such a sense of enjoyment, the kind of enjoyment a child can have when he first learns to play with words. WE DIDN'T WANT TO ASK CATHY TO GIVE UP CRITICIZING HERSELF. SHE HAD COME A LONG WAY AND MADE HERSELF MUCH MORE INTELLIGENT THAN SHE WOULD HAVE BEEN BY DRIVING HERSELF. AND SHE ONLY HAD HERSELF TO DRIVE HERSELF SOMETIMES. BUT SHE DIDN'T HAVE TO NOT ENJOY THE PROCESS OF CRITICIZING HERSELF. I WONDER IF IT'S POSSIBLE FOR A PERSON TO FAIL AT NOT ENJOYING CRITICIZING THEMSELVES. YOU SWITCH THE LAST AND THE FIRST WORD OF THOSE SELF-CRITICAL STATEMENTS AROUND. "YOU CAN PROBABLY THINK OF ANOTHER ONE," WE SAID. AND SHE'D THINK OF ANOTHER ONE. AND THEN A LITTLE SMILE WOULD COME TO THE CORNER OF HER FACE.

And we'd know at the sight of that smile that she'd been able to switch the first and the last words. A MORE INTERESTING WAY TO DO THAT IS TO HAVE THE CONSCIOUS MIND THINK OF THE STATEMENT WHILE THE UNCONSCIOUS PREPARES TO KEEP THE GOOD FEELING. OR IT'S POSSIBLE THAT THE CONSCIOUS MIND COULD KEEP THE GOOD FEELING AND LET THE UNCONSCIOUS WORK A REARRANGEMENT OF ALL THE WORDS.

And that was an interesting idea. If it's so much fun to switch the first and last words, what if I were to identify the sentence and then rearrange all of the words, in a random order? THAT COULD KEEP A CONSCIOUS MIND SO BUSY THAT THE UNCONSCIOUS MIND COULD HAVE TIME TO APPRECIATE LIFE. SHE COULD MAKE A LIST OF ALL THE DIFFERENT WAYS THAT YOU COULD SAY THE SAME SENTENCE. SHE'D DECIDED, APPARENTLY IN A CRE-ATIVE MOOD BY HER UNCONSCIOUS, THAT SHE'D ONLY CRITICIZE HERSELF WITH TWO WORDS. THAT WAY IT WOULDN'T BE SO HARD TO REARRANGE THEM. AND THEN WHEN SHE'D SAY "DUMB SHIT," ALL SHE WOULD HAVE TO DO WAS SAY "SHIT DUMB." AND IT REALLY SAVED A GOOD DEAL OF TIME, A LOT OF MENTAL ENERGY. THEN SHE REMEMBERED ANOTHER THING WE HAD SPOKEN ABOUT, AND THAT WAS THE ABILITY TO EXAGGERATE A CRITICISM UNTIL IT WAS REALLY LUDICROUS.

Over the course of therapy, we had the opportunity to observe Cathy. And she didn't know that we were listening but we heard someone just get her good, lambasting her and her self-worth and her ideas, and everything about her really, LIFE, THE UNIVERSE AND EVERYTHING. And Cathy's re-sponse was, "Don't you think you may be underrating how bad I really am. WELL, I DON'T EVEN HAVE THE RIGHT TO TAKE UP THE AIR AND BREATHE HERE AND SAY THIS SENTENCE BACK TO YOU. IN FACT I'M PROBABLY SOILING THIS CARPET WITH THE BOTTOM OF MY SHOES. I shouldn't even be wearing these shoes. Some animal had to die so that I could wear these shoes. Her assailant couldn't think of any way to improve on that.

AND SHE'D KEEP GOING UNTIL SHE MADE HERSELF LAUGH. And that wasn't the response he'd been looking for. SHE WAS THINKING ABOUT ALL THE COWS AND ALLIGATORS SHE WAS GOING TO APOLOGIZE TO FOR WEAR-ING THOSE SHOES. And we had to thank her for some of the ideas she'd had about elaborately improving on criticisms. We had to admit that we learned a great deal ourselves.

SO YOUR CONSCIOUS MIND MIGHT DECIDE THAT YOU ARE GOING TO ELABORATE ON A CRITICISM AND FIND OUT THAT YOUR UNCONSCIOUS WAS MERELY GOING TO REARRANGE THE WORDS. AND MAYBE YOU'D FIND OUT THAT YOUR CONSCIOUS MIND WAS REARRANGING THE WORDS AND YOUR UNCONSCIOUS WOULD ELABORATE ON IT. YOU CAN MEET YOURSELF GOING AND COMING THAT WAY.

But one thing was for sure and that was the more she was able to criticize herself in that new way, the more she was able to develop a new sense of understanding and appreciation for herself, even for those thoughts and things that had embarrassed her so, and left her so vulnerable. WE MEN-TIONED IN THE TRANCE THAT WHEN YOUR SPOUSE CRITICIZES YOU, CATHY, IT'S SIMPLY AN UNDERSTANDING THAT HE REALLY WANTS YOU TO MAKE THE MOST OUT OF YOURSELF, OR NOT GOOF UP IN LIFE THE WAY HE DID. SO, YOU REALLY OUGHT TO SIMPLY USE THE TECHNIQUE YOU'VE LEARNED

TO MAKE YOURSELF FEEL BETTER AND GO OVER AND HUG HIM AND KISS HIM. And "Thank you for noticing me," she would say to him when he criticized her.

AND THAT REALLY STOPPED HIS CRITICISM. AND THAT'S WHY WE CAME TO CALL IT THE "SNOOPY AND LUCY INTERVENTION." IT IS JUST LIKE WHEN LUCY WOULD CRITICIZE SNOOPY AND HE'D KISS HER ON THE CHEEK. AND THAT GOT RID OF LUCY IN AN HURRY. Blah! AND THAT REALLY CHANGED THEIR RELATIONSHIP QUICKLY.

NOW ON THE WAY HOME FROM OUR OFFICE, WOLFGANG LEFT IN A TRANCE. HE'D BEEN REMEMBERING PREVIOUS EXPERIENCES AND REMEMBERING PREVIOUS LEARNINGS IN TRANCE. Because when you leave a trance state, you keep with you a good bit of the thoughts that you're going to want to think about in a leisurely way for a longer time.

WOLFGANG GOT ON THE BUS WHEN HE LEFT OUR OFFICE AND HE WAS GOING TO HAVE A LONG BUS RIDE AFTER DARK. When a person gets onto a bus and finds a seat, there's often a great sense of relief to just settle down into that seat and know that you don't have to do anything. HANDS ON THE LAP, JIGGLING IN TRANCE. And know that you can enjoy the ride and look out the window, look at the sights.

WOLFGANG CAME TO REALIZE THAT A TEN-MINUTE BUS RIDE REALLY MAY TAKE A GREAT DEAL LONGER THAN THAT BECAUSE HE WAS IN TRANCE. HE COULDN'T MOVE. HE FOLDED A PIECE OF PAPER ON HIS LAP AND BEGAN TO LOOK OUT THE WINDOW SMILING. IT WAS LIKE SEEING HIS OWN REFLECTION IN THE GLASS and occasionally looking at the scenery, the grass and the trees, a few cows AND THE LIGHTS INSIDE THE BUS, THE BLACKNESS OUTSIDE THE WINDOW. HE COULDN'T HELP BUT WATCH THAT FACE IN THE WINDOW. HIS NECK WAS ERECT ABOVE HIS SHOULDERS. HIS CHEEKS WERE FLAT, QUITE SMOOTH AND RELAXED. HIS BREATHING WAS COMFORTABLY FROM THE LOWER CHEST. THERE WAS NO TENSION IN HIS FOREHEAD.

He could even see the traces of the tear track, that warm tear that he had cried and allowed to roll over his cheek so gently, back in the trance session. It left its little mark there on his cheek. It reminded him of that feeling of warmth.

AS THE BUS PASSED BY AT VARIOUS BRIDGE PILLARS, THE SCENE SUDDENLY CHANGED AND HE REALIZED "THOSE DARN LANKTONS, THEY'VE GOT ME IN A TRANCE HERE AND I'M JUST SEEING MYSELF IN THE WINDOW, FEELING THAT FEELING I LEARNED IN TRANCE." You can be very pleased at the sight of yourself that you catch unexpectedly in a reflection in a window or a mirror and enjoy the sight of that face, memorize its details.

AND AS THE SCENE CHANGED, WOLFGANG SAW HIMSELF WITH THAT SAME GOOD FEELING THAT HE HAD HAD IN OUR OFFICE, WHILE HE WAS AT A DANCE. AND HE WATCHED HIMSELF WITH THE CONSCIOUS MIND

BEING SOMEWHAT CURIOUS AS TO WHAT AN IMAGINATION CAN CHANGE IN SUCH A VIVID WAY. AND HE COULDN'T HELP BUT NOTICE HE WAS LOOKING QUITE GOOD IN THE PICTURE, FEELING QUITE GOOD WATCHING IT. He couldn't help but enjoy the sight of himself so effortlessly dancing in that scenario, smiling. Maybe it was a bump in the road. . . .

AND ANOTHER THOUGHT PASSED HIS MIND, A POST-HYPNOTIC SUGGESTION OF HAVING ME STARING IN THIS WINDOW HERE AND THE SCENE CHANGED. THEN HE SAW HIMSELF INTERACTING AT SCHOOL, STILL WITH THAT SAME FEELING, A GOOD FEELING HE'D LEARNED IN TRANCE, TALKING TO A FRIEND, TALKING TO A STRANGER, TALKING TO A TEACHER, SITTING THERE WITH AN OPEN BOOK, A LOT OF VARIOUS THINGS, LOOKING AT HIMSELF FROM A DISTANCE, HEARING THE THINGS HE'D SAY THAT WERE CONSISTENT WITH THAT FEELING.

And in a very short period of time, your conscious mind may help as you sketch out the scenario that you're able to see yourself in, while your unconscious allows you to keep those pleasant feelings and enjoy watching how you use them in that scene that you sketch. Or maybe your conscious mind just enjoys the pleasurable feelings and you allow your unconscious to sketch out that scene and enrich it with the details of your own life and those people important to you at school.

THEN HE SAW THAT THE BUMP CHANGED THE SCENE AGAIN. HE WAS WITH HIS GIRLFRIEND INTERACTING AND HE STILL HAD THAT POSTURE THAT REFLECTED THAT FEELING. HE HADN'T REALLY THOUGHT OF HOW HE LOOKED TO HER WITH THAT GOOD FEELING AND THE KINDS OF WORDS THAT HE IMAGINED GOING ON IN THAT SCENE. THOSE ARE INTERESTING, TOO. In feeling that good watching the scene comfortably, you're even able to watch yourself remaining comfortable, even though the other person might be gently or even harshly criticizing or asking for something different from you.

HE REMEMBERED HAVING THE THOUGHT LATER THAT HE WAS GOING TO THINK THAT THOUGHT AGAIN IN MORE DETAIL WHEN HE WAS LYING COMFORTABLY IN BED AT SOME TIME. AND THEN HE SAW HIMSELF AT WORK INTERACTING WITH WOMEN, INTERACTING WITH MEN. IT DIDN'T SEEM TO MATTER. HE HAD THAT POSTURE THAT REFLECTED A GOOD FEELING AND HE WAS ABLE TO HAVE THAT GOOD FEELING AT WORK, WITH BOTH MEN AND WOMEN. AND THE THINGS HE WAS THINKING HE'D SAY WERE THINGS HE VALUED. BUT THEY WERE SLIGHTLY DIFFERENT BECAUSE THEY WERE MOTIVATED BY THAT FEELING HE LEARNED IN TRANCE.

And your conscious mind isn't sure how you are going to change the words to be those words that you would say. Maybe you won't realize what words you're going to say until you hear your unconscious supply them. But you can enjoy watching yourself interacting. Memorize the pleasantness of that sight. AND I REALLY DOUBT THAT YOU COULD FAIL TO REMEMBER SOMETHING THAT WASN'T EVEN SAID TO YOU AT ALL. YOU PROBABLY CAN.

MAYBE YOU REMEMBER THAT ALAN LEARNED HOW TO NOT NOTICE A LOT OF STIMULUS SOMEWHERE. WE DID HAPPEN TO FORGET THAT ALAN HAD BEEN ONE OF OUR CLIENTS LONG AGO, WHEN HE WAS IN HIGH SCHOOL. Your conscious mind not noticing the stimuli as we've been speaking to you, sometimes simultaneously, in no way prevents your unconscious from accomplishing what you want to accomplish.

HE CAME INTO OUR OFFICE ONE DAY WITH THAT CERTIFICATE, AND HE SAID, "YOU KNOW, I LOST TRACK OF DICK. I THINK HE DROPPED OUT OF HIGH SCHOOL AND HAS NEVER BEEN SEEN AGAIN. BUT I HAD TO COME BACK AND TELL YOU THAT I LEARNED HOW TO NOT NOTICE A LOT OF THINGS WHEN I SAW YOU." WE SAID, "GEE THAT'S NICE. GLAD WE COULD DIMINISH YOUR CONSCIOUSNESS." AND HE SAID, "NO YOU DON'T KNOW WHAT I MEAN. I really mean it. I wouldn't have been able to get through college without it. I'VE BEEN ABLE TO NOT NOTICE A LOT OF THINGS. I'VE BEEN ABLE TO SIT IN THE LIBRARY AND NOT NOTICE ALL OF THOSE GIRLS WALKING BY. I'VE BEEN ABLE TO SIT IN THE CLASSROOM AND NOT NOTICE ALL OF THOSE PEOPLE MAKING NOISE AROUND ME. I'VE BEEN ABLE TO CONCENTRATE ON WHAT I WAS STUDYING AND NOT NOTICE ANY OF THOSE PREVIOUS THINGS THAT I CAN'T EVEN REMEMBER WHAT THEY WERE. BUT I SURE CAN CONCENTRATE."

BUT WHEN YOU REMEMBER NOT TO NOTICE THOSE STIMULI THAT ARE IRRELEVANT AND UNNECESSARY FOR YOU TO NOTICE, YOU CAN BE SURPRISED HOW MANY THINGS YOUR UNCONSCIOUS ALLOWS YOU TO NOTICE, THAT YOU CAN ENJOY.

"AND HERE'S MY COLLEGE DIPLOMA. AND I'D LIKE YOU TO SIGN IT, TOO." AND WE SIGNED THE BOTTOM OF THE DIPLOMA AS A TRIBUTE TO HOW NOT NOTICING A LOT OF THINGS MAKES SENSE IN A FUNNY WAY IN COLLEGE.

NOW WE'VE BEEN SPEAKING TO YOU ABOUT MORE THINGS THAN YOUR CONSCIOUS MIND IS ABLE TO WORK THROUGH IN ONE MOMENT. We've been speaking to you and you've been having more thoughts than you can keep track of. YOU SHOULD ALLOW YOURSELF TO CONTINUE ANY OF THE WORK THAT YOU'D LIKE TO THAT YOU BEGAN HERE TODAY SOMETIME WHEN YOU'RE ALONE OR SOMETIME WHEN YOU'VE LEFT THE STAGE. There's a good bit of comfort that a person can take anywhere. MAYBE YOU'LL DO IT IN A DREAM AT NIGHT AND BRING UNDERSTANDINGS TO YOUR CONSCIOUS MIND ONLY AS FAST AS IS COMFORTABLY NECESSARY. In a dream at night you can go anywhere, talk to anybody, and do anything that will allow you to further your understandings and memorize that comfort again and again.

I THINK IT'D BE VERY INTERESTING IF YOUR UNCONSCIOUS KEPT THE LEARNINGS AND USED THEM FOR YOUR OWN BENEFIT AND YOU DISCOVER THAT YOUR CONSCIOUS MIND COULDN'T JUST REMEMBER WHAT IT WAS THAT WE SAID TO YOU THAT DAY. THAT WAY ALL OF THE LEARNINGS WILL BE YOURS AND ONLY YOURS, AND ONLY YOU CAN TAKE CREDIT FOR WHAT YOU ACHIEVED. AND DON'T GIVE ANY OF IT AWAY TO US OR ANYONE ELSE.

Waking up from a dream can be a lot like the experience of walking along a seashore, when the tide has gone out. And you really don't know what you're going to find there that's been delivered up onto the sand from the depths of the ocean. But you wake up from a dream bringing with you certain gifts from your unconscious, an ability to be comfortable perhaps. Or maybe it's an ability to not notice something we said so that you could have your own thoughts and learn something your way. And how does a person even go about coming out of a trance? Sometimes a person comes out of trance by opening his eyes and looking around. [Client opens his eyes and looks around.] And other times, even after your eyes are open, you may find you're still not completely out of a trance.

SOMETIMES THEY COME OUT BY ORIENTING THEIR BODY AND STRETCH-ING FIRST. YOU WILL BE SUFFICIENTLY OUT OF A TRANCE TO TAKE CARE OF YOURSELF QUITE WELL FOR THE REST OF THE DAY. MAYBE YOU'LL HAVE A NICE DREAM. HI, YOU ARE OUT. WELL, WHAT WOULD YOU LIKE TO SAY, ANYTHING?

Client: Sure, I just want to say that when I came in here, I was, ah . . . very ah . . . scared and embarrassed. I am relaxed right now. That's how I feel. I feel extremely relaxed.

Carol: It's an unusual place to feel relaxed. Do you have a sense of how much time passed or did you forget to notice the time passing?

Client: Very short. I wish it would have been longer. It seemed like I just enjoyed it so much that I wish it would have lasted.

DID IT SEEM LIKE A HALF HOUR, OR TWENTY MINUTES?

Client: It just seemed very short, like a few minutes.

ACTUALLY IT WAS FORTY-FIVE MINUTES, AT LEAST. WELL, I'D LIKE TO THANK YOU GUYS FOR MAKING THIS POSSIBLE. AND THANK YOU FOR MAK-ING IT POSSIBLE.

Client: Sure, it was my pleasure.

DUAL INDUCTIONS IN FAMILY LIFE AND THERAPY

We have a theory of dual induction that is very applicable to families. We'd like to talk about that and have you practice a version of it before we study in more detail the specific metaphor protocols you've now seen demonstrated. Because you have also just seen a long, therapeutic example of dual induction in a clinical setting on the Paco video, you may be wondering how this is relevant for you in a family session that may not involve formal hypnosis. The answer is that there are, of course, other contexts in which this type of thing occurs naturally. For example, what if we are two parents, arguing, saying the same thing, saying different things? There are several features of this dual induction but the easiest breakdown here would be that between the delivery and the content. There are basically four possibilities derived from speaking either simultaneously or alternately, and about the same or different content. You could deliver the *same* content and do it *alternately*. And you might hear us saying you could focus your eyes over here, and Carol saying your eyes focus this way. If you do that, you are going to *fixate* attention, and the client has some attention that is left. This is primarily the format you heard us using with Paco. The other possibilities tend to be much more confusing for the client's conscious mind and, due to Paco's anxiety level and paranoid concern about what we would be suggesting to him, we did not want to introduce extra confusion of this type.

If you talk about the same content *at the same time*, the client doesn't have any attention left. You overload the conscious mind. If you talk about *different* content, *alternately*, you create a dissociation. The client tracks both of them. This is what happens a lot in the family situation. You are sitting in the room at the dinner table, and one parent is discussing the homework, and the other is discussing the chores . . . and you are thinking about them both somehow. This happens a lot, alternately talking about different things.

This also happens during large portions of time when children are being raised but when the parents are in different rooms! Do you see that? Here's how that works. When Johnny is out in the garage working on soldering something with Dad, he's got the propane torch there and Dad's saying, "Now when you solder this stuff, you have to make sure that you get flux all over it completely and that there are no finger prints on it." And then Johnny goes in the house and sits down with Mother and they read a book, and she is saying, "Boy, you are getting really good at the way you read." Then Dad says come out and help me again in the garage. So Johnny goes out to the garage and Dad's saying, "You know you are really getting the hang of this." So you have got different content alternately delivered. The kid will develop a dissociation. And in this case it is positive.

There is a third category of *same* content delivered *simultaneously* in families. The most important aspect is the affect that is delivered with this. In that video example our affect is positive. There is affect, positive, positive, positive, which gives us our rundown of four categories (all with positive affect). And then you can duplicate this and you've got negative, negative,

negative. And to make matters worse, you could have positive, negative, positive, negative. So you could really have 16 categories but let's not, okay? All I have observed carefully is what we are doing here in therapy.

If you have *different* content delivered *simultaneously*, now that will really do it to you. What happens here is a deepening of trance phenomena created by synthesis of both. And what about when it happens between parents, who are saying to you simultaneously, "You did a good job," and, "We are so proud of you"? Here you are getting positive affect coming in on the same topic. But what if they are presenting slightly different topics?

The unconscious will synthesize bits and pieces of both. And if it is a bad experience, then bad feelings will be a part of the deepening of the trance phenomenon. Think about that for a moment. It is neither good nor bad to hallucinate. Hallucination, a trance phenomenon, can be enjoyable. Each of us uses it frequently to do some types of problem solving. But if it has positive affect attached, it feels pleasant and perhaps the hallucination tends to be pleasant. If, on the contrary, you happen to feel frightened when you hallucinate, you will have an experience that is very unpleasant—and when you tell others about it and, say, ask for help, they will call you schizophrenic. The affect issue seems to determine whether or not the dissociations can be integrated during one's life or whether they remain separate for years. Of course, when you are trapped in internal thought processing for longer periods, your trance gets deeper.

We have some rationale for what we are doing. When we see that a client can't get the conscious mind to stop monitoring, then we will talk simultaneously about the same content. And if that overload doesn't present enough to let us take the lead at that point, then one of us will switch contents and we will talk simultaneously with different contents. And one of us will be deepening the trance. So we are able to follow a very logical scheme without talking to each other about it, but simply watching the client.

LEARNING TO USE FAMILY MEMBERS AS UNKNOWING CO-HYPNOTISTS

Let's say we have any two family members, a husband and a wife, for example, and a therapist here. For the sake of this exercise, we will have a particular kind of thing happening. It needs to be something where the family member currently identified as the "client" doesn't do a lot of talking. So let's say the husband is getting sad, and usually doesn't. So we want to encourage him to stay with the sadness. You can say, "Please stay with your sadness, Jim. Go where that takes you." Shape the congruity of the expressional behavior. And you are going to do something else as well. You will also ask the other family member, the wife, to tell the client member how useful that would be for her, how she would feel about that, and how she would encourage him to do it. The only thing you need to do is make sure that she doesn't talk nonstop. So you say, "I want you to tell him how you feel about his beginning to cry." Presumably you know she is going to say something positive. You've been there, where the wife would like this guy to show his feelings. So simply ask at that point, as you might do in a normal therapy session, "Jeanne, will you tell Jim how you feel about it when he shows his feelings?" And as you do, pause as you speak and let me say some things too. And keep talking when you hear me talk." And then you say, "Continue to stay with your feelings." Now you have dual induction with a naive co-therapist and total control. Part of your control, of course, will involve occasional needs to reframe or relabel certain bits of communications coming from the other family member which may seem somewhat negative despite their positive intent.

Before you do that, I'm going to show you a spot on the Erickson tape (see p. 58) where Monde mouths off and accidentally says the wrong thing to Nick. And you'll see Erickson responding to her uninvited comment. You'll hear how Erickson handles it. He is using the same understanding of dual induction to unravel what Monde has just begun by inadvertently acting as a co-therapist.

> E: It will take you a while Nick, to put yourself back together again . . . and that reorientation to your hands, feeling them again. And getting your legs, your arms back together, your head back on . . . getting acquainted with your body. I think it's too comfortable in here.
> N: I'm still in a trance.
> M: You don't want to come out.
> N: Uh huh.

To begin we see and hear Erickson *ending* his reorientation with Nick. The trance is over at this point—except for one thing. Monde speaks. And in speaking she bestows an attribution onto Nick that is, in my viewing, contrary to what Erickson's work with Nick has been. That is, Erickson is helping Nick face reality and end his pattern of retreating. Monde, to the contrary, just by stating the obvious in the way she did, gives Nick further self-concept suggestions about his desire to avoid! And, of course, this is during the highly suggestible stage of hypnogogic trance reorientation. So, if this is no blunder, we should expect Erickson to end the reorientation or make no comment but instead what he does is surprising. Let's watch and listen more.

E: No, you don't *want* to *come out of* a trance. You don't want a charming movie to end, you don't want a flower to wilt, but you do like reality.

Well, Nick *does not* like reality. So I am surprised by this. It sounds like a typical Ericksonian communication pattern: Meet them at their model of the world, communicate in the same form that was offered, and, finally, suggest what you desire for the client to reach as the next goal. That is, he agrees that one doesn't like trance to end, flowers to wilt, and so on. Then he makes an attribution just like Monde made an attribution. And this is the only time such an attribution is made by Erickson on this tape. It is very direct considering the degree of metaphor, anecdote, and indirect suggestion we hear on the rest of this tape. What stands out for me is that Monde attributed "You don't want to come out" and Erickson, speaking alternately, entered a different topic, "You do like reality." Now let's just explain that he continues the trance for a while and then again reorients. In other words, he was done with the trance, Monde spoke, and now he is going to continue the trance and reorient later.

E: And all you can do is *wonder* how charming you will be at 40, 50, and 60 . . . I can *wonder* at all the new things you will *find* at 40, 50, 60; and I'm looking to find out how nice things are at 80.

E: One of my sons told me, "I will be eternally grateful to my grandparents. They taught me that, of course, they had good old times in the past, but the really good times are yet ahead of them."

E: The first time I learned to ride a horse, I didn't know I'd ride a jet plane; I didn't even know there could be a plane. Now I'm letting you *awaken slowly*, because it's necessary—all people—to *awaken slowly*, and to *let the trance learnings* and thinkings *set*, just like plaster of Paris takes a little while to *set*. And after your learnings *get set*, then they will *accompany you* all the *rest of your life.*

E: Now for the rest of the day, be unconcerned if you don't seem to be totally in touch with things. You will be adequately in touch for your own welfare and protection.

Well, this continues for another few minutes, at which time Erickson comes to the following conclusion of the trance.

E: And now say goodbye to our unconscious, and let's talk and respond to each other at the conscious level. Hi. Hi.[20]

---

[20]Erickson, M. H. (1976). "The Artistry of Milton H. Erickson, M.D., Part Two." Herbert Lustig, M.D. (producer). Philadelphia, PA.

I hope you get the point here, which I think is obvious: Erickson had to do two reorientations and he returned to the trance in order to counter the potentially adverse effects of Monde's offhand utterance. Do you see that?

Now, back to the exercise. What happens if you speak alternately about the same topic? You fixate attention on that topic. I want you to try that first as you rotate around, letting each person in your triad have an opportunity to play each role. So person one is therapist, and person two and three are spouses (or two other family members). Then rotate. And then person two be the therapist, and the other two be the family members. Then rotate again, so everyone gets a chance to try saying it and doing it and feeling how it feels to be in that situation. I also want you to try the other things. Inform the person that you may speak at the same time and that he or she should continue talking if you do. Spend 50% of your time talking alternately and 50% of your time talking at the same time, about the same and/or different topics. You are going to talk for about three minutes here for each rotation, but that will be enough for you to compare your experiences with the different roles and different possibilities. I am prescribing that the client begin to show sadness, the reason being that if the client were feeling happiness he might have to talk about it. This way the client will be passive.

[Exercise begins and continues for several minutes.]

It's obvious that a good bit of rapport has been established as a result of this exercise because you won't come back from your small groups. Remember, you aren't curing anyone here; it's just an exercise. Your time is up. Say goodbye to your family member, take a moment to resume your original identity, and give us some feedback. Did you discover how you can use the family in a new way? We observed some emotional displays that looked very genuine out there, so you must have been doing something right.

Many of you seem to agree that you were able to elaborate on the positive messages the family member was giving. In doing that, of course, you were not only helping the identified client learn a new role or feel a new sense of permission regarding the feeling he was experiencing, but you were also modeling and teaching a new role for the family member who was learning to be sensitive to and reinforce atypical feelings being displayed by her loved one. This was probably especially true for those messages coming from the family member which didn't strike you as totally positive. In those cases, you have to think quickly to look behind or to listen between the words of the message being sent in order to ascertain whatever positive meaning might be there. Then, whether speaking alternately or simultaneously, you reword the message to highlight the positive meaning so that the identified client gets to feel it as though it came from the other family member, and the other family member gets to learn something about how to reinforce more congruently. This is nice, though, because the family member "gets the credit" for having said the helpful thing even before she has learned how to say it.

Some of you have apparently discovered something about how readily people can and do go into a trance. Even in this very short and artificial learning activity, you found that, as clients, you were very quickly able to develop a "mini-trance" without much formal induction at all. But in that different context, old roles, frames of reference, and typical patterns of interaction were disrupted and suspended, allowing you a comfortable objectivity, while at the same time intensifying an internal concentration. This different context paradoxically fostered both a special kind of privacy, as well as an intimacy and special sharing with the family member. One woman has put it very nicely when she said, "It creates an opportunity for the family to comfortably open itself up to discover feelings, roles, and experiences that haven't been routine for them."

A few of you are bringing up the logical question of what next? You've commented that you were able to go on for the duration of this three-minute exercise, but were beginning to feel at the "end of your creative rope" in terms of content as it came time to switch. Well, that's where a treatment plan with regard to specific goals you may have for each family member, and associated metaphors, comes in handy. As you know from your client experience here, it wouldn't take much to deepen the trance you had already initiated, or simply utilize that trance which has already been initiated. Of course, you have been using it already with the permissions you have been giving with the help of another family member, but you may want to elaborate further on the new roles, experiences, communications, etc., via metaphor for the benefit of both (or all) the family members present. Now you already know something about metaphor from our earlier introduction and from viewing the metaphors we used with Paco to address the specific goals in his case. So let's go in more depth now with metaphor construction.

EFFECT AND CONSTRUCTION OF METAPHOR

Speaking of the effects of metaphor, it is almost self-evident after seeing the case of Paco and other examples here or in your practice, but your handout [Illustration 30] summarizes the basics—that is, stimulating thought and unconscious search, and allowing a broad range of individual responses. It is really quite different from assertiveness training where you specifically shape the person to respond in a certain way. A broad range of responses is okay, and it is really difficult to fail because any response is okay. Because of that, metaphor reduces resistance to considering new ideas, and it initiates a variety of subtle, mental processes like comparison

METAPHOR CONSTRUCTION

1. Define a specific therapeutic goal for this metaphor.

2. Construct a reference picture that contains the necessary components for the unfolding storyline.

3. Construct an end picture to provide closure to the storyline.

4. Check that the resources needed to reach goal will be possible.

5. Add dramatic hold using the element of metaphoric drama.

6. Observe and incorporate client's ideomotor response while delivering.

Illustration 30

and contrast, memory and congruity checking. So those are the things that we want to remind you of to justify the use of metaphor in the first place.

The next thing we want to do is learn how to construct them. So let's move on to simple construction of a metaphor. Don't do it this way. A client tells you a problem and you go, "Oh, this is just like this metaphor here." And you tell the client the metaphor. After you get the problem and the diagnosis, get a specific goal. Strategic therapists are going for goals. Now you have a target. Now you are ready to aim and shoot at it.

Construct a reference picture that will contain the necessary components for the story you are going to tell. Let's say my goal is belonging. Because I also know the protocol, I have a little edge on you if you don't know that. I'm thinking, "Okay, I'm going to have to move a positive character towards a positive character and stay stationary. So who will my positive characters be? How about that thing I know of those guys singing out there on the pier?" So in my mind I picture this man on the shore, gradually moving out to the pier to these people.

And I have some little thing in my mind that indicates to me the pier, Wolfgang, the people singing, whatever it takes in a visual imagery. I see colors. The point is that since a picture is worth a thousand words, you can instantaneously conceptualize the picture which is going to take you a good deal of time to tell as a story. And a visual picture, as opposed to saying it out in your head, is faster. It is not linear. You can have things that are completely contrasted and opposite, where to say or feel two different things wouldn't work. So the most logical way to represent the data to yourself is in an instantaneously created picture that will allow you to describe all of these details, any way you want, for as long as you want during the story. So that is why it's your reference picture. You keep referring back to it as you tell. But don't tell it yet.

Step three is construct an end picture now. In other words you know in what format the computer is going to read data. Tell it when to stop reading data before you start. Remember I said that a mentality about selecting endings before we start will apply to the way we construct metaphors. So figure out how this is going to end. You'll be so happy you did, because otherwise, you won't know when to stop. Also you are working both ends against the middle. It is much easier to figure out which components to drop in creatively to get to the end. At the very least, when it gets right to the end of your story, and you don't know how to end up, that they got married and had six kids, then you can just say something like "Time passed." But at least I know where I am going.

Then check to see that the resources are there. This is where it becomes a matter of degree of difficulty for you. It can be relatively easy, because you may simply want to elaborate upon a feeling of confidence and be-longing. So just make sure that there is a way that this is introduced in the story as an idea—take one idea and blow it up to an entire experience. That is the easy way. The hard way includes those protocols. So in that case, I would say make sure that the resources to create the protocol are in that story. Is there a character that I explain in the relationship? How can I do that? So you make a quick check, "Does my reference picture contain all that stuff by the time I get to the end of my real picture?" It is a quick check to make sure you are on the right track. And you've emphasized in your own mind the things you are going to elaborate to the client.

Then the final piece—which involves another learning we will cover in a minute—is to add dramatic hold to this thing, so that people will listen to you. And then tell your story, incorporating client ideomotor responses while you are delivering it.

When you deliver the metaphor [Illustration 31], use a range of vocal tones. Speak in rhythm with the person's breathing. Emphasize natural ambiguities of language as you talk to your family members. They will appreciate it if you do. Try to draw upon the pauses that occur . . . in the natural delivery of a sentence. There will be pauses that seem like the end of one sentence . . . which are really the beginning of another sentence.

Now what about this matter of imagery in metaphor? We promote in

DELIVERY OF METAPHOR

1. Use range of vocal tones.
2. Use pauses and speak in rhythm with client's breathing.
3. Emphasize natural ambiguities.
4. Detail images you intend client to experience strongly.
5. Use indirect suggestions and binds to detail images.
6. Observe the client's ideomotor behavior and tailor to it.
7. Be prepared to throw out your plan.

Illustration 31

Ericksonian therapy—especially Ericksonian styles of induction—a radical departure from guided imagery as a directive technique. This is also a good rule of thumb to follow with metaphor. Of course, there is a difference between "guided" and "evoked" imagery. You really can't speak without evoking some kind of imagery, especially if you are telling stories about something. But the difference here is that you are not insisting that clients picture specific images in a detailed way that you prescribe. You are simply talking about something that will bring to mind different images for different clients, depending on their particular background and on what is relevant for them to think about.

And there are different kinds of images as well. For example, the concept of "procrastination" involves an image. At the very least, the word itself is an auditory image. If your people have trouble imaging, they are dead. So they won't have trouble imaging. They may have trouble visual imaging. You generally don't want to try to get your client to do it in a particular visual system, except for self-image thinking, which is much faster if it is done in visual imagery. So we never asked Paco to picture the pier. We suggested that he would hear the humming. But we never really intended for him to conceptualize it in any particular way to suit us. You can detail the imagery and still never elaborate upon a particular kind of imagery, just by saying more about it, in ambiguous ways. For example, if I say "procrastination," it is hard to picture that or feel it or anything. It is such a digital concept. You might say that your conscious mind knows a lot of ways that things have been postponed until your unconscious is ready to do them. I have elaborated with one sentence. If I also say, "Everybody knows what it is like to do something tomorrow and not do it today," I've elaborated in two sentences. And still there is no imagery—no visual imagery, I mean. It is just detailing the images until you experience enough relationship.

Let me elaborate on elaborating here. This has to be ambiguous detail. You wouldn't want to elaborate by saying a little brown dog with a white spot on the tip of his eyebrow on his left eye, his right ear flopped over about a quarter inch behind his cheekbone, because that kind of detail forces the client's mind down your path, which really defeats the purpose of metaphor, which is to let him/her do it his/her way. It would be better to say the following: "The dog had an odd marking on its head which was located in a specific spot that can be talked about in words. Although it would take some doing to say exactly where that marking was and quite what it was that it would look like to an observer, you knew it if you ever encountered it again. The same thing was true for one of his ears." Now I can make that into anything I want. And that is elaborating with ambiguous detail, and making the client think about a spot on the dog.

Observe the client's ideomotor behavor and tailor what you say to it. For example, in the Paco tape when Paco opened his eyes and stared into the audience, one way you can look at it is: "Oh, he is resisting and he's fleeing from the moment that is in the trance being spoken about." The way I would frame it is positively. He was feeling an experience of belonging and at that moment he opened his eyes. It may actually have been his conscious intention to see if he felt better in front of this group at that point, or an unconscious wisdom to associate that belonging to a relevant context—i.e., in the presence of people. That is how we interpreted it. And at the very least, we mentioned that we would be able to link certain stimuli to other learnings.

Finally, in telling any story, you must be prepared to throw it out, in case the recipient has idiosyncratic responses totally different than you anticipated.

CONSTRUCTING DRAMA IN METAPHOR

There is one other piece I'll give you. You also have this chart in your handouts [Illustration 32]. This is something we borrowed from Alfred Hitchcock. It is his basic formula for creating dramatic hold. And we modified it to talk about clients instead of audiences.

Drama is that state of affairs that captures the person's attention, because there is missing information. Attention is being captured stimulating curiosity. You are curious because there is something not there that you know

CREATING DRAMATIC HOLD IN METAPHORS

THREE TYPES:
Suspense, Mystery, and Surprise or Shock (Humor).

TO WHOM IS KEY INFORMATION REVEALED:
Client (Audience) or Protagonist?

	Client	Protagonist
Suspense	Knows	Not
Mystery	Not	Knows
Surprise/Shock/Humor	Not	Not

Suspense: Audience knows what will happen, but wonders **WHEN?**
Mystery: Audience must guess **WHAT** is happening or will happen?
Surprise/Shock/Humor: Captures attention and begs that questions be asked.

Illustration 32

is supposed to be there. So it's a matter of who has the information, and to whom it's revealed. With that in mind, then, suspense can be created by the client knowing something that the protagonist doesn't know.

Suspense, especially, is waiting to find out how it is, and in this case, when something that you know is likely to happen is going to happen or doesn't happen, or how bad it is. So suspense is created in movies in a couple of different ways. One way in which it is created is by the soundtrack alerting you that something is going to happen now. And *you* know, but the protagonists don't hear this music. It would be real handy if they did, wouldn't it? You are swimming in the water and you hear "da-dump, da-dump, da-dump, da-dump," and you know that Jaws is coming. The audience knows and the protagonist doesn't know so you are wondering how this is going to turn out. When is it going to culminate? Now a mystery, on the other hand, is just the opposite. The protagonists know something that you don't know. But you are not trying to win a Pulitzer prize when you create dramatic hold. You are trying to hold the client's attention. That is all. For example:

"I had a teacher one time who saw me for therapy. It was very odd that he actually was able to save his life with some used bubble gum, a compass, and a piece of string. Now when he first saw me for therapy, he was pretty anxious about a lot of things in his life. We really took that on to be the therapeutic task—to help him with his anxiety." You see you want to know, don't you? It is a real mystery as to how that is going to work out. And I would have to figure it out as I got there. What comes to me is something to do with a gun. He knew a student had a gun in the school, and he was going to do something during the third hour. To make a long story short, he chewed the gum, stuck it on the side of the door, stuck a compass to it, and when the student came through the door with the gun, the compass needle swung because it detected metal. It is very simple. And that saved his life. I don't know how you missed that, it was so obvious. So you just introduce those things in the reference picture, know how it ends, and then leave it up to your creative process to place the other pieces in.

Surprise, shock, or humor is created when the client doesn't know—the protagonist doesn't know, nobody knows except the playwright. And you have examples of that. Surprise will capture your attention and require of you to define the situation as dramatic. It defies you to not pay attention anymore. You have to pay attention and ask questions. What is going to happen here? It really captures your attention. It makes you know that there is activity. And so you want to find out then what clues you can. You know something the protagonist doesn't, so that is suspense.

If you don't know what is going on you have mystery. You can only get away with mystery for so long in real life. All these things apply to real life in a very interesting way. In my character development, if I never tell you anything about my past, I am a mystery, which allows you to project anything you want. And eventually you will project the bad parts of yourself and I'll be rejected. And once you project a bad part, then you act to get rid of a person. So that is the end of it.

So if you are around someone who never talks, and they remain a mystery, eventually they are going to get rejected. This is my way of wording our theory of drama and suspense in real life—that people provoke rejection by not sharing their feelings. But this simply explains it as part of the life of dramatic metaphor. Remington Steele is a character in a television program; nobody knows his background. The woman who plays with him is always wondering if he is a good guy or a bad guy. In real life, though, she would decide at some point. Well, I'm just teasing you with some ideas about how you apply this formula to real life.

The movie, *Gandhi*, opens up with Gandhi walking down the street. You don't know him from nothing until someone emerges from the crowd and shoots him. And surprise! He didn't know it and I didn't know it. Now I really may forget about that generally afterwards but it does capture your attention at first. And then you don't remember it again until you say,

"Haven't I seen this road?" and it has been about two and one half hours. And you know what is going to happen.

We were teaching in Australia, and we cavalierly pulled a book off a shelf to prove that many people, especially authors, use these devices frequently. We read out loud the first lines of a bunch of books. The first one we pulled out and opened said in the opening line, "Bang, bang, bang, bang, four bullets tore through my chest, but I'm getting a little ahead of the story." So that is the device you use. And you simply introduce the character with that kind of surprise or whatever it takes to capture the client's attention.

Now use those ideas and embellish them with just a little drama. So you merely make a reference picture, make an end picture, and then decide whether, as you get started, you are going to take some information that the protagonist has from the middle of the story and tease the person with it up front. So your listener doesn't know what is going to happen. Then you have some elements of mystery, something about the ending.

I want to tell you about the high school reunion that we had, our 10-year reunion several years ago. We were really disappointed to find out that one of our classmates was murdered by her husband, who then killed himself, in an incident that occurred only one week before our reunion. Now everybody loved Georgia and Sally. They came from sort of different sides of the track. Georgia came from a perfect neighborhood, and Sally came from what was a battered home, on the other side of the track. And no one thought for a minute that her life was going to turn out very well. . . . Now see I've started by telling you the end. Somebody got killed and you don't know which one yet. And the characters were surprised, too. There was shock and surprise for starters. And something about the ending creates suspense. So you could use surprise, suspense, or both and then tell your story.

We generally try to end stories in a benign way. And usually they are true stories. It's really okay to use just normal, dull endings, too, because the ending doesn't really matter. It's convenient usually not to offend the conscious mind. So having a believable, natural ending is fine. Having it be too Pollyannaish is probably bad.

To be tragic or shocking is often bad. Every client is different and there will be some cases where you'll want it not to end happily. In some cases you'll want the guy to die, which will alert the conscious mind to think a lot about that. I asked Erickson about asthma. I told him I had this asthma boy who was coming to see me. He said, "I worked with a child who had asthma one time. He was taking 360 pills a month. And of course his parents asked me if I would work with him. I agreed. I saw the boy several times during the first week. I reduced my sessions the second week and saw him once a week after that. By the end of four weeks he was taking only 12 pills a month. And his parents found out he'd reduced his medication to only four pills a month. And they demanded that he resume his medication. And the boy died. Now I want to tell you a story about a client who I had one time. . . ." And then he went on to another story.

So, when I got back to Michigan and my asthma client was coming up to see me, I was thinking about the story. In the only story he told me about asthma, the kid died. Great. So there is a story where the ending is not positive and it causes you to think about it a bit. What I concluded was I had better work with the parents' anxiety, because the parents' anxiety killed the kid. That is what the story said to me. And by not telling me how to deal with this kid, Erickson let me treat the client in a unique way. I don't even know if that is the point he wanted me to get.

We are still taking each piece one step at a time. Now that we have looked at the effects and construction of metaphor, we want to go from the diagnosis to the metaphoric learnings in a solid manner. Also, I might refer you to the writing that we recently did about this in the volume edited by Jeff Zeig, entitled, *Ericksonian Psychotherapy, Vol. 1: Structures.*[21] The articles there, especially that on multiple embedded metaphor, provide an excellent summary for those of you making careful study of the protocols. Now for those of you who have not brought that book with you and have not memorized the article—and that is doubtlessly all of you—we have a handout that covers the essentials [Illustration 33].

METAPHOR PROTOCOLS

Attitude Protocol

The first goal we addressed with Paco, as you will recall, was the attitude challenge: He does not have to be like his peers' opinion of him, whatever that may be, real or imagined. Let me show you how this works with a different story first. Let's say the client thought that a woman could not be president of the United States. You are going to create a story that will essentially lead the client to use his map of experience to predict the outcome of a situation and choose a story in which the outcome turns out to be opposite of what the client was bound to predict. So you could tell him

---

[21]See Lankton, S. R. (1985). Multiple embedded metaphor and diagnosis. In J. K. Zeig (Ed.), *Ericksonian psychotherapy, vol. 1: Structures* (pp. 171-195). New York: Brunner/Mazel; and Lankton, C. H. (1985). Generative change: Beyond symptomatic relief. In J. K. Zeig (ed.), *Ericksonian psychotherapy, vol. 1: Structures* (pp. 137-170). New York: Brunner/Mazel.

CONSTRUCTION PROTOCOLS
for
THERAPEUTIC METAPHORS

1. Reorganization of family structure.
    1. Illustrate how a protagonist's discomfort (which is obviously different from the identified patient's problem) relates to a family structure (similar to that of the clients).
    2. Illustrate how the protagonist's family organization changes as a result of interacting differently (a model of reorganization suitable for the client's family system).
    3. Show how the discomfort (still entirely different than any in the client's actual family) was resolved by changing the family and **do not** provide sufficient logical connection between the disappearance of the symptom and the reorganization of the family in the story.

2. Age appropriate intimacy and task behavior.
    1. Emphasize goals and not motives and detail the protagonist's observable behavior similar to the desired behavior to be acquired by the client.
    2. Detail the protagonist's internal attention and non-observable behavior used to support the actions he or she acquires which may also be used by the client.
    3. Change the context within the story so as to provide an opportunity for repeating all the behavioral descriptions several times.

3. Attitude restructuring.
    1. Examine the behaviors and attitude in question from the protagonist's perceptions.
    2. Examine the opposite behaviors and attitude from the perspective of another protagonist or examine same behavior from the perceptions of significant others.
    3. Relate the consequence(s) of the behavior(s) to the perceptions held by both the protagonists and/or the observing others.

4. Affect and emotional flexibility change.
    1. Establish a relationship between the protagonist and a person, place or thing which involves emotion or affect (e.g. tenderness, anxiety, mastery, confusion, love, longing, etc.)
    2. Detail **movement** in the relationship (e.g. moving with, moving toward, moving away, orbiting, etc.)
    3. Detail the internal physiological changes that coincide with the building emotion in the protagonist (be sure to overlap with the client's behavior.)

5. Self image thinking enhancement.
    1. Detail the protagonist's central self-image and desired experiential resources.
    2. Detail rehearsal of the central self-image through several scenarios involving increasing difficulty or potential anxiety.
    3. Culminate with the use of an emanated image of success in a future context that resulted from reliance on the acts rehearsed in the scenarios.

Illustration 33

a story, like the one I know about a woman who started a corporation called Corporate Management. And she was dating the boss.

This woman bought all the stock around and finally owned 51% of it and fired her boss, who she broke up with, and now she owned the company. It's a huge money-making corporation. Now I could tell the story as if I didn't know what got in her head that made her think she could do this, but she fired the boss and took his position in the company. Now I've already led the listener to believe that the woman did a foolish thing. So if the client was inclined to think the woman was going to foul it up, then he'd think, "I know how that story ends." But at the end of the story, it turns out she's doing fantastically well at this corporation. And that is the truth!

Something has gone wrong with the client's projection. You've baited him to project his attitude and then you've demonstrated that it is wrong. At that point his attitude would have to be the subject of some quick rethinking, and there is not time to rethink. Where did he go wrong? What was the explanation? How could he have made this mistake? The conscious mind just can't handle figuring it out. So the best choice is just to forget it. And what he forgets, temporarily, is that part of his logic we refer to as his attitude. So you have a therapeutic moment where the attitude is being questioned. That is what we are trying to do with the attitude protocol.

Now, let's look at the protocol itself. There are three components: one protagonist needs to behave or perceive in ways that are similar, if not identical, to the client's behavior and perception. A second protagonist will most likely behave or perceive in the opposite way. Finally, the conclusions or the consequences of those attitudes are revealed. This is essentially like the Aesop fable method of making a point: Compare and contrast the consequences of actions held by two different protagonists, like the little boy who cried "wolf" and the townspeople who didn't appreciate his little joke.

In the Paco tape we had one protagonist who gave up due to peer criticism and the other who did not pay attention to the attributions of his peers. The outcome was that the protagonist who learned to ignore the other's comments and ignore many other things finished college, while the other protagonist did not.

For the exercise about constructing attitude metaphors, we want you to look at your partner's ICL graph [Illustration 8] and determine from over- or under-used behaviors what *may* be an attitude that is likely to be detrimental *in some circumstances* in his or her usual life. Then plan an attitude protocol that will challenge that attitude using this guideline [Illustration 33]. For example, if you see the friendly-submissive quadrant conspicuously empty on your partner's graph, you know that this person has, for some reason, avoided identifying with any of those adjectives. Ask yourself what type of attitude the person might hold about behaving in those friendly-submissive ways that has prevented him from comfortably developing and seeing those characteristics as representative of him in some way. Attitudes like "It is a sign of weakness if you want to be taken care of" or "If you want something done right, do it yourself!" may come to mind. It doesn't matter that you identify the exact one that your partner might voice, you'll still be on the right track. In real therapy, of course, all too often you have the opportunity to hear your clients' attitudes being clearly expressed in the clichés they use and the lectures they give to one another (or to you) about how people behave. In the exercise, we would like you to do the planning simultaneously and without consulting your partner. When you are both prepared, deliver the metaphors, one at a time. To help reduce the anxiety of the speaker, we want the listener to close his or her eyes to simulate the trance. [Exercise proceeds.]

All right, how many of you succeeded? Fine. Now, for you *as clients*, how many got an emotion? How many learned a behavior? No one? Good. How many of you had thoughts provoked or began to consider new options *as a cognitive possibility*? All right! I think you can see that this *is* an attitude-challenging procedure. We need to remind you of what we may have already stated. You can evoke a feeling with this because you can evoke a feeling with anything you say *when* the image or idea you use happens to be idiosyncratic to emotional material in the client's life. But separate that from the structure of the protocol itself! Evoking a feeling while using this protocol is accidental and you cannot always predict that in advance. The typical results of this protocol, on the other hand, you can predict in advance.

Erickson said that one of the most destructive things he saw in a family was the evangelistic attempt of one spouse trying to reform another spouse into something else.[22] We think this aspect that Erickson spoke about is a result of a pathological pattern that precedes it. This may show up as a desire to convert a spouse, but it may also show up as a way of disassociating and alienating a spouse. This is one of the most pressing and damaging problems that we find in families and I think you'll be able to say that you find this in almost every family difficulty. It is a certain form of overgeneralizing we call *caricaturization*, or perhaps a worse term is *personification-aling*. I think we may have coined those appalling words! This kind of overgeneralizing begins when one partner ascribes a *motive* to the other,

---

[22]A discussion of this by Erickson can be found in Haley, J. (Ed.) (1985). *Conversations with Milton H. Erickson, M.D., volume II: Changing couples* (pp. 9-12). New York: W. W. Norton.

based on the observation of some small behavior problem, and then equates the presence of one or more motives to an undesirable pattern that is personified by someone else. Such a situation calls for interventions of at least three kinds: disruption when it occurs, reframing when it is brought up, and an attitude change protocol when the offending spouse is in trance. Let's go into this for a moment.

Here is how it works. Let's say I see Carol biting her nails and I accuse her of being self-defeating—spending time and money to get nice nails but at the same time biting her nails. That is me attributing a motive to her. Do you hear it? I am saying she is motivated to self-defeat. Okay, that is not too bad yet. Now let's suppose she does something else that catches my attention in this way—say, losing a sweater. If I then say you are just going the same route as your mother—and this could be uncle Charlie, or aunt LouLou—then I am giving a *caricaturization*. I'm saying that a part of her is like someone else who is, of course, undesirable. The insidious part is that it is based on motives, a make-believe concept that is invisible for starters, and then laced with overgeneralization masquerading as logic. This is really destructive family hypnosis.

When the mind of the one partner frames fragments of behavior as an indication of this personification, it is like a bad psychoanalyst calling you "resistant": If you agree, you are resistant and if you disagree, you are really resistant! It separates people from each other. It stops cooperation of spouses. It scares each person into delving into a part of their map of experience in which they are stripped of resources for coping with the manufactured problem. It must be stopped so that each person can be free to be him- or herself and be appreciated for the unique person he or she is.

The attitude protocol is perfect for challenging this belief. You ought to have a few examples in your repertoire that can be molded for each unique individual you see. For instance, there are a number of incidents in life where the occurrence of a single event is certainly not like anything else but might seem that way to an illogical or ignorant observer. One is an eclipse—it is not like the end-of-the-world fantasies invented by a tribal superstition. Another is the first appearance of a green stem from a seed that appears above ground. How can one be sure it is a weed and not a flower until it matures? I trust that you can make these ideas into attitude metaphors? Okay, how? Yes, you present one protagonist who expects the worst and one who does not and you allow the use of drama to sort of engage the listener into jumping to conclusions, based upon his or her own belief system. Then, at the conclusion of the story you show that the unpredicted outcome was the proper course of logic.

Other examples come from your own practice and life. Haven't you had clients who dropped out of college to the dismay and false prophecies of parents only to become successful and respected in their chosen fields? Erickson loved to give lengthy examples of individuals, like Edison who lost his backers, Ford who was crazy enough to think that there could be a horseless carriage, the Wright brothers who were so dazed as to imagine that a machine that was heavier than air could fly, and so on! One day I recall Erickson giving over an hour of examples of impossible scientific achievements that did work in the end. These included vaccinations for small pox, the steam locomotive, the X-ray, those I just mentioned, and more. The attitude protocol makes the listener wonder if the predications he or she has made are accurate. And then Erickson would use the moments of doubt that followed to elaborate upon a more loving and constructive use of personal resources.

Affect Protocol

Now our second goal in the Paco therapy was to help him have a feeling of belonging. That was the therapeutic point that we made by telling about Wolfgang joining the group on the pier. The way to tell a story so that an emotion will be created is to first define a relationship that involves some kind of affect. The protocol that describes feelings is applicable to the study of emotional arousal in any one of several therapy or dramatic contexts. The form of human involvement in relationships suggests that a similar process is taking place in human experience whenever emotion is evoked. The process of the individual's change in perceptions and changing experience gives the only clue about the structure that evokes emotion in a variety of contexts. These contexts can include story, drama, cinema, gestalt therapy, hypnotherapeutic metaphors, social interaction, fantasy, etc.

How many of you saw *Master Harold and the Boys*? It is a perfect example. It is about the effect of apartheid on black/white relations in South Africa. There are two main protagonists. One is Master Harold, the little kid whose father employs black servants, and the other is one of the black servants. In the bulk of this play, what you have are the flashback scenes the boy and the servant create by speaking to one another about the great times they have had. You learn some other things as well about how the servant carried the boy home on his shoulders when his father was drunk in a bar. And how they flew kites together, since the father couldn't be there. You really understand that this servant has been a father to this boy.

The quality of experience in creating the character, the quality of affect and character development, will tell you what kind of relationship they are going to have. Remember *Sophie's Choice*? There the quality of the relationship was absurd. The flashbacks had absurdity to them. So we knew that there was going to be a tragedy or an absurd type of drama.

Now in *Master Harold* we have two people who are like father and son. And they had a lot of fun. But then my mind says, "Okay, but I haven't got a comparison and a contrast situation of two different perceptions and behaviors. This playwright is not going to elicit an attitude in me. I'm not learning any behaviors here. It's got to be an emotion-eliciting story. And when the relationship changes, I am going to have an affective experience."

For instance, if Lassie gets locked into an ice cream truck and goes to Alaska, Jeff is going to be sad and I am going to cry. What is another good example here? You know those shows on the Jeffersons when finally George does something that is endearing and they hug one another? They get a feeling out of that because they have been apart most of the time in their relationship and then something will happen and they come together. So we have character development. The two positive characters come together and you feel tenderness and love [Formula 1, Illustration 34].

So the point here is that step two in an affect protocol is movement. It can be any kind of movement. You can move the characters apart, they can chase one another, they can flee from one another, and so on, if you have an antagonist and a protagonist. So I will show you some formulas for that in just a minute.

AFFECT CONSTRUCTION FORMULAS

Character:	1. Pro. Other	2. Pro. Other	3. Pro. Other	4. Pro. Other
Attributes:	+ +	+ +	+ --	+ --
Change:	→ ←	← →	X ←	← ←
Outcome:	Tenderness	Sadness	Scare	Fear
Extreme:	Love	Grief	Panic	Helpless
Character:	5. Pro. Other	6. Pro. Other	7. Pro. Other	8. Pro. Other
Attributes:	+ −	+ --	+ −	+ −
Change:	→ X	→ →	->->->X	X →
Outcome:	Aggression	Anger	Success	Relief
Extreme:	Courage	Rage	Confidence	Celebration
Character:	9. Pro. Other	10. Pro. Other	11. Pro. Other	12. Pro. Other
Attributes:	+ +	+ +	+ +	+ +
Change:	->->->X	→ →	X X	X X
Outcome:	Excitement	Frustration	Resignation	Tolerance
Extreme:	Belonging	Hopelessness	Meaningless	Autonomy
Character:	13. Pro. Other	14. Pro. Other	15. Pro. Other	16. Pro. Other
Attributes:	+ +	+ +	+ +	+ +
Change:	X ->->	X >>>>	X |||| →	X-X
Outcome:	Rejection	Protective	Hurt	Safe
Extreme:	Abandonment	M/Paternalism	Hatred	Security

Illustration 34

I want to elaborate the concept for you by comparison and contrast. I don't want you to take a single example and try to make all of your stories come out that way. In affect formulas, I want to show you the different choices you might have. Let's look at belonging here. If my protagonist is positive, as in the case of Paco and the story of Wolfgang, and if the other protagonists he is seeing are positive, there is a positive relationship. At a distance then—and my character gradually moves toward the stationary other characters—you'll feel excitement or belonging [Formula 9, Illustration 34]. And you know that from movies you have seen.

We won't be able to go into detail about all of these formulas in this workshop but we can give examples of the ones we will use most in therapy. For starters, let's take what was just said about Formula 1 and interpret all of the symbols on this sheet. There are 16 formulas here. These do not make an exhaustive list but they are remarkably rich with variations. Another thing about this set of formulas is that it is our *basic* set of formulas for emotional and affect episodes in stories and in life. They are two-dimensional formulas. There are also at least two other ways of charting the changes that result in feelings. These ways include a three-character interaction instead of a two-character interaction, and also emotions that happen in what might be called a four-dimensional formula that involve certain ordering of these episodes. But that is all too advanced for the purposes of this workshop and the time we have. And, more important, the way to learn something complex is to start at the foundation. I suspect you will find this advanced enough!

The illustration (34) places each formula into five rows. The first two go together and show the valence given to the protagonist (pro.) and the other person or thing in the story (other). This is represented with a " + " and a " − " sign and sometimes with a double " − " sign to indicate very negative characters. This "positive" and "negative" character aspect must be indicated in the character development part of the protocol as you define the relationship.

Row two uses arrows to show the direction of movement in the characters and the change of the relationship. We'll speak about those in a minute. Now the rows labeled "outcome" and "extreme" refer to the bodily and cognitive component that may be elicited respectively. The arrows with tails mean self-motivated movement as in the case of the coming together we discussed in Formula 1. If there is an "X," as in Formulas 3, 8, 11, and so on, it is used to indicate there is no movement of a character. You can see then that resignation and tolerance (Illustration 34, Formulas 11 and 12) have to do with two characters that get no closer or no further from each other and the affect depends upon whether one character is a negative anxiety-producing agent or not.

That will almost explain all of them but you see some strange symbols in Formulas 7, 9, and 13 through 16. Formulas 7 and 9 use short little arrows to show a gradual movement that culminates with a conclusion of reaching the other person. For confidence (Illustration 34, Formula 7) a protagonist must move gradually towards a goal that is (at least perceived) as negative or anxiety-producing. At each step of the gradual and systematic movement, the protagonist, as in real life, will find the resource necessary to adequately proceed to the next step. That is, the goal will seem difficult but each step is actually manageable. An excellent example is the movie, *The Karate Kid*. In that movie the boy has to meet a challenge of another boy for his self-respect and the attention of a girl. The challenge has become a karate match (very threatening) and the protagonist realizes or thinks that he cannot succeed when he looks at it. But, and this is a big "but," he learns that he can do a lot of little things—polish a car, sand a deck, paint a fence, and so on. Every small step that he takes he finds easy and suddenly realizes that he has accumulated enough learnings to succeed at his goal. Likewise, the protagonist moves to increasingly more difficult tasks at each of the preliminary stages of the tournament competition. He finds he has the resources for each stage of progress and, of course, they systematically lead him to accomplishing his overall goal. This movement provides a feeling of confidence for the protagonist and viewer, and that is the kind of movement the arrows represent in Formula 7.

The only other odd notation is for rejection and protection (Illustration 34, Formulas 13 and 14). In formula 13 the positive other leaves the protagonist, and in 14 we see arrow heads only to represent the idea of the positive other being pulled away from the protagonist but not leaving voluntarily. Now that summarizes our nomenclature, so let's go into detail with other common affects as we did with Formulas 1 and 7.

In many of the current dramas, the man and the woman move toward one another. In older flicks the woman was stationed as passive and the man moved towards her. That would be a perfect example of the excitement building up. As you see Rhett Butler moving towards Scarlet, the feeling of excitement mounts. If they are both coming towards each other, it is slightly different. There is more of a tenderness going on there. If Wolfgang moves towards a group of people who are positive and finally joins them, he's accepted. There is some excitement as he moves and there is belonging when he gets there. So that is the formula here [Formula 9, Illustration 34].

It could have been different. Remember *Alien*? That is a good example of scare and panic. Here we have the protagonists, all the nice human beings, and the alien is the double negative antagonist. As the creature comes towards you, you feel scared [Formula 3, Illustration 34]. And worse still, if it comes towards you and you move away from it, you get more scared because you are admitting that you are helpless [Formula 4, Illustration 34].

If the monster went away and if the protagonist was positive, the antagonist was negative, and the change is that the protagonist stays put and the monster leaves, what a relief that is [Formula 8, Illustration 34]! The wicked witch is dead, so there is celebration as long as you are not the one who killed her. If you are the one who killed her, that is a different story; but if you are just the people in the city, then you can freely celebrate the witch being dead. If you are positive and the witch won't budge and you move towards her, you encourage your aggression. And when the troops you are chasing flee—say they are negative and you are positive—when you move towards them and they leave, then you feel anger [Formulas 5 and 6, Illustration 34]. What we are talking about is the movement of object relations in the map of experiencing in a person's head when he or she listens to a story, watches a movie, experiences real life, whatever it happens to be.

When that object relations change follows this pattern [referred to above], our theory here is that your requisite response would be to have the bodily reaction of the emotion. Define the relationship, show some kind of a movement, and, finally, focus the person on the body. *Master Harold and the Boys* is a perfect example. The worst thing that you can imagine happening happens here. I knew that I was in for an emotional change.

Now, in *Master Harold and the Boys*, what could there be that moves the servant and the boy together when they are close already? It is unlikely they are going to move together. That leads to one other choice. The author's going to move them apart and I am going to feel bad [Formula 2, 15, or 16, Illustration 34]. And I knew ahead of time that was what was going to happen. But I was surprised at what happened. They get into a little tiff. And the boy says, "You have to call me Master Harold." The servant says, "Don't ask me call you master." That will change everything. It looks as if the boy is going to say he is sorry. But they are both positive, and the movement is threatening to be moving them apart.

In this play the movement is rapid and barriers are put up. The boy spits in the servant's face. You feel hatred. It is so strong and so rapid. After an hour and a half of positive relationships being built up, wham, the protagonists are separated and you can't get them back [Formula 15, Illustration 34]. The whole audience gets spit upon.

The playwright then actually focuses on the bodily reactions just perfectly, in two ways. First of all the servant is about to punch out the kid. Another servant grabs him and says, "Don't do it." Then the main servant replies, "Think how you would feel in the same circumstances." He quickly recounts the history he and the boy have had together. And our secondary servant, listening, becomes tense and breathes more. He grits his teeth. And when the main servant gets to the part where he recounts, "Now he spits in your face" (in this rundown), the secondary servant, true to our formula, has his fist up and is ready to punch. So everyone watching gets to identify with that molding of the bodily reaction. It is absolutely nothing more than a perfect replication of this protocol. Focus the listener on the bodily reaction that the protagonist is having.

And the listeners will be having the reaction, too, a little bit. So you are really focusing it on them, too. They have an object relation change in their head; they are psychologically prepared to have a feeling, and you focus them on a small inner body reaction that will correlate. And they find some of that feeling. So if I create a positive relationship between Wolfgang and a group where he gradually moves closer to them, and they don't go away or move towards him (if they go away we create frustration [Formula 10, Illustration 34]), then he should feel a feeling of belonging [Formula 9, Illustration 34]. The protagonist should *be* belonging and have a *feeling* as well. And I can tell a story that describes the protagonist's body, making sure that I also focus on my listener's body in such a way that I blur the boundary between my protagonist and my listener. When you saw this happen to Paco on video, it was great because he is down in a slumped posture; and when the story came to the conclusion, where our protagonist ought to be feeling a feeling of belonging, Wolfgang has gotten about a foot taller and so has Paco and he is smiling.

For this exercise, I want you to look at your partner's ICL graph and determine an emotion that is likely to be used very rarely in his or her usual life and then plan an emotion protocol using one of the formulas presented on this overhead [Illustration 34]. I would like you to do the planning simultaneously and without consulting your partner. When you are both prepared, deliver the metaphors one at a time.

Behavior Protocol

The process of ensuring that listeners will make associations to behaviors and not cognitive processes or emotions is very simple. The hardest part is to eliminate any mention of motive from your metaphor. If motive is present, listeners will either disidentify or have emotional involvement with the story.

As can be seen from the overhead [Illustration 33], the requirements of the protocol are very easy to meet. Basically, the protagonist is to be told about several internal and external behaviors, and the listening client will

be told in several different contexts. This is like TV cooking shows or car-
pentry shows. No motive is given and portions of the behavioral operation
are detailed completely.

If courtship behaviors are the intended focus, the listener can be given
several explicit methods for asking for a date or for kissing or for conduct
of courteousness on the date. The entire gamut of behaviors is not needed
in detail. Most important, the motive of the learner is not given. The behaviors can then be studied by the listening client for the performance
quality and not for the value they contain.

To refer back to the Paco demonstration, our third goal there involved
a behavioral goal and a version of this protocol. We wanted to teach him
behaviorally specific ways to alter to the point of absurdity the self-critical
behaviors in which he was almost constantly engaged internally. In this
case, the detailed behaviors were ones he could use interpersonally with
anyone who actually criticized him, and especially internally in response
to his own criticism that had resulted from almost every stimulus in his
environment concerning other people and his perceptions about what they
were probably thinking of him. So we simply spoke about a protagonist
named "Kathy" and gave very little background regarding how we came
to know her or why she needed this lecture on improving the way she
criticized herself. Paco knew all about one set of self-critical behaviors and
used them regularly, but he had a lot to learn about the self-critical methods
we taught Kathy. Primarily, Paco learned some exaggerated, ridiculous,
and even humorous ways in which a person can criticize himself and respond to criticism from others.

For this exercise, again look at your partner's ICL graph and this time
determine a behavior that is likely to be used very rarely in his or her usual
life. Then plan a behavior protocol that will stress a half-dozen external and
a few internal behaviors related to this social conduct. You need to retrieve
any behaviorist training from your past so as to plan very behaviorally
specific examples to include in your story.

Remember, you are not making anyone do anything. You are not installing
behaviors or any such thing. You are simply offering the client an opportunity to expand the internal map with regard to these behaviors which, for
some reason, were not learned, reinforced, allowed, or whatever in their
family of origin and/or in the current family structure. In the safe objectivity
of just listening to a story, the client has the opportunity to consider these
behaviors and to incorporate them in whatever way is relevant and appropriate. It is important to remember for the sake of this learning experience
that delivering these isolated metaphors is not representative of the way we
are proposing you do therapy. This is just a way to learn the protocols.
These behaviors have been avoided for some reason—usually some attitude,

at the very least, that has discouraged or made the behaviors seem unacceptable. Therefore, just detailing the behaviors for the client won't necessarily ensure any integration of them into the client's actual life. In fact, as happened with one person in a workshop who agreed to be the subject in a demonstration of behavior protocol, she experienced uncomfortable conflict as a result of hearing behaviors detailed to which she had cognitive objections. In order for the behavior protocol to be optimally "processed" by the client, then, we need to make sure we have sufficiently challenged the attitude that prevented such behaviors or stimulated new attitudes that do allow those behaviors.

Self-Image Thinking Protocol

In most sessions, as was also the case in the Paco tape, we generally address attitude, affect, and behavioral goals as the first steps. We almost always want to follow that phase of the therapy with some kind of self-image update so that clients can see themselves reflecting the new attitudes, feelings, and behaviors in their own, real life situations. This accomplishes that "reassociation of experiential life" that we wrote about so often in *The Answer Within*. In other words, we want the resource experiences we have just retrieved in therapy to be associated to and actually stimulated by the sights, sounds, events, and significant others in the person's life outside the therapy session.

The self-image thinking part was accomplished with Paco as he made a visual image of himself with the new resources interacting in situations that concerned his work, his girl friend, and his peers. In the multiple embedded metaphor format, it is often useful to do the self-image protocol while using the protagonist from a previous protocol and goal, most typically the one used in the second story which is usually where new affect is retrieved. In this case, that character was Wolfgang and the feeling was belonging. After completing the affect protocol and retrieving the feeling, the story of Wolfgang was suspended but not formally concluded. We still had the unresolved drama about how he traveled across a whole continent in one afternoon. Meanwhile, attention was diverted with the next story tangent about self-critical behavior. Finally, we returned to Wolfgang still sitting there in our office in the trance he had been in while remembering the Canadian pier experience. It was at that point that we initiated the self-image protocol, mentioning that he left our office and got on a bus to go home. The bus made it very convenient to speak about the reflection of the self that a person can see in the window as you ride along.

The protocol for self-image metaphors is quite straightforward. It basically involves directing the protagonist through the steps of seeing the self with desired psychological characteristics visually reflected in some way and seeing that self interacting through a variety of scenarios involving significant others. A third, sometimes optional, part involves having the protagonist project him- or herself some years into the future when desired goals have been accomplished and then review the steps taken to make those dreams come true and arrive so successfully into the future.

So to follow this "simple, straightforward" protocol, all we have to do is to retrieve the desired psychological characteristics and include some device that makes it logical for the protagonist to be looking at a reflected self and imagined interactions. Actually, we don't even have to have a protagonist. We could just direct the client through these steps. We often do it in just that way, whether the client is in or out of trance. But for the sake of indirection, continuity, and flexibility, let's just say a little more about using the metaphor option.

First of all, it is very important to take frequent tangents from talking about the protagonist seeing himself or herself so that you tell the client in the present tense to "see yourself." You should hear yourself say, "See yourself" about 100 times during the course of one of these metaphors. One way we manage that is by saying something like: "I had to tell her to 'look carefully at yourself and notice how pleased you can be when you see that (whatever) reflected there on your face and in your posture' "; or "She was having that experience that everyone has when you suddenly catch a glimpse of your face and can be surprised at the subsequent interaction you imagine." If you are in some relationship (therapeutic is best) with the protagonist so that you can logically be saying these things to him or her, the "you" pronoun is very easily managed. Or, if not, simply make full use of poetic, therapeutic license to just switch verb tense and pronouns right in the middle of your sentence.

Having some reflecting device built into the story explains the protagonist actually seeing the self (and desired traits) reflected and only imagining the interactions with significant others. Of course, your clients will be doing both, except on those creative occasions when you might bring in a mirror and ask them to open their eyes in trance. But generally, just as we avoid the use of mechanical devices with Ericksonian inductions, we usually opt for having clients utilize the far more personal associations they can make internally in response to our suggestions about seeing the self. So we might be talking about the protagonist looking at himself in a bus window or reflecting pool or mirror, or in the sunglasses of a companion, or whatever, and then mention that a background can be added such that the person begins to see the self interacting with significant others while keeping constant the desired psychological characteristics, regardless of the others' response.

Now just a word about this matter of the desired psychological characteristics. The self-image protocol, when used with other metaphors, is designed to utilize the resources earlier retrieved. So, with Paco, we recapped
the observable indicators that both he and Wolfgang had demonstrated
during the belonging story and we mentioned in the story that Wolfgang
saw those indicators reflected in his face as he sat there looking into that
bus window. It should go without saying—but we will say it anyway—that
when these resources have not been retrieved with earlier metaphors they
will have to be retrieved and described one at a time as the protagonist and
client add them to the imagined picture of the self. This can sometimes be
accomplished with fairly direct suggestion if clients have available and
organized the resource experience you want them to put into the self-image.
It is often the case that people have a well developed resource that they use
easily in many situations but just aren't able to get into certain problem
contexts. In those cases, direct suggestion to retrieve that resource and add
it to the picture can be followed with suggestions about how to mentally
rehearse the self interacting with that resource in those situations where it
had not been previously available. Otherwise, for less developed experiences, it will probably be necessary to use the other protocols, anecdote
and indirect suggestion.

Family Structure Change Protocol

Now you didn't see an example of the family structure change protocol
in the Paco tape but it follows nicely from what we have covered. Look at
the illustration [Illustration 33]. You see that the goal is to help the client
speculate that symptomatic relief for a problem, although entirely different
than the current family problem, subsides when a similar family structure
is changed. That is to say that the family structure, which is like their own,
is in some way contributing to problems and symptom formation. We won't
have you do an exercise on this but you will see this in an upcoming family
interview.

You will recognize that with this protocol—somewhat like the self-image
protocol—you are taking advantage of or utilizing and referring back to
behaviors, affect, and attitude restructuring changes that were retrieved and
illustrated in earlier metaphors. It is as though the other protocols create
and retrieve the component pieces that the individual members will require
to implement successful family structure change. Changes in family structure
are necessarily complex and involve changes in attitudes, affect, and behavior in order for family members to congruently and comfortably play
new roles requiring different communication and transactions.

To summarize and prepare you for what to look for, one story we expect to tell to the daughter in the upcoming family interview will conform to the family structure change protocol in several ways. First, the protagonist in the story is a young woman who is living with her family of origin, as is the case with the daughter. The protagonist's parents unnecessarily control and baby her while she does none of the separating and boundary building which is appropriate for someone in her age group. This is also the case for the daughter in the client family and therefore the family structure is similar, if not identical. Now second, the protagonist in this story presents a symptom of migraine headaches which is quite different from the more low level depression symptom manifested by the real daughter. So the symptoms are different. Finally, an account is related of how the protagonist progressed in various ways to implement needed changes in family structure such as developing her own interests, taking charge, setting limits—in short, separating and boundary building. In the last step of this protocol, the symptom "just goes away," mysteriously as it were, but it is certainly implied at the psychological level to be a result of the change in family structure.

DEMONSTRATION OF THE FAMILY INTERVIEW

What we want to do in family therapy, in general, is use metaphor, anecdote, and indirect suggestion—interventions that, as we stated on the first day of this seminar, are largely taken from hypnosis. We have been stressing the impact of these interventions upon different levels of the system in such a manner that you should be able to see the effects are quite logical, and in certain ways these effects at each level are predictable. The next thing I want to do in the remaining time is have some people come up here and be a family. I don't want you to get together ahead of time and plan to have a child be a mass murderer or something. I just want to demonstrate the interplay of these techniques.

You, you, and you come up. And we need a female or two—come on up. This is a couple and two children. Names? "Elenore." "Doug." "Leonard." "Janet." Who is married to whom—Elenore and Doug? Leonard: "I am 17." "And how old are you, Janet?" "I am 13." Ordinarily, of course, I would have already gotten the interpersonal checklist. I already would know the problem and the family background. So I would know how old the people were and, of course, their names. So I'm a little bit behind here and have had to ask questions that I wouldn't normally have to ask.

I could proceed with something like, "I'm so glad each of you has finally made it here to the appointment. I know we had some difficulty setting this up and I'm real pleased that you have all shown enough motivation to make it here. I can't remember who made the appointment now. You did, Elenore?

Would you be willing to refresh us on why you've come. I would like to talk to each of you a little bit and find out how you feel about the things that are happening and what you'd like to accomplish. So let's start with you Mom, since you called.

Mom: Well, Janet has been skipping school and I just found out about it the other day. And she has begun to stay out all night. She is defying us. We can't get her to stop. Isn't that right, Doug?

Dad: We try to talk to her and she just storms out of the room and locks herself in there. It's either bang her out or wait till . . . well, that's why we're here, to try to get something resolved so we can talk about it at least.

Therapist: And you've exhausted your abilities at home, so you thought that perhaps a third party would make it possible to keep the ball rolling in the direction that you value since you really want the best for your children? You want to understand things about your children that you are still in the dark about? You thought that maybe a third party could help?

M: Actually, we want the ball to roll in a different direction.

T: Different than the one I suggested?

M: Different from the one we've been in.

T: Well, that's good because usually I notice that so often people fail to play hockey and have the learnings from that. . . .

T: And your name is Janet and you are 14?

J: Thirteen, but I'm really more like 18. I mean, they just don't give me credit. It's everything for him, I mean . . . it's all for him.

T: Well, one thing that 13-year-old kids can frequently learn is the importance of having their own opinion about things. So I'm glad you disagree with the opinions of the group about some things because otherwise you wouldn't be an individual. And I know your parents value that and want that despite the difficulties they've had bringing that about in a successful way. And she was talking about you a little bit there, Leonard.

L: I just want to finish high school and get on to college.

T: When do you graduate, this year?

L: No, I wish I did but it will have to be next year which is something I don't like.

T: Yeah, it will be nice for you to get out of this house and go ahead and . . .

M: [interrupting] He's a very good boy.

T: [addressing the boy] You wanted to say something else?

L: Well, my parents are real good but the thing is, I like to study in peace and quiet in the house.

T: Before you say anything more, something just occurred to me. [addressing Mom] Would you do me a favor? Uncross your legs and get a little bit more comfortable in the chair. And have you ever noticed that uh . . . we have a thermometer that is hooked up on the outside and the inside. And the outside thermometer doesn't work worth a damn and I don't know why. If it's really 50 degrees it will say 30 degrees. So what I do is I hold the button down and I watch it flip around and I sort of take the average. You have to be real sensitive to the internal environment and somehow the cold weather screws up its sensitivity. And I think oftentimes in families there is a good bit of environment that could be warmer. And so I'd like you to concentrate just a moment in a more relaxed state, and just concentrate on your stomach. In fact, close your eyes if you would. And concentrate on your stomach as if you were a thermometer. I want to ask your opinion about something that your son is saying when he is done speaking. And you probably have some idea but you're going to be wrong. So withhold your judgment on what it is I'm going to ask you. You'll probably be surprised.'' So (to group), what will happen here is she will shut up and she won't interfere.

[T addressing son now] Okay, so I wanted you to hold that thought. Now go ahead, you said you wanted some peace and quiet.

L: Yeah, I did. Well, you know I don't get into a lot of trouble. It's not asking too much to be able to come home and be able to study at night, study my algebra and my biology because, you know, I just want to do well and make good grades. But the problem is when I'm concentrating and trying to study, I hear all the screaming and yelling in the house, sometimes with Dad, sometimes with Janet. I get confused. I don't know what is happening. I feel like maybe I should be out of the house. I think maybe I should move away. I don't know why.

T: This is one of the really difficult decisions that a person may make in his or her lifetime. [T addressing Dad now] You've learned to stand on your own two feet and be an independent man. Oftentimes this is done without fathers telling the child the way they really feel about things. And while your wife is listening and being a barometer for something that she thinks I'm going to ask her, would you think back and just take a tangent for a moment so that everyone will be able to feel a little more comfortable here. Think back to how you learned to be an independent man and what it was that was present or lacking in things that your father mentioned to you. Don't tell me what it is, I just want you to think about it for a minute. [to son] While he is thinking about that, watch his face. The more sincerely he remembers that, the more his face will tell a story.

Now, Janet, while everyone is sitting here doing little tasks, I wonder if you can feel how you feel. Are you relaxed in a situation where Mother is calm, breathing nicely, and father is thinking about something? You like the silence? Is there anything you'd like to tell them? You were thinking that something is nice and I often wonder if your parents recognize how you like their company. Sometimes a person says something . . . I know I had a client one time who said to her husband, "I like your sweater." And her husband said, "You mean you didn't like the one I wore yesterday?" So when you say it is nice that it is quiet, it would be useful for everyone to realize you are not saying something negative. You are saying something positive. So think about how you might say that. But wait before you speak here. You've been in a lot of trouble in this family and I don't want you to jeopardize your situation by speaking too soon.

[T still addressing Janet, primarily] I worked with a young man one time who came to see me. He wanted to go into business for himself. He wasn't real sure what he wanted to do, but he knew that being his own boss would be a useful thing. And of course everyone has their own ideas when they hear stories about how people succeed. And each person learns something different about it. But there is a certain learning I am aiming at here that I want to share. And any other learnings are fine, of course, but what this young man did in therapy . . . well, I got him to be very quiet in the trance sessions for a couple of days and to just let me talk. And while he was listening, I explained the way you go about showing someone that you appreciate them. It's so important in the business world. You can compliment people. Everyone knows what a compliment is. You can praise another person. I don't have to tell you . . . I said to him, the way that you say "I like you" to somebody or "I feel good about something" to somebody. Now oftentimes children growing up have good feelings that they are afraid to share with their parents. And they bring this fear with them into adulthood. So it was obvious that this young man had learned a problem in childhood. [addressing Mother briefly] I hope you're listening to some of these ideas from the standpoint of how your barometer feels, Elenore, because I'm going to ask you in a minute to say something about it. And what I noticed was how this fellow had grown up depressed because he had so many good feelings he wanted to share but didn't know how to make his parents understand the good feelings that he had. And I don't know how a person can fail to learn how to praise and compliment.

 Your father now has been thinking about things that you were told or weren't told when you left home. And in the vein of what I was just saying, I wonder if you [Dad] have some observations. You might want to share them with your son at some point because it is imminent that he will be leaving the house. And I know that you want him to capitalize on your past learnings. [addressing wife now] Now while your husband is talking, I want you to listen to how things feel. [to husband] So what I am asking you is, do you know what I am asking you? You're having some thoughts and I want you to tell me what you're thinking about.

D: I was thinking about my early jobs to earn some money and buy a car.

T: How early?

D: Oh, 16, as soon as I got my driver's license and it made me feel real good that he trusted me with that responsibility so I could earn money.

T: How do you think you would have felt if he hadn't trusted you with it? Do you think that would have retarded your separation a little bit? I know you don't want to have that kind of hurt shared with your daughter, so a real concern here—and I know you would agree—is how you can demonstrate trust for her, especially since. . . . Did you ever wonder which comes first, the chicken or the egg?

[T addressing Mom now] All right, now I've been saying a few things to different people here and I just wonder if you could share your feelings about yourself as they have spoken.

M: About the things I want to say?

T: How did that make you feel that you weren't getting to say them?

M: A little bit mad, shut off kind of.

T: You look a little sad saying that you are shut off.

M It is not a new feeling. T: Being shut off? From whom?

M: Everybody does it, they all have their lives. I'm just here.

T: Everybody, hmmm, there are three bodies here, huh.

M: All three.

T: Well, hold onto that for just a moment now.

And back to the group now, hold onto everybody for just a second. See what I've accomplished by getting the mother to concentrate on her problem? Mother's problem for me was that she was trying to be a negative co-therapist and get everything to look her way. But it doesn't matter if it looks her way because it is going to be screwed up because her way hasn't solved it for a long time already. So I have to change her way. One of the things about her way is that it is all external conversation about what everybody is doing wrong. So I wanted her to concentrate her attention on herself. That will accomplish interview management, if nothing else. Also, hopefully, you heard the interspersal voice tone shifts, for example, when I asked the mom, "How did you *feel about yourself* while other people were speaking?" I didn't ask her what she wanted to say or what was happening. I wanted a specific answer. I wanted her to tell me about herself, not everybody else. And then we would find out a little bit about her needs if she has enough strength to tell me. If she doesn't, then we have to stop her and (well, she does in this role play) do something different.

Now, how the daughter can compliment people is something she is going to need to do when she grows up. There may be some other things, but all I know right now is that she needs to learn how she can share her excitement. If she is a mystery to the family because nobody knows her motive, they'll project bad things onto her. So I've got to get her character development in this metaphor of this family's life. She's got to share herself somehow. And the others are not going to hear what she has got to say. So we have to turn that around. That means changing the reinforcement contingencies. I quickly noticed that the avenue to get her to do that was to compliment them. So that is my thinking so far. Now you hear my use of metaphor to interrupt them, to confuse them, and a little bit to retrieve resources. We haven't done a lot of that yet.

You are the family in question. How does it strike you so far? The son says he gets the feeling that the truth is getting aired here safely. The father has some question about whether our direction is going to get to the outcome that he hopes we are going to get to. His occupation in the role play is an iron worker. He's not dissatisfied with what is happening unless we prolong the phase where he doesn't see immediate or direct attention being paid to the presenting problem. Actually, I don't know that we would get wind of this potential dissatisfaction so soon because I would keep going with the wife telling about the feelings she has. And we are still in the part of "let's hear what all the complaints are in the family." At some point the husband would say, "I understand my wife is unhappy. Maybe we ought to work on that, too, but how does it relate to my daughter?" So then in the metaphor of iron worker or the metaphors I know would appeal to an iron worker, I need to explain how going through the back door is going to help us with what is up in the front door.

And then I might go on with something like, "Let me just add that, because sometimes I know there is somewhat of a mystery. We've been talking to your wife now for half of the 40 minutes. We've been together hearing about her feelings of sadness and I know you appreciate an opportunity for her to air them. And I want to say that I really compliment you for being flexible enough of a man. I know a lot of times people come in as manual laborers and think they are just going to chop a tree down and somehow that is going to solve the problem. And if that's not what you're doing, then something is wrong. It looks to me like you are a person who came in thinking that you wanted to deal fully with the problem of your daughter and you were willing to be open to hearing something that your wife said. I've seen so many men who are such fools that they won't take a moment to listen to what the wife's feelings are. I don't know if that is why she loves you or if she's thought about it that way recently, but her recognition that she can use this session to talk about the feelings of sadness she has, and some needs she has in the marriage, means she knows that you will listen. And I hope you take that as a compliment from her.

"But the importance of dealing with your daughter is important, too. And I know sometimes in a plant, for example—and I don't know if this has happened in your plant—management takes steps to solve a problem, but it doesn't seem apparent to the people on the line. You know, they order a new computer system, and what you really need is an extra man beside you there, or some new tools that aren't fraying out. And you think, 'What the hell, what I need here is a new pair of crimping tools, not a damn computer that's gonna cost thousands of dollars. Why don't they give me a raise or just buy me a new set of crimping tools?' And the long-term goals of management, if it is a successful company, actually are taking care of the needs of each individual. I don't know if you saw *Star Trek*, but it's like Spock saying that the needs of one are sacrificed for the needs of many, and I don't want you to sacrifice the needs you have, in helping your daughter change. But I do want to remind you of the logic that sometimes escapes people in a plant when they are on the line and they are dealing with the difficulties all the time, and sometimes the solution solves 100 problems but it is not apparent that it is even going to solve one of them at first. I wonder if you have ever noticed that in your plant. If you work in a successful plant, I know you know what I mean.

"I think one thing that is going to happen is the communication is changing. You came in with nobody talking about anything except difficulties with the daughter. Now, in the session, your daughter has told you that she loves you, that she is really pleased to be around you sometimes when it is quiet. Maybe Mom has a little bit to learn from you kids about sharing your feelings more often and in the open, especially with everyone's ability to respond favorably. And maybe you have a little bit to learn from her about a discipline that you have imposed on yourself even when you feel badly. And so what I see is a little bit of understanding beginning to happen between your wife and your daughter, and between your son and you, and between you and your wife. That is how I see it relating, even in this short session."

I want to say two additional things about that demonstration. What was seen in this family pertains to some overall points we are trying to make here. The more rigid the family is, the more the symptom will have two aspects to it. One, it will be carried by a single individual. And two, it will be symbolic of all problems in the family. I think I can probably make some conjectures here that will make this clear. So the more rigid the family, the more this is true and the less rigid the family is, the less this is true. I never came across that anywhere in print and I think it is a good thing to share. It's easy to pick up these little phrases that come floating along like, "a symptom is symbolic of the family." Well it is, providing the family is extremely rigid.

So by the term "rigid" we mean that in the family structure, the following occurs: Structure sanctions roles, roles limit communication, communication produces belief, and belief precludes the conscious use of unconscious resources. The more rigid the family, the more everything you see is only what you are going to get. The roles that are being played are the only roles that are going to be played. The communications that you see aren't going to change. Let's elaborate on what we mean.

In this mother's case, she came in sort of critical and controlling and tense, and then she showed us another side. She also had some anger that was apparently covering her sadness. She could focus on herself and not just be critical of others. So in other words, Mother is not as rigid as she could be. There is more role flexibility, perceptual flexibility, affect flexibility, and this is significant when using those original six diagnostic parameters. Remember that during assessment we asked ourselves about the sensitivity and flexibility of members to one another? Here is where the answers really matter. If Mother weren't less rigid, if these things weren't something that she would do, then we might expect the daughter to have an additional difficulty here. Perhaps she might be sexually promiscuous and getting caught at it: That would also be a part of the presenting problem.

Father, we see, was not just a person who said, "Let's get down to business, let's get this thing solved. You are wasting our time." That was part of where he was coming from, but he was also able to listen to the other people speaking. He was able to tolerate time being shared for other people's problems. And in the role, even though we didn't give him time to live it out fully, it was clear that he was going to listen to his wife's concerns. And he was also able to dig into his past memories and be kind of nurturing to his son. So if Dad weren't doing those things, he would be that much less flexible and this would be that much more of a rigid family. And the daughter would still have other components of the problem. See, Dad was willing to tolerate more thoughts than just that limiting line of thoughts.

Perhaps if he wasn't this way, we would find in the daughter a thought process that disintegrates when she speaks. That is, she would not stay on a single topic. She wouldn't stay on target at all. So her problem would represent that somebody else in the family needs to be able to loosen up his/her thinking and concentrate on more topics. And if that person won't do it, then a quick learner in the family will learn how to do it and try to compensate. The symptom carrier often, in an odd exaggeration, helps to strike a balance. This is not done in a purposeful or conscious way. When we observe this we are not saying that they are responsible . . . in fact, when people do this they are responsible for *not being responsible*! They are being controlled by system dynamics and not individual will and ambition.

And what if the son had some anxiety, too, so he wasn't just a wonderful kid? He had some problems that he wanted to talk about. Say he had some anxieties that he was uncomfortable with the noise. And he had some of his own perceptions and judgments that disagreed with one another. That is, let's say he had observable emotional conflict. If he had some difficulty so that there was more than just the superficial lack of problems, then there would be more rigidity there. And again, it would be a more rigid family.

Then from the daughter we might see a real hostility of some kind designed to remove herself so that the anxieties she felt would not be produced by action done around anybody else. She would need to use hostility to disaffiliate. Then instead of just a girl who is not going to school, we would see a sexually promiscuous, hostile girl who seemed to be having some thought disorders. But instead of all of the problems in this family being localized in one individual, it was a less rigid family. And so each person took their fair share. It was a United Way kind of family.

The more rigid the family, the more a symptom of one member is symbolic of all problems in the family. The more rigid, the more close that symbolic connection. But it doesn't matter if the son has anxiety; the father could have this anxiety and that would get rid of this aspect in the daughter. If the son was the one who couldn't stay on track, then she would still have these other problems but the son would take over the one problem of the father's. It doesn't matter who has the real problem in this discussion. I think the matter of who gets the difficulty first is just a matter of the family of origin and that these are the people coming together making a synthesis of some kind—and how smart the children are in consciously learning it and putting it together. In either case, I am just saying that it depends upon whether the better hynotists in the family are limited parents or creative and healthy parents or whether the best hypnotists are the children.

There is a dual induction tape we have that demonstrates unconscious learning. It was made to illustrate those dual induction variables we discussed earlier and that you practiced. Carol and I are talking about different things at the same time. She is talking about growing a garden and I'm talking about age regression. And the man who is our subject comes out of trance and he reports, "Well, I was having a marvelous time. I wasn't listening to either of you. I was walking down this pathway holding the hand of a little girl, down this garden path holding the hand of the little girl, and sometimes I was the little girl and sometimes I was holding her hand. It was really wild, but I wasn't listening to you guys." This is simply a synthesis of what we were both saying.

So how do you know exactly what unique synthesis this person comes up with? That is a good question. But I guess that is a matter of the subject's personal experience and ability to have the trance phenomenon under discussion. I think that is analogous to how a certain child will have that particular problem when these two parents get together and explain reality as he is growing up. Will he or she synthesize it as they intended or synthesize it a different way? So when he synthesizes it one way, he gets one problem and if he synthesizes it slightly differently, someone else gets a slightly different problem.

Basically this is what I wanted to demonstrate: How I would perceive that and the logic I'm using here. There is something to gain from sharing that with you and letting those seeds grow. Another point is if the individuals have more severity in their problems, what you tend to do is to build and organize resources for each of them. In this instance, when the mother had her eyes closed, I would have worked to help retrieve more resources for her. We take the person who is the most distressed consciously and, generally, have him use trance to get more of the resources he needs, or become prepared by means of the trance to learn the experiences and transactions needed in homework after the session.

If, for instance, a mother was also getting tense and beating a child infrequently, then when she had that kind of trance I would use it as an opportunity to go on into the realm of the kinds of experiences and resources she might want so she wouldn't have to substitute trying to calm the environment down by beating it. Now I don't know what that might be. Each individual family will have different requirements. These might be feelings of security or change of an attitude that she will not get rejected if there is a problem for which she seems to be responsible, or whatever it happens to be that is important for that unique individual. But that would be what we do with her at that point *in the session*.

And if the father was an alcoholic, while the mother was sitting there thinking about those trance learnings, I would use a paradoxical approach to explain something like this to him: "Go ahead and continue to deny reality. When there is a good deal of stress it's important for a person to operate well in a stressful environment, to do the best one can to deny *unnecessary stress*. But you don't need to deny stress by hurting yourself. Let me explain to you how you can deny stress more effectively." He may want to close his eyes during that. Probably at that point I would have Dad in trance learning how to use resources to deny stress, which will help him feel more able to cope. And that brings us to paradox.

CHAPTER FIVE

Increasing Role Flexibility: Paradoxical Prescriptions

PARADOX

We have mentioned paradox several times and we now need to take it up and examine some ways of constructing and delivering it. There are different levels of paradox. We haven't figured out a schema that is satisfactory to categorize all of them. There is paradox that deals with the immediacy of the moment and there is paradox that is of essential truths: "You are free to feel secure to the extent that you are free to experience your insecurity." The paradoxical symptom prescription is yet a different category. We think the latter is useful and important to use with almost every client, as we will explain. So we think our breakdown here is very useful and complete.

One of the things that tends to be underemphasized is the keeping of therapeutic leverage on the part of the therapist. That is step number four on the outline [Illustration 35]. You don't see that step at all in much of the other written material about paradox. Another thing that seems to be missing from most paradoxical approaches is building resources for a client so he or she is more likely to succeed at the developmental task in question. That is represented by number five here that says, "Present metaphoric or anecdotal illustrations of the needed resources. Digress into multiple metaphors to address treatment goals."

Now there is one other thing we especially value, and it doesn't get shared very often either. Usually what therapists do is they formulate the wording for the symptom prescription to *only* continue the undesirable behavior. In other words, an example might be, "Well, keep ignoring your

PARADOXICAL PRESCRIPTION

1. Empathically reflect an understanding of the family's or client's difficulty or utilize client's orientation with resistive clients.

2. Formulate the wording of the symptom prescription.

3. Present a reason within a positive framework for the prescription.

4. Create an alteration: splitting, adding on, or modifying intensity, frequency, or location of the symptom's occurrence.

5. Present metaphoric or anecdotal illustration of the needed resources. Digress into multiple metaphors to address treatment goals.

6. Deliver either first or last in the therapeutic session.
   Take an interpersonal posture that is not "one up" as it is delivered.

Illustration 35

son for the next couple of weeks." When therapists don't modify it in some way, they send the parent or whoever it is out without having any therapeutic leverage whatsoever.

Our first point of importance, the first step in therapeutic modification, is to present the reason for the prescription in a positive framework. Now that needs to be explained a little bit. You've got a diagnosis, right? Let's say you take Elenore's role from our demonstration and you know from quickly sizing her up that she is a woman who feels that people aren't going to respond to her sadness. She feels alone and abandoned, left here to do all the work. She wants a little help, but she doesn't know how to say it. Rather than saying it, she gets critical of other people. And if there is a problem that she can't solve by keeping silent about her own needs, she begins blaming. Well, how could you say all that about her in a positive way? That is the first important aspect that prepares for the paradox in a palatable way.

You would *not* say it from a psychodynamic framework. You wouldn't want to say, "You have a good deal of hostility that was probably originally aimed at your parents but now is being transferred on to your family, and it is so good that you are holding that inside of you and, instead, being only slightly critical of people." You wouldn't say that because it is not positive. It is psychodynamic. Also, of course, the proper use of insight type statements in analysis is a matter of very careful timing and is not dictated by the moments of the therapist's brilliance.

Think about what you are going to want to do treatment-wise with each person. One of the things you are going to want to do with Elenore is help her feel comfortable having her feelings and expressing them to other people. Actually having her cry and learning to ask for people to be close would be a very useful aspect for her. And maybe then you would want to start talking about sexual closeness, which she has probably not been having either. You would, in other words, have some sense about the direction in which it is going to go. Do you follow this so far? You know some of the components and therefore you know where it would be handy to go. And since you are strategically directing the show, speak about those things that relate to her needs. Maybe it's crying, maybe it's talking about sexual matters and closeness. You don't need any more time than we had here in order to make that judgment about her. Well, in some cases you do. In some cases you have people who you can't figure out what they are getting at, because you don't understand them enough or they are too obtuse. But most of the time you will. But if you don't know, then it is not the time to proceed with a paradoxical prescription.

So the point here is that it's not just using a symptom but using the whole person and where you think therapy will most likely go that will give you the way of positively framing this thing. You could say, "You are a woman with a great depth of sensitivity and feeling and I know that you know the value of closeness within your family. And no doubt it really distresses you to notice that there is somebody in the family who is disturbing the degree of closeness that is there. Because you are at that stage of development in the family where you appreciate that it is time to put the struggles of the economic past behind you and to embrace the adulthood that your children are having as they can hug one another and embrace one another. And you can smile at each other and ask for help from your husband and have him respond. And you can increase the degree of intimacy in your family in a number of ways. You are on the threshold of enriching the sexual life of your marriage here and understanding your children as adults. It must really distress you to realize that is in jeopardy right now when you see your family moving apart." She won't disagree.

You've just reframed everything exactly to tell the truth but in a completely positive way. The other truth of the matter is, from the daughter's perspective, "Mother is always riding my back and she won't let me alone. She doesn't recognize me and she thinks that everything has to go her way." Well, there is nothing wrong with her way as long as we emphasize the positive qualities of her way. And that is what we are doing here.

So when you say she is on the verge of doing those things, what is she going to say? "I'm not on the verge of improving my family. I don't want to get anybody happy or closer here." If she said that, then say, "Well, fine, call the session off." You've just spoken about all of the difficulties that she has that she has been unable to speak about, in a positive frame. But you've really not only helped her save face with these issues; you have helped bring them into the open in a framework that is acceptable. You've induced a learning set within the therapy session. And that is what we mean by putting this whole thing in a positive framework.

Now there is reason for saying, "I want you to continue to be extremely sensitive to people moving apart and being less than satisfactory in their performance at school and family. I want you to really be critical of deviations from what you know is the ideal, because your attempts to achieve that ideal are really the motivation for making you that full human being right now and bringing to you the closeness, sexuality, and tenderness that you deserve to have at this stage of your life."

You are not putting a trip on her. She could not say, "No, it's not that, I just want my daughter to stop running away from school and I want to remain a nerd." She is not going to say this (although, of course, she is free to do so if that is really necessary). So you've given a positive frame and, by doing that . . . well think about it. What is the point of doing that? The point of doing that is that your job will now be easier. That's all. Because you have done this, it is now going to be extremely easy to talk about any of those issues in therapy. When it gets down to this step about presenting metaphoric and anecdotal illustrations of the needed resources, and metaphors for treatment, the foundation will be very well prepared.

There is something else you want to do. You want to have therapeutic leverage. You don't want to just say to Mother, "Go ahead and continue to be critical of other people not living up to their optimal." You don't want to just say that, because if you do you don't have any control over how she does it. So you want to create an alteration in the symptom. The three ways that we put it are splitting, or adding, or modifying. Splitting and adding are especially useful. Modifying is a broad category where you increase the frequency, change the location, or increase the intensity of what occurs.

So how can we change the symptom while prescribing it to help ourselves get therapeutic control? Try this: "But I don't want you to just criticize your daughter randomly all day long when she is not listening to you. What I would like you to do is carry a pad of paper with you and jot down during the day when you have specific complaints. And keep a list so that at supper time we can take three or four minutes to choose the one or two important things that you'd like your daughter to listen to. In just a minute I'll tell you how I'd like you to tell her about them. But I think this will be much more efficient. It will make sure that you are giving yourself credit for keeping track of the infractions that you notice. And you won't be not heard because your daughter is off to change her makeup or something." We have only modified the location of the problem behavior and the frequency of it and Mother is not losing anything here. She is gaining a lot and I am gaining even more. I have opened up this whole area as therapeutic. And you have a contract. If she accepts that, unconsciously she is saying that there is something about that it is right, "I agree." And so you have a contract at the level of psychological communication to open into those areas in therapy. And if you are wrong, the client will correct you and help put you on track. The client may say, for instance, "Well, it is not that so much. You know, our sex life is good. It is just that he's not there enough." So, excuse me, we'll just cross that one out.

The next and perhaps most important step is to present metaphoric and anecdotal illustrations. And usually the way it goes is you say, "Let me show you the way I mean. . . ." Now you have to be able to use metaphor to make your point. So what is the point here? The point is that spreading things out is not as effective as putting them all in one spot. Well, I can think of several anecdotes to make that point: that things are different if they are spread out than if they are in one spot. For example, you can take medicine that you have and you can take it every three or four days to make sure it lasts longer. But then it won't work because you haven't taken it regularly enough to keep a level intensified. Another example is in blowing glass: "I don't know if you have noticed a glass blower at a shopping mall and how, when he works, the flame is intensified in one area," etc. Another example is keeping your tools in one spot so you don't need to look all over when you need to do a repair job. Another is: "A bird would be very foolish to place its eggs in six locations rather than in one nest. It would wear itself out trying to keep them warm."

So first you are using little anecdotes to illustrate exactly what you mean. You may then take a digression into the next metaphor. The next metaphor has to do with the importance of being close . . . apparently that is what she is trying to accomplish with her criticism. After all, you just informed her of that. So now we move with our anecdotes into closeness. It is an issue. So it won't seem irrelevant and Mother will still be with you. She is getting what she wants: something to train her daughter a little better. You just happen to be a little verbose and you will be speaking about and retrieving an experience that comes from tenderness. She will be crying at this point.

Well now, the next thing to talk about is people who are afraid to speak out and tell people what they are afraid of: "It would be a shame if a girl grew up in a family and didn't learn from her parents how to do that." And so you are still talking about what she needs to do with her daughter that is going to be helpful. And you have given her new tools. So now you have a behavior metaphor on how to ask for help and reach out and accept it. Well, you can let her think about that and go on to the next thing.

Now, back to altering the prescription of the symptom in various ways. What about those abusive or violent behaviors? Splitting is our preferred option there. Splitting means making certain that the behavior somehow goes into a dissociation. You want to do something with abusive or violent behaviors to stop that behavior. The way we do this is take the violent situation—let's say it is hitting for our example. Now we first track it backwards a couple of steps. Either ask the person or make some reasonable judgments about it. Before the person hits his children, he shouts at his children. Before he shouts at his children he gets tense. Before he gets tense he is preoccupied with work. So we are going backwards on the chain of events. In the forward sequence he gets preoccupied, then hears disagreement in the family, then gets tense, then starts shouting, then hitting. These are five steps that we can easily see. We don't have to get mechanically and mathematically precise here and he'll either agree with those words or he will just tell it to you.

The other angle of this is you are going to say, "Go ahead and do this (x) but you don't need to do this (y) anymore." You don't want to say, "You don't need to hit the kids anymore" because you don't want to sound like you are taking choices away. We have to offer something that he is going to be able to continue to do but it's not going to be to hit the kids.

So in this case again, you start your paradoxical prescription by formulating the wording of the symptom prescription. And thinking ahead will give a positive reason based on your diagnosis: "You're a man who knows that life is really difficult. There's no mamby-pamby getting by. A smile won't get you through anymore. Money is tight and times are hard and you need some discipline in order to survive. And I know that you don't want your kids to have the same kinds of difficulties that you had. You want to be able to run the household maximally and there is a lot on your mind. And you need ways of easing your tension. And you want to teach those to your kids. Well, I want you to continue to think of ways to discipline your kids or help them learn to survive difficulties more quietly, but you don't have to have that preoccupation with work that leads you to the tension." I think of the stage of providing reasons as involving a sort of a poetic license. This man is not going to say, "You mean I can still hit my kids but I don't need to be tense?" And unless he is a real nut, he doesn't want to be hitting his kids and getting in trouble.

And you are helping him not be tense but you are not taking away what he'll agree is his motivation. You don't usually want to directly ask him his motivation. It's best to suggest a likely one. He may correct you, however, if your guess is wrong. He'll say, "I don't really love those kids. I've agreed to take care of them, that is all. But you are right. I do have concerns about discipline and I don't want them to get in trouble." So two out of three is not bad! So, he will correct you if you are wrong, and if he does not have a map in his conscious mind for these categories you have listed, he'll indicate that with, "Nope, I don't have that spot in my map, sorry." But if he does have a spot in his map, it is much better than you help him find it.

You know, if my son loses a sock, it is better that I help him find the sock because he doesn't even remember that he had a sock. My son lost his crayons the other day. He's pretty smart. He is like Lassie a little bit. He is at the stage where you can say, "Lassie, where did you put your bowl," and Lassie will go find it. He is at that stage now. But the thing was Carol took the crayons away from him and was talking on the phone and put them in her "outbox" on the desk and forgot where she put them. And she said, "When I was talking on the phone, he put his crayons somewhere." So now we are looking all over the house. And I asked, "Shawn, where did you put your crayons?" And he answered with some sounds. Shawn got up and grabbed me by the finger and led me down the hallway and he realized it was a fun game and I was going to keep going. And he could see that he had Dad, so he kept going.

We finally got to his room and he pulled out the toy box and he looked in there very intently. And I said, "Oh, they are in there." And he made more sounds. So we pulled all the toys out and they weren't there of course. See, if I let Shawn hunt for his crayons he'll make a good shot at it. And he'll get all distracted by dragging Dad down the hall and things that are of interest. And if you ask the child abuser what his motivation is for hitting the kids, he'll do the same thing. He'll get all distracted on things that are interesting to him, like how life is miserable and communists are taking over the country and how the free-love generation let everything hang out. And we'll never get to the crayons.

What I am trying to do is give you an enjoyable and believable reason for framing the motivation rather than asking for it. And clients will correct you if you are wrong. If you're not wrong very much, you'll gain some extra credibility. They'll think, "Man, this guy understands." And you are helping them save face. So you are gaining a little bit of an ally in therapy. You know, if you ask somebody "Why," there is always an implied challenge.

So we are back to splitting and we've gotten our reason. We are asking the man to continue to have that concern and the knowledge of the importance of discipline that he'd like to impart to his children but he doesn't need to (and we can pick any one of these things) ". . . get so preoccupied that it is uncomfortable for you," ". . . get so tense that it is difficult for you." But I try to nip it before it becomes an external behavioral expression. Don't try to take these resulting behaviors away because it will look to the client as if you are trying to take something away and he/she will usually challenge you about that.

So let's look at alcoholism as another example of self-destructive behavior. Any ideas? Okay, this woman suggested that we would use splitting and help the client by removing or reducing tension. Right, if he has tension in his chain of events that leads to the drinking, removing tension will stop the sequence. But then she said, "We could work on why he gets tense." How about working, instead, on how he gets calm. The way this woman put it is a very useful example of what is wrong with a large part of our profession: Trying to find out what is wrong with everything is wrong. We should have a whole psychology . . . I'd settle for a set of books called *The Anatomy of How People Have Talent*. I don't want a set of books on how they get schizophrenic; I want to know how they become healthy and talented and capable and a genius. I think we need to turn psychology upside down and do that.

Let's change our point of view for a moment. We are looking at para-doxical prescription as one component of our treatment plan. Other goals will include behavioral changes, attitudinal changes, affect changes, struc-tural changes within the family, and social network. We are looking closely at this tool right here and we presuppose that you have the movie to know what behavioral changes you are going to make. So don't lose track of this whole picture. When you get stuck here in the trees, see the entire forest.

Now, drinking—let's go back to that a little bit. Somebody criticizes the person. Prior to that he is trying to make a good impression. After somebody criticizes him or he perceives a criticism, he starts getting angry; but he only does it in words inside his head. After that he finally may have words with somebody. And then he says to himself, "What the hell, I'm going to go have a drink." And then he goes and starts a binge. But you'll find out because you'll ask him what happens and how the events unfold for him. And he'll tell you. Or else if he doesn't tell you, you can find out through metaphor.

Let's look at a quick example about finding out diagnostic information through metaphor. There was a woman we were told about whose parents had both killed themselves. She was sent by her friend to see Erickson. She basically thought Erickson was senile and that there were some pretty stupid people around who were just hero worshipping this irrelevant old man. When she sat down in Erickson's office, he apparently said something along the following lines from the recount we got. She initially became angry that her friend had told Erickson about her past history. In fact, no one had told him anything about her. He said, I suspect, something along the lines of, "A lot of people come to visit with psychiatrists for different reasons. Some of them have anxieties and some have inadequacies. Some of them have sexual difficulties or marital problems. Some have difficulties with their children and some have problems with authority figures.

Why should a person be tense around an authority figure? There are lots of kinds of authority figures in our lives. All of them cause difficulties at different times. There are teachers, doctors, lawyers, fathers, mothers, parents—they are always wrong in some way. They are always too fat or too heavy. They are too rich or too poor. They expect too much or not enough. Or they are always in your hair or they are never around.

And how can a parent be absent? A parent can be absent because of work difficulties or due to the war. They can be absent because they prefer to withdraw because they are crazy or they are dead.

And parents can die in a number of ways. They can die in auto accidents or die in the war or because of murder or suicide. It can be one parent or both parents. I had a client one time who came to see me and both parents had killed themselves.

This woman had a difficulty thinking that her friend had told Dr. Erickson that both her parents had killed themselves but no one had. He apparently just proceeded in his customary getting-down-to-business manner. You know, "Is it bigger than a bread box? Okay." And then Erickson dealt with what was obvious, her attitude (conveyed nonverbally, most likely) of "I don't want to be with this old person here." He surely investigated the magnitude of that, watching and guided by the woman's responses. You could do the same kind of thing if it's worth it. If the person won't talk to you about the problem and you really want to help in some way, you continue trying that 20 questions metaphor maneuver and closely monitor the ideomotor responses of identification or disagreement evidenced by the people listening to you.

Now, with this case about substance abuse, I would actually use the word denial here—denying stress and trying to have some enjoyment in life. The person is a 36-year-old who is at that age where he expects a lot out of life and people expect a lot out of him. I would say, "You are at the age of your life where you expect a lot out of yourself. People expect a lot out of you. You really have to perform. There is a good deal of money at stake here. There is a family for whom you are responsible. And there are people at work who are asking you to solve problems that probably no one has ever told you how to solve in the first place because you are a self-made man and nobody has ever tackled these problems before. Who do they think you are anyway? If I were you I'd be under a lot of stress. I'd be trying to deny that stress and be wondering how the heck I'm going to have enjoyment. At 36 you ought to be finding out the enjoyment of being a man instead of the stress of being somebody's puppet. That must really upset you and drive you to distraction. So go ahead and keep trying to have some pleasure, but you don't need to keep worrying about making a good impression on others." Or "You don't need to have that discomfort when somebody criticizes you."

And then if you can stop the cycle there, at the discomfort that begins it, the symptom won't develop. The more rigid a symptom is, as we said, the more it will disintegrate when you change a component of it. An abusive symptom, like the example here, is usually very rigid and routinized. The same thing is done in the same way over and over again. Often the cycle has not been examined and so the person may not realize that it is so patterned.

So that is splitting. We are going to compare and contrast that with some other things. Basically, the therapeutic job is to identify the sequence and interrupt the sequence. It is also to find something that has to do with the motivation which you've attributed, usually as the positive reason for why you are going to give clients this assignment to do exactly what they are doing.

We've mentioned modifying. This means changing the intensity, frequency, location, and timing involved in something. Here is an example from Erickson[23] with a 17-year-old boy who had an IQ as low as 65. The boy had this repetitive arm movement. He was in juvenile detention for delinquents. And he couldn't stop his arm movement. The psychiatrists had decided that this was some kind of masturbation enactment due to guilt about same.

So Erickson asked the boy to continue doing the hand movement and move it about but with a change. He had an intern count the movement. It was 135 times a minute. Erickson suggested to him that it would increase 10 times per minute. At the next visit, a day later, the count increased to 145. During the next few days it was increased and decreased five to 10 per minute and varied each day. This fluctuation continued under Erickson's direction until the rate was down to 10 per minute all day long and then it was increased to 50 per minute.

I think that continued two or three weeks. And the next time Erickson saw the boy, he complimented him on doing quite well—only 10 times per minute. He was then to "increase" it so it would be "as much as 20 or 25 times per week" and the boy was asked to guess on what day there would be no uncontrolled behavior. He was also given the job of kneading bread dough at the training school later, and his adjustment continued to be satisfactory.

So that is a gross example of changing the frequency. And you notice that he didn't begin to change the frequency by decreasing it but by increasing it. He did that with a number of overweight people. They were to

[23]Erickson, M. H. (1980). Special techniques of brief hypnotherapy. In E. L. Rossi (Ed.), *The collected papers of Milton H. Erickson on hypnosis, volume IV: Innovative hypnotherapy* (pp. 158-160). New York: Irvington.

eat enough to remain at exactly 317 pounds, or whatever weight they began with. Then they were to eat enough to weigh exactly 320 pounds. By doing that increasing first, do you feel how the clients take responsibility for their eating habits? The problem that had not been under their control comes under their control. What had been a symptom controlling them is something they now control. So the role changes. The client might think, "I'm not a victim of my eating anymore. I'm controlling my eating."

We recently saw a couple and the wife complained that the husband wanted sex too often and made unwelcome advances nightly. So we asked that the wife make advances at least five times in the ensuing week between sessions and that the husband, upon being approached, turn her down. This is leaving the behavior intact and changing its locus. We didn't split it; we didn't add on to it; we changed the location of the problem in the sense of who enacted it. By the way, two weeks later the wife and husband had a greater frequency of sexual contact and both were satisfied. There was remarkably little in the way of other interventions, except, of course, for the metaphors and anecdotes that followed the paradoxical prescription, metaphors to illustrate and elaborate upon how a woman can gain a sense of power and control when she takes advantage of an opportunity to initiate the romance.

We did give them an ambiguous function assignment to change the location of five pictures on their walls every other day and tell us what they thought we wanted them to learn. And we did about two and a half hours of metaphor with them. Some of this was in trance and some was out of trance. The goals had to do with the normal growth demands that a couple, each 25 years old, with a three-year-old child might be expected to encounter. But nothing else exotic was done. The paradox, surely, was the decisive intervention for the correction of the sexual advance and frequency problem.

Someone has just asked for some alteration examples. Certain people tend to get migraine headaches and they try to stop them when they begin. Well, you might have them try to not stop but rather to bring on the onset sooner. Or the pain that is in their back—they might have it while they are driving rather than when they get home so they can have more time at home to relax. Or they might move the location of the pain to be slightly more to one side or the other. I've had people have pains in shoulders hurt more so that they could get over it more quickly. And you can do combinations of these alterations. You might say, "Why don't we have it hurt more when you are in the shower and out of contact with people? You won't be disturbing them. And maybe you'll be getting over it more quickly by having it intensely for five minutes in the shower rather than spread out randomly at half the intensity all day long."

You have to look at the family members and listen to them because what you say depends on the uniqueness of people. Oftentimes the overweight people are not getting gratification from social interaction. And part of the reason that they are not getting gratification is because they are not asking for it and they are not putting limits on other people's demands on their time. That is usually part of the syndrome we sometimes hear referred to as "pleasing others." In this type of family every member has come to expect the mother, for example, to put her needs aside to serve them. Usually, the mother does this cheerfully. No one is aware of her pain. Sometimes the mother is not aware of her pain. She fails to put limits on how much of herself and her time she gives away. This expands into the neighborhood, the PTA, the cub scouts, the fund drives, and so forth. But you can't expect us to generalize about what you say when the mother gives a reason for what she does or what you set as a goal.

For instance, how old is the person? Let's say that she is 30 years old, single, lonely, and obese. She needs to be involved in courtship and socializing of some type. Your appeal might be to the sense that at 30 years of age, a woman really needs to understand gratification. She is not getting very much of it and you might note, "Your parents had to survive economic hardship—their parents surely struggled through the war and the great depression. They could not have learned enough about enjoyment to pass it on to you. You certainly need to learn to have and savor enjoyment now that you are on the brink of beginning your own family. Sooner or later you will grapple with that pleasure and secure it for yourself."

Before you tackle this problem of getting the woman's weight under control you need to deal with the developmental task of learning to enjoy—enjoy herself, enjoy her future, enjoy her opportunities for friends, enjoy food. Perhaps it might be important to use what she's got right now that she is doing effectively *and can enjoy*, which is eating, and for her to find that she can get the maximum amount of pleasure out of it. So you want her to eat enough to gain two more pounds. And teach her to *really enjoy* the experience of eating that food. And that may be a real important precursor.

If the person in question is a 45-year-old woman, who has four children at home and a husband, you might, for example, still mention the difficulty her parents had with enjoyment, but then appeal to the woman's need to teach her children what they will require in the way of enjoyment. Let's not forget that you need to continue the therapy to hold the therapeutic leverage as we've shown and you will need to follow up with your promises to help her elaborate an experiential understanding of enjoyment.

You always have one silly "ace in the hole," which I wouldn't suggest you use unless you absolutely want to admit that you have no creativity in a particular case. And that is to say, "I don't know the reason, but your unconscious must have a good one, so why don't we keep the behavior up for a couple of weeks and see if we can find out." And that just means that you've thrown away your opportunity to frame the developmental area that therapy will address *with the client's implicit agreement.* You can always state the areas later but there is a loss of punch and with that loss of punch a loss of rapport. In the case of the 30-year-old obese woman, you see, I could say, "Close your eyes, go into trance, and now let's talk about how you get gratification." And she'll agree that is right up a therapeutic alley of importance and relevance to her. But if I'm using the last resort method, I'm not quite so justified in saying anything about gratification because I have indicated that I have no idea what she needs.

Now "adding on" is an easy method of having leverage with paradox. Basically what you do is prescribe that the person do the symptom just about the way it has been done but prescribe the symptom plus something new here. For example, let's say we have a young woman who is getting depressed and saying things to herself like, "Boy, I shouldn't be in college, I'm not college material. My husband is right, I should be staying at home. I wonder what he *really* thinks about me being gone. I have a right to be gone, but I'm not doing any good here anyway." She is obsessing along that line and getting depressed. And again, you have to figure your diagnosis for the person and ask what it is that you can say in a positive framework about that depression and obsession for this person who is at that stage of development where she has to find the self-confidence to change the direction of her life. If she is going to do that, she has to be seen as somebody different by her spouse. And she has to be willing to be seen as different. The person has to be flexible enough, that is, she must have the transactions and experiences to see the logic of the positive frame and respond to it in some way. And the symptom may have a good deal to do with the person's learning structure or, in other words, the altered state in which learning occurs. She may be pestering herself unnecessarily for lack of a motivation strategy.

That is how most of us are trained as children. "Did you do your homework? Go do your homework. You don't do your homework, then you can't eat dinner." So you pester yourself into doing your homework because that is how you learn to do it. That is how that altered state is created. So it may be a perfectly reasonable thing for her to do to motivate herself. Given that, I might say something to her like, "So look, you are 25 years old. You only have a limited number of ways of making sure you keep on the track of things that are important. And you know there are a lot of important things. You are changing your priorities right now. You ought to keep hashing them over in your head and figuring out what is the most important. And besides that, as soon as you determine your priorities, you are going to be a powerful woman who's decided where she wants to make a stand. And when you do that you are going to be asking your husband for some new ways of responding to you. And I know you don't want to put more stress on him that necessary. You are a sensitive person. You don't want to ask for "x" today, when it turns out to be "y" or "z" tomorrow. So it's good that you are not asking your husband to treat you in a different way and see you in a different way. It is good that you are withholding your power right now because I think that you appreciate the importance of getting it right the first time. And you need to sort of keeping going over that and obsessing it. And keep your mind concentrating on the variety of issues at hand, part of which is your school and whether you are capable and whether your husband is right or not."

So you see, I've said that what is going to happen real soon is she is going to be real powerful and make an impact and demands on her husband and she is a good person, so she doesn't want to do it wrong and then take it back. This is helpful. Not only is it true in the family structure but it helps her save face, helps her to understand the problem, and gives her a reason, especially to back up the stance, "I want you to keep on obsessing." and now you are going to add on:

> Every time you start having those repeating thoughts or obsessions, every time that you notice yourself having that depression, I'd like you to sit down, pull out a notebook pad, and jot down three things you wouldn't dare say to anybody. And don't show it to anybody. This is between you and me for now. Make sure that happens at least twice a day. When you start feeling depressed and obsessing, pull out a note pad and write down three things you wouldn't dare tell anyone—but identify who it is you wouldn't dare tell. If it's your mother, I wouldn't dare tell her or if it's your father, I wouldn't dare tell him, "I can go to college if I want to." If it is your husband, you might not dare say, "Would you just be on my side sometimes and quit making me have these doubts." And write it down for me.

Now what we've got, you see, is the symptom plus an add-on: "Do exactly what you are doing but make sure that some beginning expression is taking place." Now what is happening is you are making the depressed behavior, which is a person turning inward and not expressing her feelings, an intermediate step to expressing her feelings. She is bringing her feelings into the foreground and looking at them and accepting the fact she has something to express. But it is very subtle.

It is not exactly the same thing as, "Put your husband in a chair and tell him you don't want to talk about this. Tell him that you are afraid that he is right, that you should not be college material." You get to the same place—not unlike being in a gestalt exercise à la Fritz Perls, but you just don't have to train your client to talk to empty chairs or quickly force material into their consciousness. It is just more gentle. It is easier and people will do it more readily because they don't have to overcome the oddness of, say, doing that gestalt therapy form of intervention.

You are not stopping at this point of therapeutic leverage, of course. You are going on to no. 5 on the illustration [35] (use metaphors and anecdotes to illustrate resources and treatment goals), which ought to convince you otherwise about any doubts you might have about clients having the resources or motivation for pulling off the suggested alterations. This paradox part may take you seven minutes in your hour, and this resource retrieval may take you 35 minutes in your hour. And together they may count for nearly the whole session. If you really have been speaking to the needs of the person, and you've been speaking about those real needs for 35 minutes, you've got a lot of allies on your side within this person's personality.

You've touched pieces that are really personal. See, nobody is following your suggestions because of compliance. If they are doing it because of compliance you have not been getting them to generate answers from within their own experience. So my families are not going out to do assignments because I said so. They are going out to do them because the assignments make good sense to them and have personal meaning for them. Just as when you did the ambiguous function assignment, it came from you and it made a lot of sense. I don't ask the question, "What if my client doesn't do it?" I ask the question, "How am I going to make sure the client does it?" And they do it. I can't remember a client who hasn't done an assignment. Now it is possible they wouldn't but it still doesn't mean you lose therapeutic leverage of course. That doesn't mean you should consider that an option or let them consider it as an option.

Well, let me tell you this for a minute here. Erickson did an interesting research study with his graduate students when he taught at Michigan. He had well trained, deep trance subjects who could do all deep trance phenomena. He sent each of these well trained subjects to his groups of graduate students and I think there were six graduate student groups. He told each group slightly different versions. As I recall what Erickson said, it went something like this, "I'm going to send these people in to see you today. And the first subject can do all of the trance phenomena except age regression, but go ahead and try to get age regression, too. And the second subject can do all of the trance phenomena but apparently can't do negative hallucination but go ahead and try for it." Then he went to the next group and said, approximately, "Now the first subject who comes in can't do amnesia but go ahead and try. And the second subject who comes in can't do posthypnotic suggestion but go ahead and try." And he went around to each of the groups and he told them something different that the individual subjects presumably couldn't do. And then guess what? The students couldn't get the subjects to do that portion that had been suggested as impossible when the students hypnotized them in the groups.[24]

So Erickson's conclusion was that minimal cues from the operator signal the other person about the expectancy. And that was so important that despite the fact that the subjects could do it, the subjects couldn't do it. I wanted to tell you that story in regard to the question someone asked me about what to do if you couldn't get your client to do the paradoxical prescription. The point here is if you mean business, you've got to act like you mean business. Erickson said a couple of times to me when he'd presented a case, "What do you do with this case? You are going to have to do something. You can't just be pussyfooting around." And I got the impression that I would have to expect of myself that I would actively do something regardless of the client, and even if it were difficult.

You have to be willing to send somebody home sometimes. You have to say, "You didn't do that? Then we're really not going to be able to use this session are we? So go on home and I'll see you next week at the same time. Anything else you need to know about this before you do it?" And when they do come back, when they failed to change to some other therapist, they know that you mean business. You have to do that sometimes.

I've told this story to my clients sometimes. When I was in karate, I was with Master Sel. He was the highest ranked nonoriental in the world. He was the best person around Ann Arbor for doing and teaching karate. So I went to him and I said, "Look, I travel a lot and I'm not going to come to all these classes where people are here for their mothers, or because they are jealous of their neighbors, or want to be kung fu champs, or something. And I will be the fastest learner that you have ever seen. I will probably be a faster learner than you, in fact. I want to do the learning when I am in town and so I want to be a private student. What do you say?" He said that he liked my attitude but he didn't know if I could live up to it. Unfortunately, I did live up to it and so all the black belts wanted to spar with me because I was the aspiring young man with good form. And they wanted to see how good I was. And Master Sel did, too.

When you first come in and you take your shoes off, you bow to the mat, you cross the mat, and you go downstairs to the locker room. But you come back and you bow again to the mat. You always bow whenever you ap-

[24]Erickson, M. H. (1980). Expectancy and minimal sensory cues in hypnosis. In E. L. Rossi (Ed.), *The collected papers of Milton H. Erickson on hypnosis, volume II: Hypnotic alteration of sensory, perceptual and psychophysical processes* (pp. 337-339). New York: Irvington.

proach or leave the mat. I changed into my gi and returned to see if another student was there. Here is Master Sel standing *right* in this guy's face. Master Sel taught the military police in the marines. He was made of iron and didn't take any excuses. And he is shouting, "If you want to be my student, you do your homework. Is that clear, boy?" He answered, "Yes sir." "Is that clear?" "Yes sir!" [louder] "Is that clear?" "[LOUDER] Yes, sir!" "If you fail to do your homework again that is it. You are done. Is that clear?" And the young man said, "Yes sir." "I can't hear you!" [louder] "Yes, sir!" [LOUDER] "Is that clear?" [LOUDER] "Yes Sir!" Now occasionally I tell that story to families. And they do their homework because they don't want me to say that to them. And they know I am capable of doing it.

Another story I tell on the heels of that is the time that I was sparring with Master Sel. He told me that I was leaving myself open after my high block. He said that he would show me on the third transaction. Soon I was leaning up against the wall with the wind knocked out of me. And I was wondering, "Why did he knock the air out of me?" He is trying to teach me and he knocked me out of breath. I'm up against the wall thinking that this man is sadistic—that is why he is in the marines teaching martial arts to the military police. I'm thinking I'm going to quit. I was not going to continue to pay this man to beat me up. I didn't get it. I thought, he's just sadistic and there are other people who could be teaching me who are not. I didn't need this abuse. It hurt. I felt like a fool.

Then it dawned on me. Part of my problem was that I was thinking this man was thinking *I* was terrible. And I had come on to him and said I'm going to be the greatest learner you've ever seen. Obviously. I wasn't that great, I was up against the wall there. But *then* it was dawning on me, he's always going to beat me because he is better than I am. No wonder I am losing every time . . . he's better! That was very important. I'll always remember that. And he didn't think any worse of me when I lost . . . because he already didn't think much of me! It didn't matter if I lost or won, he still thought he was the best in the world, and that everyone else was crude. So he didn't think worse of me when I lost and he'd always beat me! I didn't feel so bad anymore. You might share that with your clients. That has some meaning to your unconscious, I'm sure.

So try this. Get a partner. Now you have to do this right or it won't work. Pick a problem which is tangible. A psychosomatic problem is really good for the exercise. You know, "I've got this pain right here." Please don't do this . . . someone always has to be different and present a problem of vague anxiety that the universe is expanding. Please don't do that.

What you really want to do is make sure that this a good learning experience. And the way to do that is to start easy. You learn to shoot a bow and arrow at a target that is stationary and not very far away before you go pheasant hunting. Let's pick a stationary target that is not very far away for this. And you can make it up. If you don't make it up, it will put just a little bit more difficulty on your partners because they will want to say something that is really true about you; when they get to the stage of making a reason, it will put them in the position of being candid. It will make it a little tougher for them. It is okay if it is true, but you'll have the extra degree of tension. It *will* make it a better learning, but you may have to say to your partner, "Look you are slightly overweight and 30 years old . . . ," and you may not want to be that candid. The best solution is make this a role play.

Do role play with one of you being the therapist and one of you being the client. In the role play, tell your partner right away your role-play age and relevant information: "I'm 36. I'm divorced and have three children. I have these migraine headaches." Then role play for about two or three minutes. But make sure they (the therapists) know where you are coming from so that they get some idea of the developmental problem that might be going on here. And then your role play should be clean enough that they can tell if you are a different kind of person. You realize, I suppose, that the same content will require an entirely different response if it comes with a fast-talking, histrionic affect versus a slow, depressed affect. Role play it clean so they get a vision of what kind of person they are dealing with. Then (the therapists) formulate the reason and the prescription.

Now when you deliver it, you are going to do it with some kind of alteration, splitting, adding on, or modifying. And then stop. Don't do any metaphors to make your point. If you feel a sense of incompletion, that is good. Go ahead and feel your urge to continue even as you force yourselves to stop. That urge to continue is something that you can memorize and look forward to gratifying in your real therapy outside of this workshop.

In the exercise, you want to make certain that, as a first step, you respond to the problem with empathy, which reflects to the client how much you understand that it is a problem. That is what empathy is. If I come in with headaches and you tell me to keep my headache, I won't be sure you quite got the point. The point here is I have a headache and I don't want it anymore. You want to make certain that you are genuine and that there is no trick here. You really do need to understand my problem—the client's problem.

If it is the kind of thing with which you can't empathize—if they are coming in challenging you, or if they are being hostile—then utilize the behavior. You might be able to empathize with the hostile. You might be able to say, "Well, you have a good reason to be angry and you probably have more anger than you are justified in showing." But there may be some hostility in just listening to what you are saying. In that case empathy is just going to make you look like you got "social-worked," as they say. So then you are going to utilize, "I don't want to work with you; you don't want to work with me and so we are even. But I'll tell you one thing, you are a man who thinks for himself and that is the way you have gotten by and you are damn good at it. And that is how come you are able to keep away from other people and do things your own way. And you should continue to do it that way because you know that you do that better than a lot of people can."

So I am starting to formulate my reason but I'm being able to utilize in an enjoyable manner. I'm asking the client to push away and then I'm moving in to the rest of the outline and drawing him in with the following steps. So we want to put empathy or utilization in here. In this role play, it is probably going to be that you empathize with the family member.

So let's do one quick example. Somebody pick one of these tangible things and let me hear what it is. You've got a 30-year-old client who has back spasms. She has children and her marriage is okay but it could be better. Remember to keep these facts simple for your partners. Now role play this for us.

> *Client*: Well, I have this back problem and I've been talking to doctors and they say it's just in my head. But I don't know what to do about it.
> *Therapist*: And how is it now? Is it hurting you now?
> *Client*: Well, it was when I was coming in.
> *Therapist*: And is it a sharp pain or is it dull? How would you describe it?
> *Client*: It's sort of a dull pain and I have it a lot of the day.
> *Therapist*: Does it stop you from doing anything?
> *Client*: Yeah, yeah. It, you know, stops me from kinda being able to pick up my kids when I want to and hug them and hold them.
> *Therapist*: And then do you lie down or does it in any way incapacitate you?
> *Client*: I can't stay in bed. I've got kids, you know.
> *Therapist*: So you just keep going even though your back is hurting you?
> *Client*: Um-hum.
> *Therapist*: Do you take medication for it?
> *Client*: I don't like to take medication much.
> *Therapist*: Do you take Tylenol or anything?
> *Client*: Yes, sometimes.
> *Therapist*: Does it help?
> *Client*: Sometimes Tylenol and codeine.
> *Therapist*: And, does it help?
> *Client*: Nope, a little bit. No not much.

Therapist: Uh-huh. And you've been to a lot of doctors and they say come here because it's something that's eluding them.

Client: Uh-huh. They said come to you because they can't do anything about it.

Therapist: That must be really distressful for you to be 30 years old and to think that these folks are holding you responsible for these pains in your back and you don't even know how to stop them. And like you say, it's a time you would like to be enjoying family and enjoying your children and having a little bit of freedom now that the economic hardships are probably about over in your life. And it's a shame that you are the kind of person who can recognize that times are changing and that you could use a little bit of backup support. Instead you are having this pain.

I think it is important that perhaps you keep that kind of dull awareness in your back that there is this chronic lack of the kind of support you really would like to get in your life as a signal to you of how important and urgent it is to be able to lean back in a way that you know is going to be comfortable for you now in your life. But I don't think it should be necessary for you to have the feeling that you can't stand up and that you can't do things and that you have a pain that is keeping you down.

So, I would like to recommend for the next week that you continue to have that kind of throbbing dull awareness that there is something missing back there . . . in your family. You need to be able to feel a little bit more pleasure that you can lean back on in your life. As a dull awareness it doesn't have to involve the difficult aching discomfort you are having. Let me tell you how we can go about that.

That is an example of splitting, in which case my idea would be to show the woman how she can keep the sensation but not have the pain. I don't know if any of you have been injured or not but you may know it is possible to have the sensation and not the pain. Perhaps if you have been rolfed—that is sort of like being injured greatly—and in that experience you repeatedly learn how to have sensation of pushing and not pain.

Another way would be adding on the following:

Therapist: You know you are the kind of person who is quiet. I see you sitting there and being certain that you don't take up more room than you think is due you. You are a woman who obviously realizes that everyone around you has needs that are important. And we don't want your needs to get in their way. I think that is real valuable for a person to know. It is important to know that you have needs and others have needs and there are some compromises necessary in the family. And as you find more ways to find support for yourself and express your needs and stand taller it is important that you keep an awareness that you want to hold yourself back and not get in other people's way, especially at this time in your life when you are probably beginning to get on a really solid financial basis. So in that regard your symptom is a very intriguing way of keeping you from imposing your needs too much on other people. And since it is not totally debilitating, for the next week I'd like you to continue to have the problem in just exactly the same way without even giving a thought to trying to change it. But I want you to make an interesting addition. Every time you begin to notice the throb, I want you to sit down and jot down something that seems kind of dull in your life that you wouldn't dare tell anybody about . . . something that is just a little dull that is really a pain. And jot down, let's say, only one thing each time you really have to sit down because of the pain. If the pain gets worse before the end of next week, call me up and we'll do something different. But as long as it is not debilitating, let's let that be something that you continue to use to remind you that you don't want to get in anyone's way. And when the pain starts to happen, I want you to sit down and write down something that is pretty dull in your life and then bring that notebook in for me to see.

So, there were two examples. One is splitting so the woman wouldn't actually have the pain. The other is adding on so that you get her to start making an expression of things she is not making an expression of in her family. You only have to do one of the possible alterations in your exercises with each other.

All right. Your time is up and let's discuss the results. I hope you had at least a few problems that we can use to identify and clarify any remaining confusions about using this technique therapeutically. Reactions from your partners will give you the very best feedback about whether your prescriptions were delivered congruently, whether your reasons seemed positive and genuine, and whether or not your alterations somehow got at the therapeutic heart of the matter.

Someone has worked with less than ideal results with a woman who was stealing things and can't stop. Here is a single woman who is 35 years of age. You might have said the following:

Therapist: It is appropriate to be wanting to possess the things that you find valuable in your friends. And you may have some insecurity and discomfort in doing that when no one's ever showed you how to tell people what it is about them that you value. And you've lived a life where people wouldn't listen to you when you said you valued them or be responsive to the things you've found important. I think your trying to possess the things you value in others and would like to have for yourself is real important. I want you to continue to have that kind of thought, that kind of value. I sure wouldn't want you to give that up for a minute, but . . . [this is a case for splitting] . . . you don't need to let an impulse or urge like that chip away at your self-esteem and make your life more difficult.

So now you get to talk about closeness.

So this is the kind of thing you split. You often want to split pain and, as we said before, the class of symptoms that involve violence or antisocial and illegal behaviors. As for pain, there is no reason your client has to leave the office with debilitating pain. Now the responsibility becomes a little bit more urgent and you put yourself out on a limb when you say, "Continue to have that value and you don't have to have the impulse. Let me tell you what I mean." You are not really stuck if you think about it for a minute. Why? Because you transit from this portion of the paradoxical paradigm to any one of the metaphor protocols in order to retrieve and organize the needed resources.

Somebody over here had anxiety when they heard noises. It is not very creative, but it would work to say, "It's important for some reason or another for her to notice the activity around her and to notice the noise but she doesn't have to have the anxiety." Or the same thing is true with the woman who steals and we tell her she can keep the value but she doesn't have to have the impulse. And you say, "Oh, sure, but how do you do that?" Is that what you are saying? Let me go about answering that by telling you this for a moment.

When I'm doing any particular chore involving muscular activity, I've noticed Shawn emulates my muscle movements. We are in the garage fixing the high chair the other day. I took Shawn out and sat him on the chair and explained to him what I was doing with the screwdriver. He watched for a few minutes and then started trying to do what I was doing. I also noticed that he had his tongue in the corner of his mouth . . . and I noticed that I did, too! Children learn to walk by watching. And that is how come you see children who walk like this [emulating the swaggering shoulders, stiff bottom, macho walk] because their fathers walk like that.

The point here is that when we learn to walk we learn a whole slew of things, some of which make it easier to walk than others. Some people end up graceful and some people end up clodhoppers. And that is not genetic. If you learn to walk kicking your foot, then that is the way you train your kids to walk. You learn these subtle muscle movements and they stay with you for a long time unexamined. But you can forget that learning for a new learning.

I worked with a woman in Canada in 1981 who had both of her legs driven through her pelvic sockets due to an automobile accident. She was, of course, in great pain. Her husband was a doctor and I think that she had received proper medical treatment. My work with her was only for 45 minutes, but the outcome is that she has not had any pain since—the last time I inquired was in mid-1985. This case is written up with the entire transcript in *The Answer Within*. How could this have been so successful? My idea is that she learned how to properly walk as a child and the accident begged her to relearn how to walk by monitoring the pain stimuli from that area of the body.

The new learning is, "My legs have been driven here and any movement at all is going to be a threat to me. So I'll be very sensitive to any muscle movement at all and my posture. And, oh, there was a feeling, was it pain or not? No, that is pain. This is not pain. This other thing was pain. So I am always vigilant for the pain. I am always cautious about how I move. I'm tensing myself up so I don't move too much so that I'll hurt myself."

If that is not enough, she had to relearn to walk, making sure she pay attention to the pain. She took time to remember how bad it was. She was anticipating how bad it was going to be. She probably learned some superstitious behaviors in the process. I mean in the sense of muscle tension. She may have thought, "Is my husband going to hate me because I can't have children now because I ruined my pelvis? And I'm not really going to be a real woman if I can't grow up and raise children like I had planned to do all my life. Is it even worth being alive if I can't have sexual pleasure anymore?" So she would have psychological self-image problems, anticipated pain, remembered pain, a lowered threshold to sensitivity to pain, overgeneralization to stimulus, superstitious muscular habits that interfere with walking. And it is simply learned behavior.

So why can't we have the person learn the old behavior she already learned so well the first time and forget about this learning that is not necessary? It is just a bad habit that was learned. In the previous example of the woman who was impulsively stealing, it is a learned response to a set of impulses. She learned she could not control it. So let's just unlearn that the way everyone else unlearns it. You unlearn it by all the trance phenomena. And the use of trance phenomena in family therapy or any therapy is so important that we put a chapter in *The Answer Within* about it. You might want to consult that because I believe that is the best writeup I have seen that documents the occurrence of trance phenomena in non-hypnotic therapies.

TRANCE PHENOMENA TO RETRIEVE RESOURCES WITH PARADOX

The trance phenomena we are primarily interested in are dissociation, amnesia, negative hallucination, age regression, and time distortion. These are some of the trance phenomena that you use all the time. You use them to walk. And you use them to get rid of mosquito bites you don't want to pay attention to. You are using negative hallucination right now so you don't notice your bladder and how rotten your bottom feels sitting on those chairs. You use amnesia to not think about the problems that are waiting for you at home because to not have amnesia for those problems would mean you were preoccupied and not all here. You are time distorting to varying degrees depending upon your learning style and how much stimuli you need to take in per second. So why couldn't you take these things that are naturally occurring and say to the woman who was impulsively stealing, "Here is an impulse and let's make time go faster or slower." And then when I say to her, "You can have that motivation and all. That is a real good value to have that you want to take a symbolic part of what you treasure in your friends," and so on. "But you don't have to have that impulse take over your life."

Now I have two major goals. One is to stop the impulse from taking her over. That is what I'm talking about here. The second goal is to help her be able to grow by acquiring those things that she values in others. I want to help her feel like she belongs. She doesn't have to own a spoon in order for her to be like that person. I want her to notice the things that are in herself that are like that. I want her to be comfortable around other people being who is she is.

There is an attitude change in that as well: She really is valuable already, even if her parents didn't respond to her when she tried to share things with them. (An extra intuition was tagged on there.) I want her to have the behaviors of asking for help. I want her to have a feeling of joy sometimes and I want her to have sexual joy as well. And she doesn't have these things now, I imagine. That is why you have heard that stealing is a sexually related behavior and a symbol for that.

So I have a whole bunch of things that are goals. I can use metaphors to help, and indirect suggestion and binds to help build those. Before we look at suggestions and binds I want to bring into focus the tools of trance phenomena. The trance phenomena are going to get this woman who steals to stop the response to the impulse or relearn it. I want her to stop, replace, or redirect the impulse. Now I can address these issues about her maturity because we established that it is good to want to acquire things from your friends, and how you feel good about things you've got, and how you have to go tell people. So these things are all justified by the reason we gave in our paradox.

Now, how would you help her control the impulse? Well, time can go slow. So how about the moments when she does not have the impulse? She could let those seem even longer. And the moments when she has the impulse could go by very fast, providing we let her unconscious experience time distortion—not just talk about it, but have her experience it. You could do this with indirect suggestion and anecdote, too. So, now the impulses are getting to be a little bit shorter. Then she could dissociate from the shortened impulses. She could put a little bit of distance between her and the impulse, which is shortened, and it will be easier when it is a shorter impulse. It is easier to tolerate discomfort if it is short.

At that point we would have shortened impulses that are somewhat diminished by their distance. So next, she could not notice a portion of it by negatively hallucinating, just as you go through the day with a little bit of tension in your head and you don't notice all the rest of the tension in your head—you are negatively hallucinating some of it, and noticing just some of the tension. Then the woman could have amnesia for the remaining portions of the shortened, diminished impulse that she happens to notice. And while she has now forgotten about the shortened, diminished impulse—which she doesn't notice most of anyway—she could be experiencing these other things: joy, feelings of belonging, saying positive self-statements to herself. That would be a behavioral way of approaching the self-esteem, after having thoroughly confused and challenged the whole logic of her previously held attitude that there is something wrong with her if her parents didn't find any value in her.

Now, it may take more than one session, maybe, but you can certainly touch upon all these things. In the case that you split something, you really need to make sure a major part of your impact is to carry through your promise that the anxiety is going to be grossly diminished—or that the impulse won't take her over.

We've taken a similar approach to the one I've described here in the case of a bulimic woman to make sure that she walked out of the office with some confidence that she could change. She had lied to us, saying she did not have money to pay for the session. She wanted to buy food instead, so she went to the grocery store after the session. But she walked right past the fritos and forgot because she was negatively hallucinating the junk food. And the time in passing that aisle seemed awfully short and she had amnesia. And she left the store and drove half way home and remembered she forgot to buy all the junk food. She called us up and said, "Hey, I'm overcoming the impulse."

So I'm saying you can use these techniques with clients who have strong symptoms. What we did might be construed as real good hypnosis aimed at removal of a symptom, which, although inaccurate, would still be an improvement over classical hypnosis. But symptom removal per se is not the Erickson way. We want to help people get relief from distressing symptoms because we have compassion for their difficulties, but the real way is to build the resources that people need in order not to have the problem in the first place. This is accomplished in a variety of ways, not necessarily with trance, but also with homework assignments, metaphor, and indirect suggestion in or out of trance.

In negative hallucination I can be looking right at the person and I don't see them. In amnesia I don't even look at them because I forget that they're even there for me to look at and not notice. If I have a pain in my arm and I have negative hallucination, I'm aware of my arm but it doesn't hurt. But if I have amnesia, I'm unaware of my arm. I have forgotten about my arm.

UTILIZING PARADOX FREQUENTLY

You want to do a paradox with everybody. You just don't know it yet. Let me show you what I mean. Remember the Paco case? Here is Paco's interpersonal grid [Illustration 26]. Everybody's personality has aspects that will somehow interfere with the therapy. Paco will interfere with therapy because he will try to be too cooperative. If he thinks that we don't acknowledge his cooperation or he's not doing enough of it, then he'll criticize himself. And that will interfere with the therapy. So if he gets the drift that he is supposed to have the feeling of belonging—"I really want to have a feeling of belonging, I should have the feeling. I heard a joke the other day . . ."—he's trying to hard to belong that he's not belonging. So he will interfere by helping too much. Would it not be handy then to prescribe that very behavior since he's going to do it anyway? Then it comes under therapeutic control. And if he has doubts that he is doing it correctly, then it would be a good idea to prescribe that too. So no matter what your family members' personality orientations are, it would be really wise to prescribe them. For example:

"I want you to concentrate and be responsive to everything we say and do the friendly responsible thing and try to use every single suggestion including the suggestion that you think for yourself and do things for yourself. And it is okay that you doubt that you are making progress because only by doubting that you are following suggestions correctly do you really get an opportunity to do things your own way. So go ahead and doubt that you are following our directions completely as much as you can so that you have an opportunity to do things for yourself. And that is the best way to follow all of our suggestions to the 'T.' "

Now if you have a client who is real competitive instead, then what might you say to him? "Improve upon everything I say because the suggestions I make are really only stimuli for you to do a lot of thinking. The thinking you should do is to know that no one can do better than you. And I am aware of that and you are aware of that. So improve upon all of my suggestions so they fit for you as a person and allow you to cooperate with other people." If a client is really managerial, say: "Take over and improve upon the way I aim this therapy by really taking control. And do everything so well that you really learn how to let people help you in various ways."

Or if the client is really dependent, then you might say that you want him or her to let you take the lead in every possible way. And you will add a "so that . . ."; and the phrase that you add should frame the direction in which you will want to move the client. So rebellion is kind of a similar thing here: "It would be foolish for you to trust me and follow my suggestions. I wouldn't want to suggest anything to you that presupposes I know what is good for you because surely I don't. And to the degree that you get the impression that I think I know what is good for you, I want you to do the opposite. There is no reason to relax when I talk to you. It will be fine for you to retain that degree of tension."

And then the client will relax because he or she is rebelling. "You can keep your eyes open while I talk. And you should concentrate on everything I say and all of my words. And don't let your mind wander. I might mention a college that I went to and don't let your mind wander to a college that you went to. And if I suggested something about a client of mine who experienced fear, don't be thinking about your own confidence and power; I will be wanting you to think about fear. But to the degree that you recognize that I'm not saying something that is relevant for you, then don't follow my suggestions and listen to them; have your own thoughts."

So you should be able to use paradox for everybody because of its importance in interview management. You've got interview management issues because everybody has a different way of listening. And second, you've got symptoms. So we've really got a huge and important tool here. We've got ambiguous assignments for diagnosis, homework assignments for skill, ambiguous assignments for interview management and disruption of the family system. We've got drama through metaphors to hold attention, and metaphor protocols for emotion, behavior, and attitude. Now, regarding paradox, you really need more practice on and we'll work with it—paradox for interview management and paradox for symptom prescription, which disrupts either the individual's role organization or the family organization.

Now what we want to also cover is indirect suggestion and double binds. Some other things we need to keep in mind are diagnostics and therapy goals which precede all of these techniques. And we also want to use hypnosis to help create therapeutic trance in families.

CHAPTER SIX

Stimulating Unconscious Resources: Suggestion and Hypnosis

SUGGESTIONS AND TRANCE IN FAMILIES

You already use suggestions with families. You really can't communicate verbally and avoid using these language forms. So all we have to do now is show you how you do it and help you improve on it by acquainting you with some options you may not currently be doing automatically. We're going to talk first about using indirect suggestions and binds in the context of achieving general-purpose, nonhypnotic goals in family therapy; but we will work our way into suggestions and binds for use in creating trance and for specific learning goals in the family. They are really the same language forms and all that varies are the particular goals being addressed.

So take a look at the three handouts on the use of indirect suggestions in families [Illustrations 36, 37, 38]. There is really more here than you could absorb in the workshop, so these are intended to be study sheets for later as well as work sheets for use now. We've written six typical goals that you may encounter in any family therapy session. Then we recreated them in each different category of suggestions with examples from that category, so that you can compare and contrast.

The first six categories are indirect suggestions. The rationale for using these is probably pretty obvious by now. It is the way of making sure family members get the understanding that has personal meaning to them rather than simply getting their compliance to what you've told them to do. So it reduces resistance and it warms up their mind to deal with issues. You

Indirect Suggestion

1. OPEN ENDED SUGGESTIONS

Beginning therapy: "You can learn in many ways."
Gathering history: "There are a number of ways of drawing together facts and information to help us direct our actions in any quest."
Making contract: "Formal ways of agreeing on the direction of conduct have been a foundation of social gatherings that enhance the way people make a productive use of time."
Bringing spouse: "Some creative methods of motivating others to participate in things that influence their lives always result from necessity and desire."
Learn from experience: "You can develop a line of thought for your own use."
Use learning at home: "And keep your learnings and memorize them and use them in your own family in various places in your home."

2. IMPLICATION

Beginning therapy: "Since you began when you arrived in my office..."
Gathering history: "The first thing people do when they explain their past..."
Making contract: "Since you want to use your time here for certain gains...please tell me when you'd like to begin."
Bringing spouse: "While you think about getting your spouse in therapy, let's talk about what you can do."
Learn from experience: "Which lesson do you imagine you will learn first?"
Use learning at home: "The more you find ways to use the learnings now the more you're likely to use them with each other."

3. QUESTIONS OR STATEMENTS THAT FOCUS OR REINFORCE AWARENESS

Beginning therapy: "I wonder if you experience yourself ready to begin."
Gathering history: "You probably couldn't say what part of your history is the most important facet of this current problem."
Making contract: "I just wonder what you'll eventually decide to work on in the therapy."
Bringing spouse: "I doubt that you currently know how you will best go about getting your spouse to join us next week."
Learn from experience: "What can a person learn from an experience?"
Use learning at home: "Have you decided when you'll use this learning?"

4. TRUISMS

Beginning therapy: "Chairs were intended to be comfortable and serve a function."
Gathering history: "Everyone knows that we understand things best when those things are placed in their rightful historical context."
Making contract: "Sooner or later you decide what you wish to change."
Bringing spouse: "Everybody knows how two heads are better than one."
Learn from experience: "Experience is a great teacher."
Use learning at home: "Everyone knows the importance of doing some homework."

Illustration 36

5. SUGGESTIONS WHICH COVER ALL POSSIBLE ALTERNATIVES

Beginning therapy: "You might be able to get right to work or you might warm up to it gradually; perhaps you will suddenly find yourself in the midst of therapy or maybe you will pinpoint a starting date; possibly your start will be entirely different."

Gathering history: "You can go into your history slowly, gradually, quickly, with feeling or with a sort of detachment or not at all."

Making contract: "You can either work on something that comes up or you can think it through carefully; or you might let it change each week or you could identify something that is important and stick to it; maybe you'll have a unique way to go about it."

Bringing spouse: "A time to bring your spouse may be selected, or it may be prescribed; it may come to your mind or only intuitively occur to you; you may not know at all how you'll bring it up."

Learn from experience: "You may learn some or all of the material, and you may know what you learn or not know what you learn, and you might learn nothing at all."

Use learning at home: "You may not use this or you might use this learning; you might modify it when you use it; and you can use all of it or only part of it; or you might mix the distinction between what you learn and what you invent."

6. APPOSITION OF OPPOSITES

Beginning therapy: "It's fine to take a long time beginning as we may get to the solution with less waste."

Gathering history: "The more you notice the immediate situation, the more you have a capacity to concentrate on the important part of your past."

Making contract: "The more things you can think about being up in the air, the easier it may seem to get down to earth as you decide where to start."

Bringing spouse: "The more you feel alone in this matter, the more you'll feel like bringing your partner."

Learn from experience: "The more you have been in the dark, the more enlightening a learning may be."

Use learning at home: "Since you waited so long for relief from the problem, you are entitled to use it throughout your vast future."

7. BINDS OF COMPARABLE ALTERNATIVES

Beginning therapy: "Would you prefer to have me begin talking or would you prefer to begin talking?"

Gathering history: "You may go into your past immediately or gradually get to it."

Making contract: "You might decide on what to work for in therapy or you may just want to explore many issues."

Bringing spouse: "I don't know if you will want all of your family present or if you will only want your spouse here."

Learn from experience: "You may learn from the experience or merely use the experience."

Use learning at home: "You can select the way you will use this after therapy or discover the way you will use this at home."

Illustration 37

8. CONSCIOUS/UNCONSCIOUS BINDS

Beginning therapy: "The conscious mind may not notice when the unconscious mind is beginning to work toward a solution."

Gathering history: "Your conscious mind may think you need to share some part of your past while your unconscious mind desires to share some other portion of your past."

Making contract: "Your conscious mind may not notice how your unconscious will single out something you want to start changing."

Bringing spouse: "Your conscious mind may be doubtful of how your unconscious mind can figure out how to get your spouse to come to the therapy."

Learn from experience: "An unconscious learning from the experience may be developed in the conscious mind as well."

Use learning at home: "Your conscious mind might already have some ideas of where you will use this while your unconscious handles the job of doing it correctly.

9. DOUBLE DISSOCIATIVE CONSCIOUS/UNCONSCIOUS BINDS

Beginning therapy: "Your conscious mind may have begun with the aid of your unconscious or perhaps your unconscious is ready to begin with any aid you can offer consciously."

Gathering history: "Would you prefer to let your conscious mind lead your unconscious into the history related to your problem or let your unconscious lead your conscious mind into a recounting of important information?"

Making contract: "Your conscious mind didn't know that your unconscious would choose the right thing to begin therapy, but your conscious mind could wonder which topic your unconscious would choose."

Bringing spouse: "Your unconscious may let your conscious mind know how you will get your spouse into therapy or your unconscious may not even know what your conscious mind is coming up with."

Learn from experience: "Your conscious mind can be interested in what you learn from the experience and your unconscious mind can take care of really learning from it, or perhaps your unconscious mind only allows you to develop interest as your conscious mind develops a learning."

Use learning at home: "And one might let the conscious mind select the site for using the learning while the unconscious is trusted to carry it out, or one may allow the conscious mind to carry out a learning and let the unconscious select the location, and time."

10. NON-SEQUITUR BIND

Beginning therapy: "Let's begin now or use the time constructively."

Gathering history: "You will be able to either tell about your past or else you'll just go into the relevant part of your personal history."

Making contract: "You will come up with what you want out of therapy or you will decide what to work on."

Bringing spouse: "You'll probably want to get someone close to you into therapy or you'll want to bring in your spouse."

Learn from experience: "You can either learn from this experience or understand yourself differently."

Use learning at home: "Will you use these learnings at home or change your maladaptive behavior?"

Illustration 38

don't, by the way, have to always talk with indirect suggestions. You can talk with indirect suggestion about a topic for 20 sentences and then say what you mean in one sentence. It beats saying what you mean directly 20 times because after the indirect suggestions, family members will be prepared to hear the one direct suggestion. We think there is too much *direct* talking going on in this world in many cases anyway, especially in families. I realize that may be an unpopular opinion.

When Johnny comes home from school and Mom says, "Go mow the lawn. I'm really mad at you for not doing what you were supposed to do. And I noticed the lawn wasn't mowed today—go mow it!" That is direct and George Bach might be proud of Mom for confronting the issue head-on. But wouldn't it be better if Mom said, "You know everybody's heard the phrase that two heads are better than one. And the first thing that we do when we figure out how to use our time is we formulate some ideas. Now all groups of people make social contracts with one another in order to function more easily with one another. Everyone's heard the term *law* or *rule* or *contract*. Well, I don't know if you consider this a contract or if it is just something that you decided to do or if it would be fair to call it a law or something else. But the harder everybody works as a team, the easier it is to play together as a team. Sooner or later you are going to be thinking about mowing the lawn. Before you mow the lawn maybe you want to share an excuse with me. I doubt that you really have an explanation that is going to be really satisfactory to you. So I want you to go out and mow the lawn that you didn't mow this weekend."

So you get around to saying it after the 20 sentences of indirect suggestion. The child may have gotten to that thought first because you have warmed up the cortex for the thoughts. See, Johnny may have come home from school thinking about how the third grade teacher gave him a B instead of an A on the test and that someone stole his favorite pencil from the pencil box. So he is over here and you are over there. Indirect suggestion is just a way to exchange ideas.

Again, it is impossible to talk without indirect suggestion. You just *think* that you are talking without it. All we are going to do here is make it impossible for you to talk because we are going to focus on all of your words—at least, briefly. So temporarily it'll be impossible to say anything.

Let's look at what these individual categories of suggestions and binds are before we find out how you can use them in family therapy. All you need to do is understand how they work, how you can formulate them, and then you'll be ready to practice them a bit. And then you've "got it." We have some formulas that we use for this. These categories of suggestion were taken from Erickson and Rossi's *Varieties of Double Bind and Forms of Indirect Suggestion (Vol. 1).*[25] They have a few more breakdowns than the six we are teaching here, but this seems to be a sufficient number. We don't want to learn them all pedantically. We just want to learn that there are a whole variety of ways of saying things. In fact, I don't even care if I can say it is this one or this one, but at least I know there are four other ways I could say it, if not five.

Open-Ended Suggestion

Now, "open-ended suggestion" means that you are going to say something that is abstracted. And you can't get the response you want with an open-ended suggestion. If you have a response that is pretty clear in your mind, it will definitely not be clear in the listener's mind. That is exactly what you are after here. You talk, but you aren't saying anything yet. So if I want a husband to come in for therapy, then I go to the next higher level of abstraction. I know what I want to say: "Get your husband into therapy" and I find words that are abstractions for that. I won't say "husband," I won't say "therapy." I will find words that are abstractions for that. I'll say "primate" and "problem-solving context." So just take more words to say it and do the exact opposite of what you have tried all these years—to be concise in your talking. So you'll say something like, "It's important in any group of living organisms that resources of the entire unit are applied in any problem-solving context." And that says get your husband to come into therapy. But it's only one of the things that a wife might think of to get her husband to come. She also might come up with another unique way that might solve the problem in a better way than the one I have in mind. We're all thinking and brainstorming a little bit, which is allowing a broad range of responses.

If what I want to do is have the person spend more time with his children, an open-ended suggestion about that could be—what? (Participant): "Siblings can find benefit when they spend more time with adults." Good try. You got almost all of them abstracted. That got a little bit specific, didn't it? But that's fine because you didn't say which adults, and so it's an open-ended suggestion. Personally, I would make it a little more abstract. You don't have to say whether they spend more or less time. You could say, "when the degree of contact with adults undergoes alteration." Then it's even more abstract. But you did exactly the right thing and there's no one

---

[25]Erickson, M., & Rossi, E. (1980). Varieties of double bind and forms of indirect suggestion. In Rossi, E. (Ed.), *The collected papers of Milton H. Erickson, M.D., volume 1: The nature of hypnotic suggestion* (pp. 412-429). New York: Irvington.

way to do it. That's the formula—find a way to jump it up one level of abstraction. And then my way would be slightly more obtuse than the way we heard here. The husband says, "You mean I'm supposed to spend more time with my kids? Is that what you're trying to get at?" "No, I didn't say that, but don't you agree that it is true that . . ." and then you'd want to rephrase it in another way: "Everyone knows that two heads are better than one." So that's open-ended suggestion.

Implication

"Implication" is presupposition without anything else attached. If you add too much to it, it will look like one of the other suggestions. You want to enter into the sentence one of the words for presupposition like "after" and "since" and "during" and "one of the" and so on: "Since you are going to be spending more time with your children, . . ." or "When you discover a way to get your husband in for therapy, I want you to think about it." You don't need to go any further. You could go further and add something to the sentence that would be more therapeutic, but you have accomplished an implication at that point. "Begin" is a good verb to use, too. "Since you're beginning to think about ways to get your husband in for therapy, we'll want to have some time to talk about that" or "After it has begun to occur to you that the presence of your husband would be beneficial, let's talk about it."

You do this anyway, but you just don't think of it as implication. You just think you are talking. I'm simply alerting you to be cognizant of how you're moving psychological experience around. What was the other example we used? Spending more time with the kids. You could say: "One of the first things you've begun to do in order to spend more time with your children is to come here in the therapy office and sit down together." This implies that what they've already accomplished is the thing you're hoping they are going to accomplish more of.

Questions or Statements that Focus Awareness

"Questions or statements that focus awareness" is a form you usually use and you don't think of it at the psychological level, especially the questions version. You say, "Can you tell me how your father fits into this?" And you think you are asking a question for which you are going to get an answer at the conscious level. But at the unconscious level, what you've done is you've pushed associations over to the father. You have focused their awareness there. You can do the same thing without a question. You can do it with a statement, and it is a little bit more fun. The statement is a much more unobtrusive way: "I don't know whether or not you've begun to think about how your father fits into this equation. Probably you couldn't really say how your father has influenced you in having this problem." So clients think about it and they are not really being asked by you to think about it. In order to speculate about it, they have to think about their father though, right? I doubt that you can tell me which clients you'll think about using these techniques on. I'd be really surprised if anyone in the room can tell me which of the techniques they are going to study tonight when they get home.

Conscious/Unconscious Double Binds

Now, to skip ahead for a moment into the binds section, "conscious/unconscious double binds" is an interesting and very useful category. You also have "conscious/unconscious double dissociative binds" but that is definitely getting too far ahead of the story. Our formula for creating the conscious/unconscious double bind is to introduce the terminology "conscious mind," "unconscious mind," "the front of your mind," "the back of your mind," or whatever, and then to place in the equation a verb of consciousness and the outcome that you want the person to do. That is the easiest way to make that happen. Your conscious mind might really be surprised to find out that your unconscious has allowed you to remember and study these things at night. If you have two goals, then you can put the second goal here. So I could say, "Your conscious mind might attempt to spend more time with your child in some way, while your unconscious mind comes up with ways in which you can make your child feel good while you are together." And what you really accomplish is a gluing together of those two outcomes.

That brings us back again to the definition of change we have been referring to, by the way—the reassociation of the client's experiential life. To make it easier, it is a reassociation of experience. Or to make it even easier still, it is associating experience together. That is what you are doing here. You are retrieving the experience of thinking about spending time with the child and retrieving the experience of making a child feel good around you, and then linking the experiences together. That could also happen using the double dissociative conscious/unconscious bind, simply by expanding the formula slightly. For example, we could begin with the single conscious/unconscious bind we just used and then add another section to the sentence in which we reverse the roles previously "assigned" to the conscious and unconscious parts of the parents. So that would sound something like this: "Your conscious mind may be thinking of ways you can spend more time with your child while your unconscious creates ways of making your child feel good when you are together; or perhaps you'd prefer to consciously identify ways to increase your child's pleasant feelings and allow your unconscious to automatically find ways to spend time with your child." While the parents are trying to follow this convoluted thinking in order to make the appropriate "choice" at the conscious or social level, the unconscious simply associates together the ideas of feeling good and spending time with children. If they don't spend time, they are not wrong and you are not wrong. They just did something different.

Truisms

Getting back to the indirect suggestion forms, "truism" is something that is true, usually culturally true, or true across cultures, transculturally. Or it can be something that is true in time. So you could say, "Every child has the experience of being born." This we know is true, so that is true, across cultures. Or you could say, "Everyone learns to use money to buy the things that they need." And that is true in our culture. Or you could say, "Sooner or later (that's time), sooner or later you'll have an impulse to spend more time with your child." And sooner or later, they will. It might be a hundred years from now, but it is still true. So you are covered. "Everyone has their own way of going into trance"—that is a truism. "Everyone has their own rules in the family"—that is true. Now you notice what happens if I say, "Everyone has their own rules for family conduct." That is a truism, right? But is it not also an open-ended suggestion? It's about having the time set for going to bed, for example. That is an open-ended suggestion about that. And isn't it also focusing awareness on the family conduct?

So it gets a little hairy sometimes if you try to decide that one of them is one category or another. The ones that will goof you up the most are the differences between truisms and open-ended suggestions. Because anything that is *really abstract* is *true*. So the difference here is whether it is a fairly specific goal you have in mind: "Everyone has times at which they have to eat meals." Well, that is pretty specific; we are talking about eating meals apparently. If it is real vague and general: "All living organisms need to consume quantities of energy on a regular basis," then that is *not* specific. So you would call it open-ended if it is not specific.

Suggestions Covering All Possible Alternatives

"All possible alternatives" is self-explanatory. This category involves identifying and offering numerous alternatives of response, including the alternative to not respond at all. The "not" option can be phrased positively, however. For example, if we're still talking about spending enjoyable time with children, we could suggest that the parents might just want to spend normal time with their children enjoyably, select certain times to spend, discover unexpected times, create times for special occasions, or proceed in some unique way that you couldn't possibly guess. So we've given an option for responding in some way that has not been specifically named and that could conceivably include not responding at all, but we've stimulated the parent's thinking in quite a few different ways along the lines of spending time together.

Apposition of Opposites

The last of the suggestions on our list is "apposition of opposites" which is a real useful category for utilizing or reframing the seemingly negative things your clients report or say. The simplest formula for creating it is "the more you this (something negative), then the more you can that (something desirable)." A client irately demanding to know what in the world possible benefit a person could derive from performing such a ludicrous act as the ambiguous function assignment you've just given, for example, might be told that "the more you doubt that any possible benefit can come from doing this, the more significant and personal your learnings are going to be once you discover just what they are."

Binds of Comparable Alternatives

Now, let's consider the category of "binds of comparable alternatives." Do you want to do it this way or do you want to do it that way? The "it" in question here is the only part of the sentence that is, in fact, not in question. In other words, somehow doing the "it" is presupposed, while the conscious mind is asked to choose between two comparable alternatives which are both subsets of "it." So, would you prefer to spend that special time with your children on Monday or Tuesday each week? Or, "I wonder whether you'll prefer to take your children to the beach or to the circus that's coming to town?" Of course, if neither of the comparable alternatives is relevant for the clients, they can ignore the illusory bind and say, "Neither, thanks." But this is rarely the case for binds presented in a therapeutic context where target goals and associated experiences have been selected based on careful observation and assessment of the individuals and the system they comprise. And if we have adequately retrieved the resources necessary for the family members to respond to relevant, action-oriented suggestions, then we can expect that they will respond.

Non-Sequitur Binds

A non-sequitur juxtaposes two things that don't logically follow one another. We are using the term non-sequitur binds to cover a type of phrasing that clearly states a goal you have in your treatment plan and then rephrases it. I'll say this again in another way. State your goal and provide a choice that is, in essence, a rewording of the goal you stated. By rewording the goal, you disguise it and provide an apparent choice. Our formula for this is "A and A'," (or A and A-prime).

If the goal is to go into trance you might say, "Would you like to go into trance or just alter your consciousness to be more inwardly concentrated?" If the goal is to get the husband to come into therapy, the non-sequitur bind might be, "Would you rather get your husband in therapy next week or just have him attend with you at your next session?" You hear this as a difference when it is, in fact, not a true difference. And thus it is a non-sequitur because it isn't logical to present a "choice" when in effect, the variables to be chosen between are exactly the same. It is not quite the same as classic non-sequiturs like, "Do you walk to work or carry your lunch?" It is a pseudo non-sequitur, but, as such, it creates the binding effect because choosing either of the two seemingly different choices results in the same outcome. This is the formula we use, though there are other ways to use non-sequiturs. Erickson gave an example of a non-sequitur he used with his son that goes approximately like this: "Would you rather take a bath before bed or put your pajamas on in the bathroom?"

Now we have the whole group of them and, as you can see from your written examples, there are a variety of ways in which these can be used, no matter what the phase or the modality of therapy. They will help you bypass resistance to considering new ideas, whether you proceed with hypnosis, metaphor, or more conventional conversational therapy. You've seen a couple of demonstrations using hypnosis, both in family interviews and with individuals. You're going to see a few more shortly, but first let's look in a little more detail at the structure of hypnosis as a tool you may want to add to your repertoire.

HYPNOSIS

The trance induction outline [Illustration 39] we use is a seven-step outline, and we'll just skip steps five and six and call them therapy. Step seven is to reorient the client to a waking state. Some kind of hypnosis has been accomplished in the first four steps. We want you to have some idea of how we explain induction. Apparently induction can only happen with four

INDUCTION SEQUENCE OUTLINE
Conscious-Unconscious Dissociation Induction

1. Orient the client to trance.

This step involves making certain that the client is physically and psychologically prepared for the trance.

2. Fixate attention and rapport.

Most frequently the client's attention is fixated on a story, on his or her body sensations, or on an external object.

3. Establish a conscious-unconscious dissociation.

The client's attention is dissociated and polarized by using "conscious/unconscious dissociation language," including the possible use of anecdote and education about the function of unconscious thought processes.

4. Ratify and deepen the trance.

Ratification of the client's processes of unconscious search is easily accomplished by focusing awareness on the many alterations that occur in face muscles, reflexes, respiration, and skin coloration. Deepening may be facilitated by several means including confusion, offering small incremental steps, or indirect suggestions and binds.

5. Establish a learning set.

The Ericksonian approach emphasizes an associative learning model. By contrast, this learning set differs most radically from those models in which motivation is accomplished by punishment, compliance, or fear.

6. Utilize trance to elicit experiences and associate experiences.

Erickson's therapeutic use of trance included using those unconscious processes stimulated by induction. Metaphor provides an altered frame of reference that allows the client to entertain novel experience. The experiences needed are determined by the diagnostic assessment and contracted therapy goals. They are elicited with indirect suggestion and anecdotes, and binds. Finally, the elicited experiences are arranged into a network of associations that will help the client form a perceptually and behaviorally based map of conduct.

7. Reorient the client to waking state.

Reorientation may be rapid or gradual. At this stage the therapist has a final opportunity to assist the client in developing amnesia, post hypnotic behavior, and/or other trance phenomena that are part of the treatment plan. The techniques of metaphor, indirect suggestion, binds, confusion, and paradox are also used at this stage.

Illustration 39

steps, then, and actually that is stretching it. You are really unpacking reality a bit to get four steps out of this.

Step three, conscious/unconscious dissociation, is really quite interesting. This step is the major or more important step because it educates the person about the positive nature of the unconscious, presupposes a whole set of resources that have been largely taken for granted, and creates a duality of thinking that allows the person to understand that the trance and possible benefits can proceed despite any limiting ideas, doubts, or analysis that the conscious mind may be engaging in. You already know how to do it if you can do the conscious/unconscious binds that we were using earlier. Actually, it's a little easier than that. All you have to do is give several compound sentences commenting on, comparing, and contrasting the possible, simultaneous activities of the person's conscious and unconscious mentation. For example, "Your conscious mind may be distracted from listening to the things I say, but your unconscious is able to pay attention to what's relevant. One part of you is aware of certain changes you think you want, while another part of you is able to place a variety of events into a larger perspective. You may not consciously know how to develop a trance, and yet your unconscious is in no way prevented from automatically creating the proper depth of trance for you to have a unique learning."

Now there are only three other things and one of those (step four) is ratifying the trance that has already been created, largely as a result of the conscious/unconscious dissociation sentences you've just been using. Ratification is just a fancy word that means you convince clients that they are in an altered state. And that is pretty easy to do if they happen to have a lot of physical alterations, like arm levitation or something, not to mention the other changes they have in their body. It's like you heard Erickson do with Nick: "While I've been talking, your cheek muscles have flattened, your eye blink reflex has changed, your breathing is lowered, and I know from previous experience that your heart rate has changed. That is ratifying the trance to show the person that something *has gone on here*. So that is not very hard.

Step one is to orient the person to trance. One part here could be really hard and that is getting rid of the little boogie men that clients may have brought with them. These are things like the myths that they are going to get ripped off like Charley's Angels did, that it is the work of the devil, that they will be made to do foolish things, that things will happen against their will, that their awful experiences will come crawling out of their unconscious, out of their control, and affect their personality, etc.—pretty much those things. Therapy with hypnosis can be pretty hard if your clients bring along these myths.

If that is the case, then what you should do is tell your clients the truth.

That they hypnotize themselves, that your words are suggestions, and they do it all day long, anyway. You are going to help them in the clinical context, which means that they won't make fools of themselves. It is a different motivation to be in a clinical setting and to be in trance than to be in front of a group of people, in which case there is an entertainment implied somehow . And tell them that they will be in control and can come out of trance at any time because they put themselves into it, that basically they attend to what's relevant for them. The only other thing that gets a little harder is to convince them that *they* have a package of positive experiences there.

So you need to do some educating there about what is the unconscious. And that happens a little bit here at step three, as when we were looking at Erickson with Nick and he mentioned the front of the mind and the back of the mind. That was to introduce the concept of the unconscious, to attribute positive characteristics. Then there should be some dissociation of thought processes, and some training and education about what the unconscious is. So that will help demystify the notion of trance.

Now there is only one other myth that is really difficult. And that one is held by the folks who think that it is the work of the devil. They are a little paranoid probably and using biblical references to back up their fears. I would suggest that you talk it over with them. Let them go home and think it over. When they come back, you'll abide by their decisions rather than try to talk them right into it and steamroller them, because that will make them more paranoid than ever. One thing you can do, if it is within the religious context that you can be comfortable with, is quote the New Testament, *Acts* 10, verse 10. That whole piece of *Acts*, Chapter 10, is all about Simon Peter going into trance. And he is not the only one. He sees four-legged creatures and it is all symbolic. He doesn't know what it means. So it is clearly two things. It is clearly Ericksonian indirect suggestion, because he doesn't know what it is he's being told. And it is clearly trance. In *Acts* (*10*, 10), they even use the word trance. So that ought to take the wind out of some paranoid people's sails. If the Holy Spirit can use it, then it can't be all bad. That is the point. So you have them go home and read that and come back and tell you if they can feel comfortable, knowing that there is something about it that got into the positive religious framework as opposed to the negative one that they have entertained. You don't have to use that religious example very much, but it sure is nice to know that if you need it. And if you're in Tulsa, Oklahoma, you really need it. Some of you know what I mean.

The other part of orienting clients to trance is getting them physically oriented. Make sure they take their glasses off, their contacts out. If they have pain of some kind, you may have some special needs there. Make sure their head is going to be all right. It is a good idea to have the legs uncrossed. Those body parts get real heavy if they are crossed over one another. So orienting to trance can be as simple as one sentence. Anybody who doesn't have a lot of these fears about trance, and is already sitting down in a comfortable position and not wearing contacts, can be oriented to trance in one half of a sentence. Or if you're in Erickson's green chair, it can be two syllables—when he says, "All right"—and you know the time has come and that's all it takes for orientation to trance there.

What is left is fixation of attention and rapport (step two) and that can be accomplished in a couple of ways. You can ask the person to find something to look at like Erickson did with Nick. This works fine if there is no problem with getting compliance.

With Paco, we said maybe *he'd* be more comfortable closing his eyes. That would help him shut out the reality of all those people looking at him since that was a problem for him. Another way people get fixated is with stories. So the actual fact of telling the person a story that engages their attention accomplishes that. And within that story, if you start dissociating conscious and unconscious experience, like with indirect suggestion, then doesn't that accomplish fixation as well? Yes, it does. So in other words, if you are story telling, once you start adding indirect suggestion it is going to create trance in some degree. And the degree to which you can help ratify it is the degree to which it is being stabilized and deepened.

So given that this is the outline for trance, you can do a sort of *formal* induction by virtue of the fact that it goes through these steps. They overlap a bit, of course. In fact, they overlap throughout, because you can begin doing conscious/unconscious dissociation with your first sentence, as a means of orienting.

Essentially, what you have here is that all of these things are happening at *all* times. This is not really a rigid outline. The steps overlap. But the outline is valid because it represents the order of the major thrust of the first few phases of induction. After orientation, the major thrust shifts clearly to this: fixation of attention. And then the major thrust becomes the dissociation part. Once that is established, the major thrust at step four is to glue down the resulting dissociation and ratify it. And then the major thrust is your therapy, although you may have been doing some therapy earlier. But you can count it sentence-wise. It might have been one sentence of therapy here at orientation, two here at fixation, three at conscious/unconscious dissociation, none here at ratification, and five thousand sentences here at steps five and six. So that is how the induction overlaps and kind of blends together. We will show this in the following induction examples.

In this transcript, "M" represents Jack Moser (Ph.D. [cand.]) and the "C" represents his client. This client was seen by Mr. Moser at one of our advanced supervision workshops and, although the goals and needs of the client were used to design the treatment plan, we won't relate them here. The portions of interest are the exemplary induction and significant example it provides of the use of indirect suggestion. Here's the induction first.

> M: It's good to see you smile and laugh. That would be a good gauge at the end of our session. You know, how you feel at the end of the session might be a good criteria for figuring our progress or whatever.
>
> C: [sighs deeply]
>
> M: So why don't you just go ahead and get comfortable—and it already looks like you are relaxing—and we'll get started. And you know, we've spent time in the past just relaxing in trance, finding a comfortable position, getting your feet comfortable. Just breathing and relaxing. Yet consciously there is a natural kind of uncomfortableness about being on tape, just being here and knowing that something different is happening. And yet, your conscious mind may be already relaxed and interested about what you'll be doing or what I am saying or what you'll be saying and I'm doing. And you've relaxed before and gone to the favorite spot in the yard where you like to sit outside and you can feel that comfort of letting go.
>
> C: [moving hand on lap somewhat]
>
> M: And you may be thinking of the courage that it took to come today. It took a lot of courage to just come in here, not knowing what really was ahead of you and yet knowing that you've done good things behind the steps that you've taken and will continue to take.
>
> C: [moves head to the right on cushion]
>
> M: And as I talk about many things you may allow your conscious mind to just think about anything or nothing while your unconscious mind just continues to listen and learn about yourself at a different level of being. And you know that many times your conscious mind listens and forgets—your unconscious mind learns and understands—and there are other times when your unconscious mind listens and understands and your conscious mind learns and forgets. It really doesn't make any difference as long as you, Connie, listen to the sound of my voice and find that place of comfort that is right for you. That's right, for you know that you've relaxed deeply in the past and you can do it again. You know that it is unnecessary not to forget the things you can't remember so you might as well let yourself go and continue to find that depth of relaxation and profound peacefulness.
>
> C: [heavy exhale]
>
> M: Breathe deeply. Just swallow and relax. Enjoy the relaxation and quiet time.
>
> M: And just driving out here might have been an enjoyable experience.

Driving here, following directions, just stopping at the traffic light, turning left and then right. When I came here to the Windjammer [conference room] I came in the opposite direction. I took a right instead of a left and went into the wrong motel. And I had to come back out and I took a left into Howard Johnson's and found out I was on the wrong side. I came back out and I took a right and came back the way I was going. By the time I found out I was going in the wrong direction and turned around to come back, I decided I'd just [heavy sigh] pull over to the side of the road for a second and just turn off my engine . . . and try to figure out if I could spend a minute of quiet time just listening to some unconscious directions.

C: [swallows]

M: I swallowed, listened to those directions and [client moves head] kind of moved my head into a more comfortable position. I just asked myself where I was, where I'd been, where I wanted to go. But as I did, I counted down slowly from 20 down to 1. I, 20, listened to my unconscious mind as I, 19, and as I listened to my unconscious instructions and felt the lightness, 18, and the comfort, 17, I allowed my unconscious mind to Ann, direct yourself in the upcoming minute. I wasn't really sure that 16 . . .

Now I will stop this here and point out that the induction has many elements that we consider important to a typical Ericksonian induction. We see the use of confusion in the form of triple negatives and left/right confusions. We heard a conscious/unconscious dissociation with binds including the double dissociative bind. We heard the incorporation of several incidents of the client's ideomotor behaviors into the induction. Moreover, I think you can see that orientation to trance blends with the fixation and the dissociation stage and then the whole thing moves into the deepening stage. We, of course, went into this aspect of treatment in depth in *The Answer Within* and in our hypnosis workshops, so that I don't believe you want us to analyze it further now.

Also, we liked the example that follows. We have skipped ahead quite a way into the treatment to show you this fine example of the use of indirect suggestion. You will see, in what follows, that the use of indirect suggestion and psychological implication is essential to this style of treatment. Look at the impact this makes.

M: . . . I thought about that a lot in the month that I was with her—just trying to hold in a different way or touch in a different way—or just somehow have her remember the sound of my voice or trust that sound when she heard it. You know how there are some voices that you hear and there is a trusting sound to them and you remember that voice and you may remember it again in the future.

That is what I was hoping, and when I left I really didn't know what to expect.

C: [Her posture is slumped, her head is reclined back on couch, she is breathing in gulps through her mouth with her lips softly parted and her neck stretched. Her legs are parted, knees separated by one to two inches, her hands crossed at waist, and skirt hiked up several inches above knees. This posture paired with her partially see-through blouse, heavy eye makeup and hair softly flowing over her shoulders—as well as the high rate of swallowing and breathing—gave a distinct erotic and sensuous tone to her presence. It seemed like his soft voice and imagery were potentially conveying an erotic, and definitely, therefore, unwanted message]

While these aspects were discussed with the observers in the training group, Mr. Moser completed the above metaphor and judged from the client's ideomotor behavior that his goal was met. He then proceeded with a therapeutic point that would be accomplished with the story of the Washington zoo. During this story, we (Stephen and Carol, in discussion with the observing participants) opted for calling him with instruction.

M: It is like those birth experiences those Pandas had up in the Washington zoo. I was in Washington when the Chinese government sent those two pandas over, Ying and Ling—who'd ever have thought they would give them Irish names?—and they were in the zoo and I went over to see them and took all the kids. It was funny because they were sort of wary of each other. They would sort of walk following each other, and one would sort of swipe at a pole and you know how bears do. I knew everything wasn't black and white when I saw those two! But I knew also that getting to know each other and that sort of wariness was the way bears sort of do sometimes.

M: [pauses while listening to intercom]

C: [interrupts on the intercom (connected by earphone to Mr. Moser) to explain that he should continue his stories but introduce his wife as well as his children so that the seductive content would be removed]

M: And my wife even mentioned when we were standing there that she could understand the way that these two bears needed to [client straightens head as he continues] take a look at each other and get to know each other.

C: [lifts chin upward to put her head more vertical on the couch, swallows, smacks and pushes her lips together thus removing the softness they had displayed]

M: And my wife is the kind of person who looks at relationships and tries to step back and see the roles of each, the proper roles of each—the male and the female. I even remember when Brian, my seven-year-old was born [client opens and closes mouth and tilts head] and my wife would spend time with Brian every day. And we realized quickly that there was something wrong with Brian. [Client shakes head gradually, swallows pushing lips together again, leaves lips closed together as she continues to listen.] And I think my wife noticed it first because mothers are so observant about those things with their children or maybe it is intuition or maybe it's just a sixth sense that things aren't right. Maybe you have noticed that with your children, that things aren't right or they are just not acting properly. [Client continues to move her jaw as she swallows. This posture of head and face is much less sensual and erotic than it was only moments ago before Mr. Moser started introducing his wife.]

Now here, Mr. Moser goes on about how he and his wife take the boy to the doctor. You will see that the client adjusts her dress down to her knees after only another one-and-a-half minutes. And, of course, when she does, he incorporates the movements by saying that his protagonist moved around in the chair in order to get more comfortable.

Now there has been some research I've read that favors the use of direct suggestion over indirect suggestion. The psychological implication of this type—the introduction of the image of Mr. Moser's wife in order to stop the sexual content associated with the trance—is perhaps the best advertisement for using indirect suggestion. Nothing direct could have done this any more quickly without alerting the conscious mind to the potential and without alerting Ann to the projections of the therapist about her. Thus, this has eliminated the difficulty without increasing any resistance.

I want you to see, too, this next fine example of reorientation of a couple in marital therapy with us who were also seen in an advanced supervision workshop by Dr. Susan Vignola. She has been working with them in trance for about an hour at this point and I think you'll see a reorientation that is very respectful and smooth, very well suited to wrapping up the work done with two people in a family at once. Listen for the way she validates the learning of each spouse and how she still uses confusion, anecdote, and indirect suggestion. She is able to brilliantly weave this into the fabric, interspersing direct suggestion as well. The result is a solid closure for the trance learnings and an orientation to future learnings. They did, by the way, have amnesia for the content of the trance.

In the following transcript, Dr. Vignola is identified as "V" and is talking here to a couple (the husband is "R" and the wife is "B") who she has in trance. She is now reorienting them from the trance after completing a set of metaphors.

V: And you may wonder in your own minds about people you might have known—the Eds and the Nancys, the Billys and the Williams, in your own life—and what learnings you can bring with you out of trance from their experience and learnings you are yet to learn from your future. What you learned here today is not what you are going to learn tomorrow or all of your tomorrows-tomorrow. And at some point when tomorrow has become today and today has become part of last week or last year, you may not remember any of what was said here today or you may remember something.

Occasionally, you may remember bits and pieces or you may not remember, for unconsciously you know that you have it stored forever and at any point in your future you can tap into your unconscious learnings knowing that they are always a part of you, as much a part of you as your fingertip or fingerprint that is uniquely yours, that no one can ever alter or take from you. No one can take your learning and your knowledge. And just as your fingerprint stays the same, the protective covering of your finger nail can grow and continue changing. Even when it breaks it grows back again. And your conscious mind will break off different pieces of learnings and new ones will grow in their place, as you associate new things and new information, sometimes old things and old information in new ways.

And I don't know what you are going to bring with you out of your trance today, but I know what you bring with you—today's learnings—may be different for each of you and you need not be concerned that what you have learned, Betty, is different than what you learned, Robert. You can simply appreciate the fact that for all your living days you can continue to learn, and the more you can be different the more you can continue to learn from each other. And I hope that you can learn to love the difference in each other because it gives you a beautiful gift.

Just as we can share and appreciate and value the uniqueness of each rose petal as it's different from another and one day is not like another day. Yesterday is different from today which is different from tomorrow. And your experience of today is different from your experience of tomorrow and you don't know what you're going to know tomorrow until it's yesterday when you now know what you knew then but you don't know what you are going to know someday in the future.

And as you hold on to some or all or none of your learning you can bring yourself out of trance as you once again allow your conscious mind to focus and hear the sounds of the waves and notice that the rhythm of the waves has altered as we've sat here together. And our breathing is now going to change as you begin to adjust your posture and sooner or later . . . that's right . . . and there will be more movement in those hands and feet . . . that's right . . . and your eyes will open. And take your time.

R: [stretching, opening eyes]

V: Hi. What are you going to do on your day off, Robert?

R: [leans head back, stretching arms over head] Take my little boy fishin' for one thing.

V: Oh, does he like to fish?

R: [smiling, looking toward wife] He's fixin' t' see if he likes it, [puts arm around wife] that's for sure.

V: Oh, great. Are you a fisherman?

R: Well, let's put it this way, I go fishin' but I hardly ever catch anything.

B: [puts hands to neck as if awakening]

V: Well, a lot of fishermen that I know don't go just to bring home dinner.

R: It's a good thing I don't [wife uncrosses legs].

B: We'd starve to death [still rubbing mouth, yawning].

V: What do you do before you go back to work this morning?

B: [garbled]

V: Well, this is a different opportunity for you this morning. I'd like to thank you both again for the opportunity of working with you.

It is time to bring the workshop to a close now. And we want to impart this final idea. In order to integrate the material from this week of training, you will need to practice each of our interventions both alone and in combination. We previously used an analogy of learning to juggle as a way to illustrate learning complex material and the analogy is worth repeating. Just as one must learn to toss and catch each of the three or four juggling balls independently, each form of suggestion, bind, goal setting, and metaphor construction pattern can be learned and practiced one at a time. Then, one must learn to control two in combination; then three, four, and so on.

We've presented many powerful therapeutic interventions and a framework for applying them in the course of this workshop — it is understandable that they must be processed and repeatedly practiced to be of greatest value. You've experienced how well these frameworks and interventions work for us, so now we invite you to do that on your own and in your own time. Finally, feel free to contact us with any questions and come to study with us further in other advanced training workshops.

Index

Abstractions, 251-252
Acceptance, feeling of, 159
Active behavior, 140, 143
Adding on, 221, 230, 237-238
Adolescence, 95
    as psychological age, 89
Affect, changes in, 76
Affect construction formulas, 199-203
Affect protocol, 198-203
Age regression, 216, 241
Alcoholism, 126-127, 217, 224-225
Alien (movie), 155-157, 201-202
Alignment, strategic, 63-64
Alliance, therapist-client, 63-64
Altered framework, 154, 155
AMA Journal, 9, 11
Ambiguity, 147, 148
    in metaphors, 187, 189
Ambiguous function assignments, 21, 23-
    25, 52, 136-152, 228, 232, 244, 255
    components of, 142-144
    indications for, 147-152
    rationale for, 146-147
    responding to, 144-146
    task vs. purpose in, 143
American Society of Clinical Hypnosis, 9,
    11
Amnesia, 13, 14-15, 32, 241, 242, 243, 264,
    266
Anecdote(s), 7, 14-15, 24, 40, 222
Anger, 109-110
*Answer Within, The: A Clinical Framework
    of Ericksonian Hypnotherapy* (Lankton),
    71, 79, 82, 205, 240, 262
Anxiety, 58-61, 126-127, 158, 160-161,
    162, 182-184
    amnesia in treating, 14
    parents', 193
Arthritis, 86-87
Assertiveness training, 185
Assessment parameters, 73-75
Assignments. *See* Homework assignments;

Ambiguous function assignments
Asthma, 192-193
Attention, focusing, 153
Attitude, changes in, 76, 92, 159-160, 241
Attitude metaphors, 49, 50, 193-198
    constructing, 195-196
Attributions, 3-4, 17, 45-47, 121-123, 183,
    196-197
Automatic writing, 8, 12
Awareness, focusing, 30, 247, 252-253

Bach, George, 250
Back/front of one's mind, 41, 259
Back pain, 84-92, 228, 236-238
Beck, Aaron, 50
Behavior
    changes in/modifications of, 11, 76
    client's, noticing, 40, 81, 84-85, 255
    ideomotor, in trance, 187, 189, 226
    prescribing, 53 (*see also* Paradoxical
        symptom prescription)
Behavior metaphors, 80, 203-205, 222
Behavior modification, 25, 76
Belief(s) and belief system(s), 45, 47-48,
    50,76, 87, 136, 215
    changing, 54
    challenging, 197
Belonging, feelings of, 111, 159, 165-166,
    171-173, 189, 198, 200, 203, 243
Berne, Eric, 10, 48, 49, 94, 118n
Bible, trance in, 259
Bind(s), 6, 7, 138, 246
    in ambiguous function assignments, 143-
        144
    of comparable alternatives, 248, 255
conscious/unconscious, 249, 253-254,
    258
    double, 9, 249, 253-254
    double dissociative
        conscious/unconscious, 249, 253,
        262
    illusory, 255

About the Authors:

Stephen R. Lankton, MSW, DAHB, is a licensed Clinical Social Worker practicing in Phoenix, Arizona. He is editor of the *American Journal of Clinical Hypnosis*, executive director of the Phoenix Institute of Ericksonian Therapy, and a recipient of the Erickson Foundation's Lifetime Achievement Award for Outstanding Contribution to the Field of Psychotherapy. Mr. Lankton is also faculty associate at Arizona State University, Diplomate in Clinical Hypnosis, and past president of the American Hypnosis Board for Clinical Social Work. He is the author of 16 books with translations in several languages regarding techniques of hypnosis, family therapy, and brief therapy.

Carol Hicks Lankton, M.A., is a licensed marriage and family therapist who operates a private practice at the Wellness Institute of East Hill in Pensacola, Florida. Internationally recognized for her role in the development and growth of an Ericksonian approach to family therapy and clinical hypnosis, she is the coauthor of three books and author of numerous chapters. Carol conducts training for mental health professionals worldwide. She is passionate in her desire to rapidly facilitate therapeutic transformation that is both brief and deeply healing. Visit her website at www.answerwithin.com for more information about her orientation and programs.